BIG MUDDY BLUES

ALSO BY BILL LAMBRECHT

Dinner at the New Gene Café

BIG MUDDY BLUES

TRUE TALES AND TWISTED POLITICS
ALONG LEWIS AND CLARK'S
MISSOURI RIVER

BILL LAMBRECHT

THOMAS DUNNE BOOKS ☒ NEW YORK
ST. MARTIN'S PRESS

THOMAS DUNNE BOOKS.
An imprint of St. Martin's Press.

Excerpt from "The Dry Salvages" copyright © 1941 by T. S. Eliot and renewed 1969 by Esme Valerie Eliot, reprinted by permission of Harcourt, Inc.

"Ode to Diversion" reprinted by permission of Don Sondrol.

www.stmartins.com

Map on page viii-ix by Jeffery L. Ward

Library of Congress Cataloging-in-Publication Data

Lambrecht, Bill.
    Big Muddy blues : true tales and twisted politics along Lewis and Clark's Missouri River / Bill Lambrecht.—1st ed.
      p. cm.
    ISBN 0-312-32783-8
    EAN 978-0312-32783-5
    1. Missouri River—Environmental conditions.   2. Missouri River Valley—Environmental conditions.   3. Missouri River—Description and travel.
4. Missouri River Valley—Description and travel.   5. Missouri River—History.
6. Lambrecht, Bill—Travel—Missouri River Valley.   7. Environmental protection—Missouri River.   8. Environmental policy—United States.
I. Title.

GE155.M85L36   2005
333.91'62'0978—dc22
                            2004051434

First Edition: April 2005

10 9 8 7 6 5 4 3 2 1

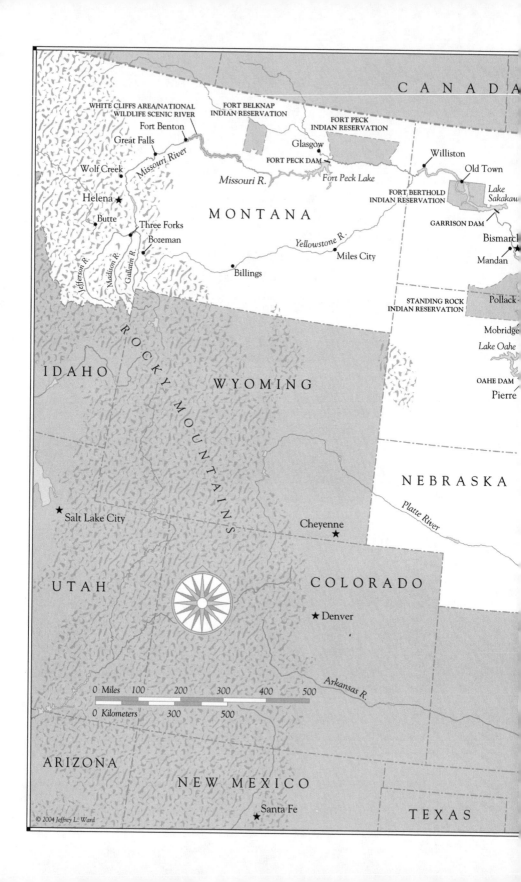

CANADA

WHITE CLIFFS AREA/NATIONAL
WILDLIFE SCENIC RIVER

FORT BELKNAP
INDIAN RESERVATION

FORT PECK
INDIAN RESERVATION

Fort Benton

Great Falls

Glasgow

Williston

Wolf Creek

Missouri River

FORT PECK DAM

Old Town

Missouri R.

Fort Peck Lake

*Lake
Sakakaw*

Helena ★

FORT BERTHOLD
INDIAN RESERVATION

MONTANA

GARRISON DAM

Butte

Three Forks

Bismarc

Bozeman

Yellowstone R.

Jefferson R.

Madison R.

Gallatin R.

Miles City

Mandan

Billings

STANDING ROCK
INDIAN RESERVATION

Pollack

R O C K Y

Mobridge

Lake Oahe

IDAHO

WYOMING

M
O
U
N
T
A
I
N
S

OAHE DAM
Pierre

NEBRASKA

★ Salt Lake City

Platte River

Cheyenne
★

UTAH

COLORADO

★ Denver

0 Miles 100   200   300   400   500

Arkansas R.

0 Kilometers   300   500

ARIZONA

NEW MEXICO

Santa Fe
★

TEXAS

© 2004 Jeffrey L. Ward

THE MISSOURI RIVER

NORTH DAKOTA

• Carrington

Jamestown•   Fargo•

MINNESOTA

Lake Superior

MICHIGAN

SOUTH DAKOTA

Lake Sharp

⚡ BIG BEND DAM

Lake Francis Case

FORT RANDALL DAM

Yankton•

Lewis and Clark Lake   GAVINS POINT DAM

Sioux City

St. Paul ★
Minneapolis•

WISCONSIN

Mississippi R.

Madison ★

Milwaukee
•

Lake Michigan

• Sergeant Bluffs

I O W A

OMAHA INDIAN RESERVATION

Macy•

DESOTO NATIONAL WILDLIFE REFUGE

Chicago •

★ Des Moines

• Council Bluffs

Omaha •
•Bellevue

Lincoln ★

Missouri R.

Mississippi R.

ILLINOIS

St. Joseph

★ Springfield

Missouri R.

Hardin

Orrick •   •
         Waverly

Columbia
•

Alton
•

Wood River

Topeka ★

Kansas City   Rocheport

St. Charles•
★   •St. Louis
Jefferson City   Hermann

KANSAS

Arkansas R.

MISSOURI

Mississippi R.

Ohio R.

KENTUCKY

OKLAHOMA

ARKANSAS

TENNESSEE

CONTENTS

CONTENTS

CONTENTS

ACKNOWLEDGMENTS

I needed every seed of understanding I could glean from authors of Missouri River books. Among them, Robert Kelley Schneiders dug as deeply as possible into the Missouri riverbed of history for his scholarly books. From Michael Lawson I learned a great deal of what the Great White Fathers did to the Sioux in the name of river improvement. The late Stephen Ambrose's outrage at the fate of his favorite river persuaded me that a new round of Missouri River reporting was in order.

I owe special thanks to Pamela Barnes in the *St. Louis Post-Dispatch* library for turning me loose in the newspaper morgue at odd hours and for sending me ancient clips in the biggest envelopes my rural letter carrier had ever seen.

My colleagues at the *Post-Dispatch* in Washington and St. Louis tolerated my fascination with the Missouri during a time when national and international news flowed as swiftly as any river.

The Missouri Historical Society let me in the door even when it was closed. Robert Archibald, president of that extraordinary institution, helped to sharpen themes in the book.

Thanks to the Chouteau County Library staff in Fort Benton, Montana, for the piles of materials they slid in front of me, and to the Renwick Gallery staff in Washington, D.C., for exhibiting George Catlin's inspiring portraits a stone's throw from my office. Art historian Linda

Claire Kulla, at the University of Missouri in St. Louis, provided insights into Catlin and his times.

Lots of folks generously put me on rivers or in the sky: Bob Freeman; Sandy Wood; Roger Blaske; Bud and Esther Lilly, Steve and Thelma Burdic; Jeff McFadden; Bob Shadwell; and David Carruth, among others. Some ended up in the book. Thanks on the same score to the Nebraska Game and Parks Commission; the Garrison Diversion Conservancy District in North Dakota; and the South Florida Water Management District.

Nathaniel Martin Knoll and Mark Behuncik rooted out some of the down-and-dirty blues lyrics. My family at *Bay Weekly* newspaper in Maryland—including Alex Knoll and Betsy Kehne—supplied me with gear to get these words down.

Thanks to the many tolerant folks at the Fish and Wildlife Service and the Army Corps of Engineers, about whom I write. I also learned a great deal from Ron Kucera, Scott Faber, Chris Brescia, Chad Smith, Richard Opper, David Weiman, Clay Jenkinson, Sara Shipley, and Joe Browder. I hurried to keep up with St. Louis filmmakers John Knoll and James Scott as they completed their fine work: *Confluence: The River Heritage of St. Louis.*

Special thanks to Dawn Charging, Faith Spotted Eagle, Pemina Yellow Bird, Tex Hall, Antione Provost, and all other tribal members who escorted me on what land and waters they still can claim.

INTRODUCTION

Away, we're bound away
'Cross the wide Missouri

JUMPING-OFF POINT:
AUGUST 2000 · KANSAS CITY, MISSOURI

The *Evelyn Rushing* rests in the gentle current of the Kansas River readying to swing upstream into the Missouri. Another day, the 164-foot-long vessel might be pushing barges laden with farm fertilizer, or perhaps asphalt. Today, its cargo is human, and they are players in an unfolding political drama.

Passengers board on a ramp dropped in the mud. I see Senator Christopher Bond, a Missouri Republican who goes by the name Kit. There's Congressman Ike Skelton, a Democrat from the tiny river town of Lexington, negotiating the flimsy ramp. Kansas City mayor Kay Barnes follows, a mother duck leading a parade of bureaucrats.

Weaving and tripping, they're about as steady as a hog thief named John Collins, who came to misfortune two hundred years ago at this very spot. Here the Kansas River joins Big Muddy, America's river west.

After tapping into the whiskey reserves of Lewis and Clark's Corps of Discovery, Private Collins got himself drunk and court-marshaled. He suffered one hundred lashes for abandoning his sentry post, leaving the mission unguarded from the natives Clark called savages.

Now, two centuries into the era opened by Meriwether Lewis and William Clark, guests are welcomed aboard the *Evelyn Rushing* by barge executives and agribusiness leaders from the National Corn Growers Association, sponsors of this outing. A handful of reporters scramble up the ramp, I among them.

A sporting way to debark, sticking a plank in the dirt. Surely, the river commerce boys behind this public relations gambit could do a better job of staging their party?

No, they couldn't, for no respectable boat landing exists in all of greater Kansas City.

As we shove off, I notice beer bottles strewn on the banks alongside plastic grocery sacks tangled in weeds. The odor of sewage hangs in the air. Abandoned barges bleed rust along a shoreline dotted with scrub trees. Downriver, a Dodge truck sticks ass-up out of the bank as if dropped from the sky.

I observe and decipher, considering the name our hosts have given to this outing: the Save Our River Rally.

BIG MUDDY

The Missouri River is not the biggest river in the United States; that distinction goes to the Mississippi, which discharges eight times as much water by volume into the Gulf of Mexico. But at about 2,341 miles (nobody can say for sure) the Missouri River is America's longest river, even after Army engineers whacked away some 120 miles. It is so long that it takes in many of America's most distinguishing characteristics and much of the bounty Thomas Jefferson gained in the Louisiana Purchase. From the Rocky Mountains, it waters the interior plains and highlands settled by Euro-Americans who so swiftly followed Jefferson's Missouri River emissaries westward.

Once upon a time, the Missouri flowed northward to the Hudson Bay. Then Pleistocene glaciers shoved it back east, as if Canada were throwing up a bulwark to keep the famously ornery river at bay. To this day, Canadians defend that barrier lest Missouri River water cross their border again.

In its sphere of influence, the Missouri is without peer. No American river basin comes near the expanse of land drained by the Missouri: 540,000 square miles in ten states; one sixth of the continental United States.

The Missouri begins in Three Forks, Montana, rising from the confluence of the Jefferson, Madison, and Gallatin rivers, named by Lewis and Clark for their president and two of his secretaries. Past Montana, it traverses or touches North Dakota, South Dakota, Nebraska, Iowa, Kansas, and Missouri. All those states claim stakes in its water and wage wars to protect their claims.

Since the Corps of Discovery climbed its length, the Missouri has been much changed. Two thirds of the river is either channelized or impounded by dams. Gone are nearly all of its braided channels, backwaters, oxbow lakes, chutes, sloughs, meanders, and islands that provided the circulating blood of one of North America's richest ecosystems.

Meriwether Lewis, the amateur scientist, weighed equal volumes of the Missouri and Kansas rivers and recorded the former as twice as heavy because of all the sediment it carried. Thus the river has long been called Big Muddy, much in the way Spaniards called the Colorado the Colored River and Rio Puerco in Mexico the Dirty River. But today its nickname is a misnomer because the straitjacketed river no longer braids its channels through miles of life-enriched bottom wetlands. Today's Missouri is an enslaved river impatient to be free.

SAVING OUR RIVER

I'd walked into Big Muddy just as a monumental ruckus brewed.

On one side, conservationists were fighting to bring back the river by recreating a semblance of Big Muddy's historic ebb and flow. The government biologists behind the plan, some on board *Evelyn Rushing*, wanted to restore the environment and save its endangered wildlife. To succeed, they'd have to undermine one of the most prodigious engineering feats in American history. That meant loosening the straitjacket strapped on the Missouri in the name of navigation, flood prevention, and restraint. So these conservationists are revolutionaries.

On the other side was a powerful establishment defending a century of control over this unruly river.

"Tampering with the river," was how our tour leader aboard *Evelyn Rushing* labeled this insurgency. Mayor Barnes, who comes from a long line of Kansas City politicians seeking to keep the Missouri clamped down, called river restraint "a matter of life and death."

"Wacko environmentalists," Senator Bond said of the revolutionaries. "This issue is far too important to be decided by some geniuses in Washington."

The establishment of politicians, farmers, bargers, and the Army Corps of Engineers wanted to save the river not just from the conservationists and wackos but also from the U.S. Fish and Wildlife Service.

If the Fish and Wildlife Service finally succeeded in its decade-long quest, agribusiness would lose out to three endangered species: two birds and one prehistoric fish, the pallid sturgeon. The changes would reach far into the ecosystem beyond three creatures. Victory would, biologists said, return the Missouri to something of the river it had been for the eons before the mid-twentieth century.

It became clear to me that the aim of the Save Our River Rally aboard the *Evelyn Rushing* was to save our river from those who want to save our river.

LOSING OUR RIVER

The enemies may be many, but *Evelyn Rushing* has the river almost to herself this summer day. Our rally comes upon only one other vessel under way, a johnboat with a home-welded pilothouse. At the helm of *Tugboat Annie* is a lone protester who has hoisted a placard sniffed at by passengers on my vessel:

NAVIGATION, $6.9 MILLION, RECREATION, $90 MILLION.

It is another message that takes deciphering.

We see no other humans until, after nearly an hour, we pass by two elderly African Americans tending fishing rods on the right bank. They had managed to goat-walk down the steep, rock-armored banks, and they affixed enough lead to their line to hold their stink bait against the ferocious, artificial current.

We are in a major city with presumably normal sensibilities, a jazz mecca where the likes of Charlie "Bird" Parker and Hot Lips Page held forth and a place with the wisdom to house the Negro Leagues Baseball Museum. But Kansas City has fenced itself off from another great American resource literally in its midst.

We're seeing the success of a long-term campaign. It was well under way in the 1930s. Back then, Kansas City's Commercial Club pressed the government to control the Missouri. Depending on the clout of its current congressional delegation, the Army Corps of Engineers would get the cash for another of its futile maneuvers to beat back the beast with rocks, pilings, and wooden blankets. Ultimately, the river would bust loose to devour buildings, roads, and humans foolish enough to toy with it. This was also the Pendergast gangster era, when more than a few Kansas Citians ended up buried in Big Muddy.

IT WAS IN THOSE DAYS that Cecil Griffith got a knock on his door.

Griffith, who went to work for the Army Corps of Engineers in 1928, used to say he had pulled more bodies from the Missouri River than anyone else in history. His claim was doubtful given wars between American Indian civilizations that have populated the river shorelines for ten thousand years. But Griffith was proud of his work, and before dying of emphysema, he wrote a memoir, including his experience with "floaters."

One of his tales is set on a boat loaded with dignitaries, which may be why I remember him now. Some poor bastard, he began, had been in the water long enough to pop up to the surface. Wouldn't you know it? *Ka-thunk.*

As Griffith told it, the dredge boat showing off the Army Corps of Engineers' latest and no doubt short-lived triumph over the mighty river had run over the unidentified poor bastard. The decaying body twisted in the propeller. You never want to break down with bigwigs aboard. And certainly not like this. Cecil Griffith jumped overboard.

He gathered the remains as best he could, and soon the engine roared. Griffith, savior of the voyage, surely was proud as he climbed back aboard. That's when he ran into a Corps colonel, who inquired if he'd like to meet the general. Sure.

Griffith stuck out his hand and the general grabbed it.

Griffith reported that for much of the trip, the general leaned over the rail, heaving into the Missouri, overcome by the smell on his hand and on the handkerchief with which he had tried to wipe it away. Griffith may have sacrificed promotion when he observed the only surefire way to get rid of the smell: Grow new skin.

OUR TRIP IS LESS eventful, and as Bond comes to the rail beside me I point out an eddy near the bank, remarking how nice it would be to cast a fly into the swirl. Bond is a shrewd politician who knows his political base, which includes farmers, bargers, and property rights devotees. He knows a fair amount about fishing, too, whether walkin' the dog with his favorite Zara Spook lure chasing after bass in midwestern lakes or hauling up halibut the size of car doors from Alaskan bays.

"A hunk of chicken guts would probably work better," he replies, suggesting rightly that a catfish might be lurking by the bank—but certainly not any upper-class fish lured by some tidbit of fuzz on a fly-line.

How dumb am I?

When I ask the senator why we're seeing so few people, his answer confuses me. "Unless you like to water-ski on mud flats, you don't have a lot of waterborne recreation in summer," he says.

Finally, a big boat presents itself on the horizon. Life! Perhaps a reincarnation of the old steamboat days captured by George Catlin in his early nineteenth-century paintings. Maybe a marina with revelers loading up on ice on this sizzling hot day, for which boating and swimming offer an unmatched elixir.

But what comes into focus is a casino gambling boat, not under way but moored. It is not even moored on the Missouri but in an impoundment behind a levee. And that is it. On the fabled Missouri River, the highway to American empire, I see no other boats or human beings during the entire trip.

ONE-MAN CORPS OF DISCOVERY

The mystery of the lifeless Missouri propelled me on a four-year quest that brought me to its banks from Washington many more times.

Back then, I couldn't have known that I would discover a saga of hard-edged politics played out from the High Plains buffalo jumps to the cloakrooms of the United States Senate.

Or that an old-fashioned water war would break out amidst a desperate quest to save species from extinction.

Or that I would meet prehistoric creatures and half-mad river rats.

Or that I would land in the midst of a struggle of wills between two federal agencies and complicated by presidential politics.

Or that I would write dozens of newspaper stories—and eventually this book—about what I found.

Nor could I have known that in seeking answers to what troubled me on this steamy August day, I would become enmeshed in a political drama with consequences rippling far beyond this heartland watershed.

As I pursue my quest across the country—from the Klamath River along the California-Oregon border to the Florida Everglades—society collides with tough questions about the role America's rivers play in contemporary life.

How we reconcile our abuse of America's river west can shape treaties for other river wars. In the Everglades, the wisdom of a massive replumbing project remains in doubt. Along the Columbia River, salmon are being driven to extinction. Along the Klamath River in Oregon, the Klamath Tribe is fighting a losing battle for water and fish that once belonged to them but disappeared as a result of irrigation farming. Decisions about the Missouri's flow and the creatures along its banks will, like Lewis and Clark's fateful journey, shape the future of our nation's precious resources.

TELLING THE RIVER'S STORY

I am a journalist, not an advocate. I fish for good stories and political intrigue. At this waypoint in the Missouri's history, the great river overflows with both.

This is a historic confluence not only because it brings us two centuries from America's greatest exploration. These are also war years along the Missouri.

Conservationists championing endangered species stand against developers, bargers, and farmers in a conflict heated up by scarce water. In legislation, position papers, and court documents, plaintiffs complain. Fish can't spawn. Upstream, lodge owners can't get water to float their fishing boats. Downstream, barge operators are failing because of so much uncertainty. Farmers want that mad beast of a river locked in its cage. Cities and towns covet the river to develop its risky floodplain. So loud is the clamor of the special interests that it drowns out the people who have lived the longest along the Missouri River. Yet American Indians are players too, rising to end two centuries of voicelessness over their own lands.

Along the whole course of the Missouri, indeed, all the way to Washington, upstream and downstream states fight over its water. In Washington, I have watched every branch of government—the White House, Congress, and federal courts—wrangling over where the water would flow, how fast, and how deep.

As a Washington correspondent for the *St. Louis Post-Dispatch*, I'd seen a fair amount of congressional bluster and maneuvering over the Missouri River. Once, a stalemate in Congress over the river dammed up the nation's entire $22.5 billion budget for water projects. By 2003, federal courts were flooded with litigation on water rights, river flows, and protecting endangered species.

But the story lacked a human face. So I headed west the way the world used to, on the Missouri River. Along America's river west, I hoped to discover for whom our rivers flow. And I did.

BIG MUDDY BLUES

1

OUR STAKE IN AMERICA'S RIVER WEST

*The object of your mission is to explore the Missouri river, &
such principal streams of it, as, by it's course & communication with the waters of the Pacific Ocean, may offer the most
direct & practicable water communication across this continent, for the purposes of commerce.*

—Thomas Jefferson's instructions to
Meriwether Lewis, June 20, 1803

IN WHICH WE SET OUT ON A VOYAGE OF DISCOVERY

Oh, we are pilgrims here below
Down by the river
Oh, soon to glory we will go
Down by the riverside.

LANDING
THE BICENTENNIAL OF LEWIS AND CLARK'S
VOYAGE OF DISCOVERY

WHEN YOU TAKE A RIDE on the Missouri River, history is all
around you sure as water. The Missouri is America's river west.
When Meriwether Lewis and William Clark pulled and polled their 55-
foot keelboat 2,500 miles upstream, against the river's most determined

efforts to dissuade them, they made America a bicoastal nation. From thirteen bumptious and inexperienced Atlantic seaboard states whose frontier was the Allegheny Mountains, America soon stretched from the Atlantic past the Alleghenies and the Rockies and all the Sierras of California to the Pacific Ocean.

Thomas Jefferson's America followed its destiny west on the Missouri. No sooner had Lewis and Clark's Corps of Discovery returned, in 1806, than the Missouri became the lifeline between the mother nation and the new territory. For the next seventy years, there was no better route west than the Missouri.

A RIVER MUCH CHANGED

A ride on the twenty-first-century Missouri River is nothing like a journey on Chesapeake Bay or Lake Michigan or Puget Sound. I saw so little life along the river during that towboat ride because there was little to see. This Kansas City stretch—like much of the 732 miles of river from St. Louis to Sioux City, Iowa—was long ago reformed by the Army Corps of Engineers into a barge canal, by bank stabilization starting in the nineteenth century and by dam-nation starting in the 1930s. Today's Missouri is a study in subjugation, its range, speed, and flow controlled and every mile monitored by Army engineers.

Even in captivity, the Missouri retains beauty and power. Still standing in Montana are the bluffs whose "picturesque and beautiful shapes and colors" inspired the American West's first painter, George Catlin, in 1832, as three decades earlier their "High butifull Situation" had inspired the Corps of Discovery. Where today tiny segments of the river in Missouri and Nebraska have been released by trial restoration projects from their tightly engineered course, the river is reverting to the braids of channels and wetlands. Catlin described that river as having "formed a bed or valley for its course, varying in width from two to twenty miles."

In nature, the river is no sharply defined highway but a bed of watercourses and wetlands, the lands cycling from flood to marsh to fields. Now the stretch of Missouri River where the vast majority of its population lives runs swiftly and in chains. Even when the water is at its lowest, the channelized river moves so swiftly that a canoeist can relive the perils the Discovery Corps faced in their white and red pirogues.

More than the river itself has changed. Along its banks, the "mighty forests of stately cottonwood" painted by Catlin are all but gone, their regenerative magic mostly lost. I have sought and enjoyed their shade, but today you are lucky to find a grove or a tree of the species that once spread out along the river's banks, their unruly boughs indifferent to white men's authority.

For centuries, cottonwood trees sustained the Indians of the Missouri, offering them shelter, fuel, transport, ritual, and feed for the horses that sped them to the buffalo. Cottonwoods supplied Corps of Discovery with masts and dugout canoes. Cottonwoods fueled the steamboats that climbed the river and opened the West for settlement. Cottonwood lumber built river towns.

In the floodplain where the cottonwoods stood, the backwaters and oxbows nurtured birds and fish. Now the floodplains are dried up and filled in, sprouting corn and beans on farms planted right up to the riverbanks. Gone, in consequence, is most of the wildlife that made Missouri country the American Serengeti. "The writingest explorers ever," as the late historian Donald Jackson called Lewis and Clark, chronicled buffalo, deer, elk, antelope, bighorn sheep, wolves, coyotes, foxes, badgers, beavers, and prairie dogs. In the river, the explorers marveled at catfish as big as men.

If the explorers were writing a sequel to their journals two hundred years later, there would be far fewer notations: of sixty-seven fish native to the river, fifty-one now are rare. And that great catfishery? A decade ago, the size of the average catfish in the Lower Missouri was thirteen inches. Take of the whiskered bottom dwellers grew so meager that five states—Missouri, Kansas, Iowa, Nebraska, and South Dakota—banned commercial harvest of the fish about which Clark wrote, "those Cats are So plentiful they may be cought in any part of this river."

I PADDLE IN THE WAKE of Stephen Ambrose. Author of the best-selling *Undaunted Courage* (1996), which relived Lewis and Clark's exploits, Ambrose had made his reputation with books on World War II; he was the antithesis of the liberal environmentalist scorned by the river's farm-and-barge alliance that benefits from status quo in Missouri River management.

I spoke with Ambrose over the phone on several occasions and later lunched with him and other journalists in Washington. He once had confessed to me a secret of his success: He needed water to write, whether it was in Montana, where he had owned a cabin in Missouri River country near Helena; at his home in Bay St. Louis, Mississippi; or, earlier in life, in his cabin in Wisconsin overlooking a still lake. He had lost his heart to the Missouri River and had pledged more than a million dollars in book royalties toward its restoration. "It's just a disgrace," Ambrose said of its misuse over two hundred years.

As historians will do, Ambrose spoke in broad stretches of time. The three best things accomplished over the last sixty years for the United States, he said, were winning World War II, winning the Cold War, and ushering in the civil rights revolution. Ahead, he saw a fourth challenge that he described as a shift toward environmental awareness. "From when I was a kid, we've evolved to the point where we have conquered nature," said Ambrose, who was sixty-six when he died, in 2002.

The last time I saw Ambrose, he was just back from giving Vice President Dick Cheney an earful about the river. It was the beginning of an administration that would move quickly in the opposite direction. Downriver in the company of mere reporters, Ambrose wasn't about to mince words:

"If Lewis and Clark looked down on the river today, they'd say, 'Man, have they fucked this thing up.'"

MISSOURI DREAMING

My Kansas City journey on the river was the first of many. I have traversed all of its length, one way or another, many places more than once. I traveled the Missouri by tugboat, canoe, kayak, johnboat, towboat, fly-fishing tub, pontoon boat, and several more motorized species.

I got closest to the old Missouri on a three-day canoe voyage along a nearly pristine stretch of Montana river known as the White Cliffs. These soaring formations rising above the river's banks have changed little but by slow-time erosion since the Corps of Discovery passed by. On May 31, 1805, Meriwether Lewis described the scene:

> The water in the course of time in descending from those hills and plains from either side of the river had trickled down the soft sand cliffs and woarn it into a thousand grotesque figures . . . so perfect indeed . . . that I should have thought that nature had attempted here

to rival the human art of masonry had I not recollected that she had first began her work.

As in Lewis and Clark's day, the mind stretches out over this section of the river. You can feel your way back to the dawn of the nineteenth century when the Corps of Discovery—sons of the enlightened generation that had created a new nation and conceived the Declaration of Independence and the Constitution—imagined the treasures that could be harvested by diligent hands from this rich wilderness. How the future called to them! Meriwether Lewis was the handpicked emissary of Thomas Jefferson, who was not only president of this young nation but also its chief seer and flush with confidence in the achievement of independence.

Those dreams have come true. The riches opened by the Missouri River have been mined, yielding vast wealth and opportunity. Seldom was it easy coming. From dragging keelboats up this unruly river to breaking the land to the manipulations of the Army Corps of Engineers, it was won by toil, daring, and perseverance.

The old dreams have come true. They have flourished and declined. Now, the mind is free to stretch out again, and many minds are dreaming new dreams that balance the old—and are just as likely to leave the next century a new legacy of mistakes to correct. In those dreams, the Missouri River's chains are loosened—even broken—and it runs free again, restoring a vanquished ecosystem.

It may be dreaming, too, to call this Bicentennial the Age of Reconciliation, as some have. Yet there may never be a better time if we want to get right with the Missouri River, its original settlers, and the creatures of its waters and its banks.

❧ PADDLING ❧

FLOODS OF PROSE

When it ran free, the Missouri River triggered floods of prose. Writers reveled in personifying the wild Missouri, imbuing it with mischievous, if not mystical, motives. In the early twentieth century, George Fitch wrote in the *Atlantic Monthly*:

> The Missouri River was located in the United States at last report. It cuts corners, runs around at night, lunches on levees, and swallows islands and small villages for dessert. Its perpetual dissatisfaction with its bed is the greatest peculiarity of the Missouri. Time after time it has gotten out of its bed in the middle of the night with no apparent provocation, and has hunted a new bed, all littered with forests, cornfields, brick houses, railroad ties, and telegraph poles. Later it has suddenly taken a fancy to its old bed, which by this time has been filled with suburban architecture, and back it has gone with a whoop and a rush as if it had found something worthwhile. It makes farming as fascinating as gambling. You never know whether you are going to harvest corn or catfish.

A half century later—in an era of Promethean and sometimes reckless public works projects—Americans turned their warmaking powers to manipulations of the environment. Writers like Stanley Vestal fed the impulse to control a river that ran wild, often menacingly so, at the very heart of a world power:

> It is the hungriest river ever created [he wrote in *The Missouri*]. It is eating all the time—eating yellow clay banks and cornfields, eighty acres at

a mouthful; winding up its banquet with a truck garden and picking its teeth with the timbers of a big red barn. Its yearly menu is ten thousand acres of good rich farming land, several miles of railroads, a few hundred houses, a forest or two and uncounted miles of sandbars.

Sadly for literature, as well as for the tribes and the native species along its shores, the Missouri River offers far less inspiration since it has been humbled by the Army Corps of Engineers.

2

THE STRONG BROWN GOD

. . . I think that the river
Is a strong brown god—sullen, untamed and intractable,
Patient to some degree, at first recognised as a frontier;
Useful, untrustworthy, as a conveyor of commerce;
Then only a problem confronting the builder of bridges.
The problem once solved, the brown god is almost forgotten
By the dwellers in cities—ever, however, implacable,
Keeping his seasons, and rages, destroyer, reminder
Of what men choose to forget. Unhonoured, unpropitiated
By worshippers of the machine, but waiting, watching and waiting . . .

—T. S. Eliot, *Four Quartets*:
The Dry Salvages, 1941

IN WHICH WE VISIT A MAPMAKER, A TOXIC WASTE DUMP, AND RISKY BUSINESSES

Some people say the Missouri River blues ain't bad
Then it musta not been the Missouri River blues I had.

LANDING
ROCHEPORT, MISSOURI

A 45-DEGREE, 250-FOOT CLIMB up the Missouri bluffs toward a legendary rattlesnake den on the Lewis and Clark Trail is like a stroll on the University of Missouri campus to Jim Harlan, who carries Kool Lights as his elixir for stressed lungs. It's no different from his days training Army troops; he'd run with them five or six miles, and when the boys would drop to their knees sucking for air, the man among them would fire up a butt.

"You knew you were doing a good job if they said of you, 'He was one tough sonofabitch,'" Harlan says.

That is roughly the description that locals along the Missouri River and a few on the Mississippi have bestowed on Harlan, the puffing, debunking ruination of 2004–06 Bicentennial plans. The centerpiece of Harlan's work is his university-backed Lewis and Clark Historic Landscape Project. By documenting how the river has changed over the past two centuries, it disrupted commemorative planning along the Missouri.

In the river town of Glasgow in central Missouri, locals had laid plans for a $300,000 riverside trail near Stump Island Park, formally designated by the state three decades ago as a Lewis and Clark campsite. Then along came Harlan, pinpointing the campsite five miles west. The news did not sit well with citizens, who accused Harlan of sabotaging their celebration.

Harlan's work was especially irritating on the Illinois side of the Mississippi River, where the state erected an elaborate monument near Wood River commemorating the campsite where the explorers waited out the winter of 1803–04 before heading off along the Missouri in May. Bulldozing forward in his project, Harlan put the exclamation point on a generally known but hushed truth: Because the Mississippi River had shifted about a mile in the nineteenth century, Lewis and Clark's Camp Dubois actually was situated in Missouri, in the town of West Alton.

YOU NEED A MAP to travel the Missouri River. In search of one, I have tracked Jim Harlan to his office in Stewart Hall at the University of

Missouri in Columbia to learn his method of locating Camp Dubois. He'd consulted early U.S. land surveys, along with French and Spanish maps that showed the configuration of the old River Dubois and the mouth of the Missouri River. Old maps by French engineer Nicholas DeFiniels brought more evidence to the table. And, of course, the Lewis and Clark journals contributed strong clues by putting the explorers on the south side of the River Dubois, looking at the Mississippi. "Every day in the winter at Camp Dubois they were sitting there looking across the Missouri at the Mississippi River and making notes," Harlan says.

A later journal entry noted that the expedition traveled four and a half miles on that first day out, May 14, 1804, to the upper point of the first island in the Missouri River, which is situated directly opposite Coldwater Creek. But when you measure from that point back to Illinois, as Harlan did, the distance is five and three-fourths miles.

"Realistically speaking, geographic truth just gets in the way. They just want tourists to come up there; that's the bottom line. A lot of people are doing a service to John Q. Public. But I'm not going to get in their arguments anymore," Harlan says.

"Stuff has passed down like a great game of To Tell the Truth; someone will say, 'Well, Uncle Joe said this.' If you're going to pick the best site where people can come and commemorate where Lewis and Clark were, that's fine. But don't put up a damn sign and say they camped at such-and-such a site on such-and-such a date."

Harlan cackles as much as speaks, scurrying about grabbing maps. He's wearing an MU Meridians baseball jersey, number 25 emblazoned on the back (he was a fine shortstop in his day). On his desk is a photo of himself in camouflage and aviators snapped during the Gulf War in

Bahrain aboard the *Love Boat*, an oasis where a soldier could get a real beer in a Muslim land.

Nor has the government escaped Harlan's revisionism. "They're off, and pretty drastically," he fairly shouts while cradling an 1890s leather-bound Missouri River Commission map that miscalculated distance along the river. He is talking of a spot not far from where William Clark noted the first signs of buffalo.

"When he said this was the first buffalo sign, it probably meant that he had stepped in it," Harlan says.

TRACKING GHOSTLY FOOTPRINTS

I pursued Jim Harlan not just for his ruckus-rousing maps but also because of his lineage as a Missouri River character, one of a tribe likely to ignore political correctness while jamming forward in their work. Harlan would e-mail me about my river policy stories from Washington to take issue with historical tidbits or laugh at would-be reformers seeking to restore the river for creatures and recreation. "Yuppies flopping around in the river," he laughed, and I hastened my journey to his mapmaking lab.

Beginning in 2000, Harlan deployed the computer technology of Geographic Information Systems to create maps of the Missouri River and its surroundings as the explorers saw it two hundred years ago. His Lewis and Clark Historic Landscape Project began with state funding and drew backing from the National Endowment for the Humanities for the daunting venture of redrawing the land- and waterscape as it had been before Euro-Americans overtook it. The book he co-authored with James Denny, called the *Atlas of Lewis & Clark in Missouri*, was published in 2003, in time to inoculate Bicentennial tourists against sloppy history hawked by cash-hungry river towns. Twenty-seven computer-generated maps and a database, also accessible on the Web, show the course taken by the Corps of Discovery with all the travel distances and campsites. All told, Harlan's project pinpointed seventy Missouri campsites from the 1804 westward trip and fifteen in the return.

Besides what Harlan terms the "ghostly footprints" of the expedition across Missouri, his maps also show the transformation in a notoriously unruly river. In the 603.6-mile stretch of the river in Missouri, the river and islands once occupied 230,279 acres, according to Harlan's computations. Today's shrunken, deepened, channelized river needs just a third of that space: 70,026 acres. Two centuries ago, the Missouri averaged just under two thirds of a mile in width; now the waterway that detractors commonly refer to as a barge ditch averages just over two tenths of a mile wide.

These are just the sort of computations that conservationists wield in their drive for flow changes that mimic the pattern of the river's natural hydrograph. Let that river out of its cage, they plead; restore just a fraction of the backwaters and side channels that show up on Harlan's map. Then the wildlife can begin to flourish anew. That's the aim of the "spring rise" proposed by biologists and advocacy groups: Let go with a June pulse of water of 49,000 cubic feet per second—around 17,500 cubic feet more than normal—into the lower river, and we can see some *real* changes in the Missouri's health, they say.

Harlan, though, is not one to throw in with the advocates. Just as he is unconcerned about irritating local planners, he has no inclination to leap into the turbid political debate about the Missouri River's future. I discerned as much from the remark about Yuppies flopping around in the river. When I visit Harlan, it is clear that he has little regard for the aims of those bent on turning back the clock on Missouri River history.

"Social construction," he huffs.

JIM HARLAN WAS BORN IN 1951 in Cairo, Missouri (pop. 210), a town so tiny that it doesn't show on some of the maps that are the tools of his trade. He hunted, fished, and roamed the Missouri River shorelines, marked forever by his boyhood pursuits. "You grow up playing Cowboys and Indians on the bluffs, it carries over into your adult life," he says.

Indeed. Harlan spent nearly two decades in the U.S. Army on active duty and in the National Guard. He was a commo chief during Operation Desert Storm in Iraq in 1991 and earlier a staff sergeant in charge of maintaining the communications network for the Army Group, CEGSWA (Combat Equipment Group Southwest Asia). He also did duty on the northern coast of Panama, about which he is intentionally vague. Later, he returned to Panama to research the Kuna Indians, producing a master's thesis recounting the success of this shrewd and industrious tribe in protecting its land and culture from invaders.

On campus, they call Harlan "Sergeant." He searches his students' papers with the vigor of a drill instructor seeking passages cribbed from the Web. He is a soldier at heart, and he allows later that old Army colleagues are after him—despite having reached his fifties—to return to some duty about which he again is circumspect. Already, he has looked into taking a physical.

The old soldier is more at home prowling the Missouri River banks than cloistered in his office. When we disembark at the town of Rocheport, he locates a baseball diamond situated where the river once spread. Along Moniteau Creek, which flows into the Missouri, he locates the precise spot where the Corps of Discovery stopped. We're a pop fly from where Harlan repeated history.

On June 7, 1804, William Clark's journal noted their arrival at the wide mouth of "a Creek Called big monitu" marked by Indian paintings on a rocky bluff. Clark wrote of having "found there a Den of rattle Snakes, Killed 3." Exploring the spot nearly two hundred years later, Harlan happened on a gathering of rattlesnakes—testimony to the possibility that not as much has changed along the Missouri as we believe.

Not far from the rattlesnake den, we hear hammering deep in the weeds and follow the sound to its source. A pair of Missouri Department of Conservation carpenters are building walkways over wetlands at the foot of the bluffs. On top of the bluffs they already have completed an observation deck over a winding vista of the Missouri River and the bottomlands where it used to flow.

The pinewood perch overlooks Overton Bottoms, where the government is attempting a measured effort to reconnect the river with its floodplain. The Army Corps of Engineers and the U.S. Fish and Wildlife Service have bought some 5,000 acres here, and the Corps has dug a chute to reestablish backwater habitat. Of course nothing will get too real, as the Army engineers continue to raise and lower the water for ever-diminishing barge traffic.

But here and now, there is much to take in, including how this soldier-geographer thinks. Harlan notes that over the years, very few people troubled to make the climb we have just conquered. "Now there'll be a shitload," he says.

Of reconciliation, too, Harlan is suspicious. "The more urban the country gets, the more they want to turn the countryside into what looks like a park. It's pretty arrogant to say you're going to restore the river to its natural state. If you're going to restore it, pick everybody up, take them out of here, and come back in three hundred years or so and take a peek. That would accomplish what you have in mind."

FEARSOME RIVER

Leaving Harlan, I head to the river for a journey.

Fish can smell my fear as I float in a kayak toward my first Missouri River boil. I have survived big lake storms in Canada, squalls where I live on Chesapeake Bay, and journeys in Alaskan coastal waters only slightly above freezing. But surely I'm about to die in the ornery, rolling Missouri River, where my folly has me flopping around like the Yuppies Harlan scorns. The tales told about this river are scaremongering, legendary, and occasionally true.

"From the mouth of the Yellow Stone River . . . to its junction with the Mississippi, a distance of 2000 miles, the Missouri, with its boiling, turbid waters, sweeps off, in one unceasing current, and in the whole distance there is scarcely an eddy or resting place for a canoe," wrote a shaken George Catlin of his 1832 passage on the steamboat *Yellow Stone* to paint Indians unspoiled by white contact.

Father Jacques Marquette's first (and unrecorded) words upon seeing the riotous Missouri pour forth as he and Louis Joliet rounded a bend paddling down the Mississippi in 1673 might well have been, "Jesus Christ, Louie!"

We know that Marquette, a Jesuit missionary, did write these words: "I have seen nothing more frightful. A mass of large trees—real floating islands. They came rushing so impetuously that we could not, without great danger, expose ourselves to pass across."

The tales are told to this day. The Bicentennial is drawing the stories out, giving them a stage and listeners. "Don't go to the river to play," North Dakota folk singer Debi Rogers crooned to a symposium of river restorers in the autumn of 2003, singing her mother's warnings about the river. "There are tornadoes under the water. A log will get caught in your hair and you will be eaten by a giant paddlefish, which is related to the Loch Ness monster."

They aren't really tornadoes. But even channelized and ostensibly tamed, the Missouri River is in constant underwater disruption, so much so in places that trespassers feel they might, indeed, be sucked down in a maelstrom at any moment. In truth, what's happening down in the "River of Sand," another of the Missouri's appellations, is the creation of dunes by the fast current. As on land, the sand dunes shift and move. River dunes are carved and reshaped as water pours over the crest of one dune into the valley below, then rolls up the side of the next dune with enough force to boil on the surface like a pot of water waiting for pasta.

Farmers spread tales of this river's evil ways, warning that trouble will come of opening the door to Big Muddy's cage. Missouri officials preparing for Lewis and Clark Bicentennial tourism broadcast their worries of submerged rock dikes ready to wreck propellers and engine outdrives. There are also lurking sandbars, whirlpools, and floating trees—not to mention the occasional tows of barges as long as football fields.

This is not a river you take to casually.

Beneath me as I paddle is a nineteenth-century steamboat graveyard. I'm near Rattlesnake Springs, where the 250-foot-long *Amazon* went down in 1849. Nearby, the *Bedford* sank in 1840, harpooned by a snag.

More than a dozen passengers drowned, and a survivor lost his trunk with $6,000 in cash. "It was a dark and *very* stormy night," began an account of that tragedy.

Then there was the *Cora*, the third of its name to go down, around whose corpse silt, sand, and flotsam gathered to form Cora Island.

FLOATING BIG MUDDY

It's no wonder I had to travel all the way to Grafton, Illinois, along the Mississippi to find a kayak to paddle on the Missouri. With so much angst floating on this river, outfitters aren't rushing into business. Nor are sightseers demanding to get on the sometimes treacherous waterway that ferried Lewis and Clark to fame. Motorboats, too, can find themselves in a bind. On the entire 553 miles of river that run through the state of Missouri, I could find only three riverside outlets offering gas.

The dangers the modern Missouri poses to recreation are different from the tree-snags and shifting unpredictability endured by the keelboats of the explorers and fur traders and then the paddlewheelers. After snag eradication in the nineteenth century, the Army Corps of Engineers' aim early in the twentieth was a channel for barges. It has produced such a channel with a dauntless, indeed obsessive fervor, dumping millions of tons of rocks in the river to form dikes that shift the force of the current to the bluff side of the river. Army engineers strove to narrow and confine the channel by harnessing the force of the river's velocity to continuously scour away the sediment and thereby deepen the channel. The engineers have more than succeeded, hastening the river to six or eight miles per hour in some places over a nine-foot-deep channel.

I paddle with surprising ease and buoyancy through the river's swirls, wondering why such a grand resource is being wasted, for the Missouri's currents harbor danger but also opportunity for canoeists and adventure seekers with moderate skills. Big pleasure boat navigation dried up long ago, and few barges manage to use the channel that was carved to their order. Later on this journey, I have a date on a towboat pushing barges to see how barge operators envision the future of their industry. Today, over an afternoon paddle, I see but one johnboat, two fishermen on the bank—and nary a floating barge, though I pass the skeletons of abandoned ones. The river is a missed opportunity hereabouts, silent but for the controlled hum of its own heartbeat and the rush against the alien rocks of the dikes.

Scholars and dreamers speak of reconciliation along the river during the 2004–06 Lewis and Clark Bicentennial, and often their wishes include returning the Missouri, at least partly, to a state people can enjoy. Conservationists argue that lowering its dam-controlled flows in summers and letting more of the river spread out into its floodplain could achieve that goal. But watching as I have the hard rock realities of river politics, I wonder as I paddle if the reformers have much chance.

I pull out just after the Missouri River's convergence with the Mississippi. A park is being built here for the Bicentennial, and a monument to the great journey has already been erected. I read a legend proclaiming that "near here" Lewis and Clark spent the winter before completing "one of the most dramatic and significant episodes in our history."

When I return to the spot two years later, I learn the Missouri River and its powerful consort, the Mississippi, have attacked the misplaced Illinois memorial so relentlessly that it had to be first closed and later moved. In early 2003, the force of the current bit off 100 feet of bank. That proved more than a small headache for the Illinois Preservation

Society. For more than a year, as celebration fervor rose, visitors were barred from the circular monument with its flagpoles and eleven stone panels, signifying the present-day states along the expedition route. Finally, with help from the Army Corps of Engineers, the Illinoisans struck the monument and rebuilt it 200 feet inland.

The gods of the rivers have reason to seek revenge on the society Lewis and Clark ushered in. Just across the road from this historic junction decays an abandoned Superfund site, with some 250,000 tons of toxic metal wastes that, I would bet, remain where they are until the day great rivers rise to claim them.

"TO HAVE FUN" IN THE FLOODPLAIN

Thomas Jefferson ordered Lewis westward "for the purposes of commerce."

The explorers packed stores of trinkets and geegaws not just to assuage Indian tribes but to tempt them with the potential of trading in modern goods. Two centuries later, the Missouri's skimpy commerce from barge navigation—roughly $9 million annually in freight—remains the congressionally ordered reason that the Corps of Engineers operate their dams in ways that destroy wildlife along the river.

Upstream, hydropower provides several hundred million in annual revenues each year. But there's little benefit to taxpayers; the receipts cover the costs of maintenance and paying back old loans, with interest, and get swallowed up in the black hole of the federal treasury.

Meanwhile, in the Dakotas, a recreation industry that barely figured into planning for the river's mid-twentieth-century reengineering has sprouted into an $85-million-a-year enterprise.

As I travel westward along the river, packing historical accounts of those who journeyed here long ago, I find myself looking at the modern river as if through the eyes of the explorers who triggered its change. Just as Americans are grasping for lessons and heroes in commemorating a 200-year-old boat ride, Lewis and Clark would have learned a great deal about capitalism, political maneuvering, and how the American psyche evolved since the Age of Enlightenment.

The Corps of Discovery wouldn't have to travel far up the river to view a staggering amount of commerce in the floodplain, brand-spanking new development that defies nature. If the Army captains were retracing their journey today, before encountering the developers' earth movers, they'd get a lesson in their nation's warmaking history since pacifist-at-heart Jefferson dispatched them on their mission.

Just across the river from where the Corps of Discovery camped, the explorers might or might not succeed in getting the Boeing Co. to part with a few smart bombs from its factory in St. Charles County, Missouri. After all, those Teton Sioux upriver are a truculent lot. Jefferson may have been a technology buff, but all of the accumulated scientific wisdom of his day couldn't prepare him for bombs with computers guiding them, with the aid of satellites, to within ten feet of a target.

Nearby at Weldon Spring, the voyagers would record in their field notes a most unusual seven-story hill, the highest spot in the land. But this hill with the splendid view is far from natural; it is a monument to the bombmaking era of the twentieth century, packed with 1.5 million cubic yards of radioactive materials and wastes from the manufacture of dangerous chemicals and explosives.

A few miles upriver, Lewis could test the true worth of that universal letter of credit handed him by Jefferson—at the new Bentley dealership, where the price of a Bentley Arnage T is roughly one hundred times the $2,500 authorized to outfit the Corps of Discovery. But Lewis might well conclude that even more startling was the fact that a decade earlier, the Bentley showroom on One Arnage Boulevard was submerged under eight feet of muddy, sewage-laden water from the Great Flood of '93.

Smack in the floodplain, developers and their local government allies have conspired to build what they proudly proclaim as the world's biggest strip mall—with more than $2 billion spent on offices, shopping centers, and a sprawling circus of franchise eateries—on land in St. Louis County that was under water in 1993. Once more, they have ignored the reality of risk and spurned growth management while maneuvering to control the fickle Missouri River.

This area used to be called Gumbo Flats, a moniker that would ring truer to that half-breed fiddler Cruzatte and the frontiersmen in the Discovery Corps than would Chesterfield Valley, its name today. Where only a short decade ago floodwaters raged, I now count the legion of big-box stores and franchises that provision twenty-first-century Americans from Atlantic to Pacific.

MY QUEST HAS TAKEN ME to Gumbo Flats on a late summer day in the company of Wayne Freeman, who is executive director of the Great Rivers Habitat Alliance, a conservation advocacy outfit in St. Louis. I'd known Wayne, a landscape architect, for his clever work saving land along another great river, the Mississippi, and designing on the Alton, Illinois, riverfront a marina that is both utilitarian and attractive.

Now Freeman is trying to rein in the sprawl kings of St. Louis, and not too successfully, I have to tell him. Not being in the sensitive wing of the environmental movement, Wayne doesn't seem to mind being called a loser in this engagement.

"Decadence, opulence, stupidity," he says, when I ask him what he thinks of one of the tonier projects being carved out of land where flood-waters had raged. In the "Axis of Sprawl," as he describes it, developers and municipalities are tempting fate while hoodwinking taxpayers into bankrolling improvements in their Monarch Levee, a massive new engi-neering feat to contain the river.

"Here's what pisses me off," Freeman begins. "The developers pro-mote development. They build the levee. Then they get the Corps of Engineers to certify the levee. We promote development, we build the levee and get taxpayers to pay for it."

In the Flood of '93—a reference point in every discussion about de-velopment—more than one thousand levees failed in the Midwest. Sev-enty thousand buildings were damaged; fifty people died. The tally of damage came in at $12 billion. Along Chesterfield Valley, a small hole in the Monarch Levee widened swiftly to a foot-long gash. Within a half hour, a swath was blown out by the Missouri River, living up to its repu-tation for explosiveness. The Monarch was regarded as a 100-year levee, meaning that it was built to hold back a flood with only a 1 percent like-lihood of occurring every year. Since then, the community has worked to bolster the Monarch, widening it and raising its height by another six feet to a point, they say, where it can be called a levee capable of with-standing a 500-year flood.

"Bring it on," David Human, who heads the local levee district, told a colleague at the *St. Louis Post-Dispatch* in 2003.

Locals protect all that vast new floodplain development that con-tributes mightily to their tax base. But those who watched the frequent flooding in the last half of the twentieth century doubt the capacity of humans to hold back the tempestuous Missouri. Even if the new levee holds, it will jeopardize landowners elsewhere on the rivers. Why? Because water backs up at a levee, heightening chances for flooding upstream. Then, after flowing by the levee, it picks up velocity.

That's a fact Missourians prefer to ignore. In 2003, the *St. Louis Post-Dispatch* hired Saint Mary's University in Minnesota, a leader in river studies, to analyze development in the midwestern states walloped by the flood ten years before. With its Geographic Information Systems—methods of computer and map analysis—the study concluded that Missouri had developed vastly more of the floodplain in the past decade than any other state: some 4,200 acres. Nebraska was second with 2,224, followed by Illinois, Iowa, and Wisconsin, each with between 1,000 and 2,000 acres of new development.

The explorers surely would take note of the political intricacies surrounding all this construction. Their report would be read with curiosity by Jefferson, who fretted early in the nation's history about land being held in the hands of too few of its citizens. He also cast a wary eye on taxation and debt, once writing:

> This is the tendency of all human governments. A departure from principle in one instance becomes a precedent for a second, that second for a third, and so on 'til the bulk of the society is reduced to be mere automatons of misery, to have no sensibilities left but for sinning and suffering. And the forehorse of this frightful team is public debt. Taxation follows that, and in its train wretchedness and oppression.

Taxpayers surely are burdened, if not oppressed, by protecting that Bentley dealership and the other new developments. To heighten the levee, local officials relied on a fiscal device called tax increment financing, allowing property and sales taxes collected in a certain area to be directed to building the infrastructure needed for development. But it's not just local taxpayers: the Army Corps of Engineers agreed to pay nearly $50 million for work on the Monarch Levee.

I am reminded of the words of the late Illinois state senator Hudson Sours, a noted conservative from Peoria, whose fiscal sensibilities impressed me when I was a young reporter in the 1970s. "It all comes from the same Jaspers," said he, referring to American taxpayers.

Seeing that much drained from the budget of their sister agency might or might not have been troubling to Lewis and Clark. But leaving erstwhile Gumbo Flats, the explorers would certainly have commented on the name of one of the companies that set in motion the frenzied development: THF Realty.

Especially Clark, who would return to the St. Louis area as territorial governor and live out the rest of his life near the Missouri, would have been intrigued by what those letters improbably stand for: The corporate name is To Have Fun.

MISSOURI'S GIRL TARZAN

In mid-twentieth-century Missouri River history recorded in newspapers and journals, one item sticks in my mind: a yellowed *St. Louis Post-Dispatch* clipping from October 1950 with the headline: "Tarzan-style Girl Reported on Steed Island." It begins:

> ST. CHARLES, Mo.—The mystery of the flying saucer has been displaced here by the mystery of the flying woman. A slim young female in blue jeans reportedly is inhabiting swampy Steed's Island and traveling Tarzan-style through the trees with a knife in one hand.

The unbylined story describes how an islander with the name of Harry Perry encountered the woman perched high up in a tree after watching her crawl through tall grass.

It goes on: "Perry, who is in his middle twenties and has a wife and several children living at his island home, said the woman moved through the tree from limb to limb. When he asked her what she was doing, he declared she let out a Tarzan-like whoop and made a threatening gesture with the knife."

The report also quotes Bennie Barnes, "a Negro who lives on another, smaller island," as saying that he had seen her swim across the river channel. Likewise, fishermen and operators of a fruit stand on a nearby road also had seen Tarzan-girl, who was described as in her mid-twenties, trim and wearing a white beret on her black hair.

3

TWO-FACED RIVER

The river glideth at its own sweet will.

—William Wordsworth

IN WHICH WE VISIT A FARMER
WITH A MESSAGE AND A RIVER PIRATE

Back water rising, come in my windows and door
The back water rising, come in my windows and door
I leave with a prayer in my heart, back water won't rise no more.

LANDING
IN FLOODPLAIN FARM FIELDS

T HE MISSOURI RIVER has been tamed, disabused of its spreading, meandering ways, disinherited of most of its islands, wetlands, and junglelike canopies of trees where flying women could soar.

By the mid-1800s, a half century after Lewis and Clark opened the way westward, signs of people and progress were visible along the river. Samuel Gardner, a Virginian, noted the rapid development in his diary during a pleasure trip from Columbia, Missouri, to Fort Leavenworth, Kansas, aboard the steamer *Ben Bolt* in 1855.

He wrote of "a most beautiful and rich county and where a few years ago, some ten or twelve, the red man roamed over a track of this unculti-vated region, now traversed by innumerable roads and dotted all over with handsome farm houses and with cultivated farms. The march of civilization is moving westward with rapid strides and this glorious country fast and rapidly filling with enterprising, useful citizens, and the poor Indian fleeing into the wind and seeking a more congenial home in the territory of Nebraska and Kansas . . ."

The farmland about which Gardner swelled with pride was owned by ancestors of Tom Waters, whose family have been warriors over the years in the fight to tame the Missouri River and keep it subservient to their needs. Generations of farmers in his family have been awakened nights by the thunderous echo of their land dropping in the Missouri River. Like his ancestors, Waters was taught to fear what he calls the "two-faced river."

"You look at it, it's pretty and awe-inspiring," he tells me, when my quest takes me to his farm in Orrick, Missouri, twenty-five miles east of Kansas City. "But that river has the heart of a tiger; it's angry, mean-spirited. Ask people who have lost their land or had their loved ones torn out of a cemetery."

Farmers I talk to along the river echo Waters's remarks. In their minds, the Missouri's turbid, muddy waters must remain controlled by levees and dams, both for personal safety and to prevent the river from swallowing their property and clogging their drainage.

The coiner of the name Old Misery for the Missouri must have been a farmer fighting to hold the river back. To hear farmers and their advocates tell it, the river is a fearsome, useless creature, to stay away from.

Early last century, Sioux City mayor Stewart Gilman told a congressional committee, "About all the river is good for now is for a despondent farmer to commit suicide in." Kansas senator John James Ingalls, known for his pontifications, remarked that the Missouri "is too thick for navigation and too thin for cultivation."

Tom Waters's ranch would be a tidy mouthful if that bad river ever really escapes its cage. It was bad enough in '93, when the big flood destroyed his soybeans and corn. Land along the river remained underwater or soggy until August, like in the old days when farmers like to say they weren't sure whether they'd be raising corn or catfish. For Waters, a seventh-generation farmer, the flood was a slammer. He farms 3,500 acres, planted in genetically engineered Roundup Ready soybeans that keep his fields hound's-tooth clean and corn that is genetically modified to kill pests and anything else with the temerity to squat in his fields. He's a farmer who believes in technology, whether in growing grain or harnessing a perverse body of water.

And to him that river's a devil. Tom, who was born in 1963, has heard about its devious meanderings his whole life. When we drive around in his pickup, he shows me the little house where his grandfather, Luman Offutt, would lie in bed and listen to chunks of his land sloughing into the river. Waters is a big fellow, six foot three, but he speaks of the Missouri like a child of the bogeyman. "I grew up learning to be afraid of the river, and I am," he tells me.

It was his grandfather who told him about its history, about the Army Corps of Engineers showing up with their pile drivers to pin down that willful river, about bringing cherry pies back from the steamboats early last century. It was old Luman Offutt who pushed his grandson into farm politics, made him go to a meeting after the Flood of '93 and went along himself, and then got Tom appointed to a steering committee that formed the Missouri Levee and Drainage District Association.

All of a sudden, Waters is president of the whole thing. When a New York television producer phones the Kansas City Chamber of Commerce looking for a farmer in the floodplain, Waters finds himself on the CBS *Early Show* as the water rises again a year after the flood. Not only does Waters remain poised on national television, he stays on message for all the groups he belongs to. "Last summer I lost my entire crop there," he told Paula Zahn. "I've got my corn planted [in the same floodplain again] so we're taking a little bit bigger risk than in a normal year. But I believe in keeping the land in production. This nation leads the world in agricultural production. And part of that leadership is . . . this fine farmland in the floodplains and the river valleys. So to ask us to take that ground out of production and give up that fertility is—it's kind of like asking Tonya Harding to skate with that broken shoestring."

Soon, reporters from everywhere are calling Waters on this and that about the Missouri River, and now he's chairman of still another organization, this one made up of Missouri and Arkansas farmers. When I visited his farm, Waters was helping out in the campaign of Republican senatorial hopeful Jim Talent, who would win. Later, I ran into him in Washington testifying on behalf of the Farm Bureau in a congressional hearing with one theme: Reel in the Endangered Species Act, a piece of legislation that farmers uniformly despise.

"I feel like a pawn in a political chess game with my land and the land of my neighbors as the prize," he says that day.

Waters approaches no fight with more fervor than the campaign against the U.S. Fish and Wildlife Service, which when we meet is finishing a plan to change the flow of the river. Send a pulse of water down the river springtime—a spring rise—and you recreate the backwaters and replenish the wildlife we sacrificed so carelessly over the years, government biologists say. But when Tom Waters hears the phrase "spring rise," in his mind he sees croplands flooded and that riverside black gold of his washing away. Just as vexing—and something nobody understands, he says—is what the high waters do to farmers' precious drainage systems.

On Waters's spread, gravity carries rainwater from hills through canals toward a gated, eight-foot-wide-culvert at the river's edge. But when the Missouri is high, the pressure of its flow holds the gates closed and backs up water in fields. More than a few days' soaking can stunt and even ruin a crop, which is why Waters and his allies are bent on blocking these emerging plans for springtime pulses of water into the river.

"This is good stuff down here. It just makes you sick when people talk about flooding it and taking it out of production," he tells me.

Good, indeed. His riverside bottomlands, thirty miles east of Kansas City, typically yield 150 to 175 bushels of corn per acre and 60 bushels of soybeans. At last count when I visited, the average in Missouri was 133 bushels of corn and 38 bushels of soybeans. So this is land worth fighting for, even if that means enduring the enmity of environmental advocates. For the reward of Waters's clan and farmers along the Missouri for all the aggravation their ancestors endured is almost too grand to hope for: thousands of acres of rich tillable land, thanks to bank stabilization by the Army Corps of Engineers and the generosity of American taxpayers.

Another bad flood, back in 1881, triggered one of the early campaigns to civilize the marauding river. Corps major Charles Suter saw his agency's prized river control bank-securing experiments washed away like Tinker Toys. It was time, he said, to get the Missouri "pegged down." By then, the Indian threat was mostly behind them and settlers along the river wanted dependable, profitable farming. Of course the river had everything to say about prosperity, gobbling chunks of land and some damn fine topsoil. In a year's time, Suter told farmers, 11 billion cubic feet of silt flowed out of the mouth of the river—enough rich earth to cover a square mile to a depth of 200 feet.

Farmers saw Army engineers as friends and protectors, as they do to this day. So they embraced Suter's plans for building dikes to cut down on the curvature of bends and concentrate the river's many streams into one flow, as narrow as possible. Over the years, stone revetments built parallel to the river for further narrowing would not just protect farm land but create more of it as silt collected.

Now, as Waters sees it, the government biologists and their environmentalist pals are trying to undo a century of progress by letting the river act like it used to. By carving chutes to let the river sneak back out of its bed. By busting holes in those dikes to make little pools for fish. Waters is a soft-spoken fellow; he learned to stay calm during EMT training for his volunteer fire department. But he gets mad, roiling inside like the river, and this anger is why he's gone so many nights at meetings, away from his family and not getting paid a nickel.

"Not only are we physically undoing what we've done, Mother Nature is trying to undo it, too. If we don't repair these places that erode, eventually those places will get out of hand. We're headed back to laying awake and hearing that river break away again," he tells me.

Waters doesn't hold much hope for reconciliation between upper basin and lower basin states as they fight with one another over not just the environment but over the water itself. The scrap for water has gone on for decades and will continue, he says. He sees more likelihood of fixing the river's environment—though that doesn't mean backing off his argument that the Fish and Wildlife people haven't proved a thing as yet when it comes to the merit of their new plans. "I don't think they have the data to back it up. I think there's a lot of science on this thing that needs to be done, and when it's finished, and if we find out what they are talking about is not a pipe dream, I think you'll see the sides moving closer together. You know what they say about Missouri. It's the Show-Me state. When somebody says you have to do something, you say, 'Prove it.'"

A MORNINGSTAR RISES

For all Tom Waters's determination, the notion that the Missouri is a malevolent force is colliding with another view: the Missouri as an untapped recreation source that could be drawing boaters, anglers, and bird-watchers. I have been hearing about this view on the good ship *MorningStar*, with Captain Jeff McFadden at the helm, which at this moment in my journey is scooting its square bow close enough to the rock-armored south bank of the Missouri River in Kansas City so that I can leap off to inspect Berkeley Park.

From previous boat trips along the Missouri River, one of them aboard *MorningStar*, I have a jaundiced view of how Kansas City has treated the fabled waterway that bisects its town. Finally, early in the twenty-first century, I hear of a few small remedies, among them a pedestrian bridge and the port authority's construction of Berkeley Park. So I'm prepared to change my mind.

There is no boat ramp or dock enabling access to the park, but that is not a surprise. Kansas City never has provided a civilized way for people to get on the Missouri River. In 2003, the city completed a single boat ramp, kept closed when I visited except to a few special people given keys.

After a treacherous climb up 100 feet of jagged rocks, I arrive to find dozens of lamp posts, a 16-foot-wide walkway, and straight rows of trees on parched grass. But something is missing: character, for one thing. For another, restrooms. Then I notice what really is lacking: life. There are no humans in any direction: no joggers, walkers, picnickers, Frisbee tossers, bird-watchers, dog walkers, stroller pushers, skateboarders. Not a soul, not even a squirrel. For a moment, I think that the park, like the boat ramp, is unopened or somehow restricted, but I know that is not true. Having been on the river all day out of the shout of news, I begin to worry that a disaster has occurred, perhaps a terrorist attack, and that people have fled to shelter.

I fairly run back to *MorningStar*. McFadden, who has flung an anchor in the mud to keep his vessel steady in the current, receives my report while perched on the bow beneath his straw brim.

"You wouldn't expect any people to be there on a beautiful Saturday afternoon, would you? This is Kansas City," he replies.

Nowhere along the Missouri is the disconnection between the river and its people more acute than in Kansas City. Among the few dedicated to remedying matters is McFadden, an irreverent, twice-wounded Vietnam veteran who marches to his own drummer.

"My goal," he proclaimed on one of our excursions, "is reconnecting people with the river, one family at a time."

To further that goal, McFadden, who was born in 1947, all but abandoned his telephone installation business, which meant nearly a 75 percent cut in pay. He assembled his pontoon tour boat with $1,800 worth of red aluminum sheet metal and roughly that much again in windows and doors with tempered glass. He earned a captain's license decreeing him a master of steam and power vessels to 25 gross registered tons. And he filed the papers to establish River Tours Inc., which, I am startled to learn, is the only such charter boat operation on his stretch of the river.

But the absence of a tour boat trade is not for want of scenery.

"It has been, heretofore, very erroneously represented to the world, that the scenery on this river was monotonous, and wanting in picturesque beauty. This intelligence is surely incorrect," wrote the eighteenth-century painter Catlin of the river that gave him many pictures.

And despite its alterations, much of the Missouri River retains its intrinsic beauty. Bluffs framing the stream in central Missouri rise 200 feet skyward. During summer low flows, sandbars open themselves for frolicking. Flying low and slow, blue herons alight to fish bar after bar. Now the Fish and Wildlife Service is buying a few swaths of land from farmers and bulldozing portions of levees to let tiny portions of the river nourish its floodplains.

For would-be entrepreneurs, the problem is attitudinal as well as environmental. People along the Missouri River have become conditioned to viewing it as a dangerous, disagreeable ditch. That is especially true of officials and entrenched interests, the sorts that McFadden has battled to set up his business.

Having fallen under the spell of the Missouri, this battle-tried veteran is in the vanguard challenging the perception common along much of 732 miles of the Lower Missouri that the river is no good for recreation. McFadden is not the joiner type who'd behave at a Sierra Club meeting or attire himself in Gore-Tex and khakis. But he's taught himself about the river and its history, and along with his charts and ship logs, he carries a bound volume of the National Academy of Sciences' 2002 benchmark report concluding that the river's ecosystem needs emergency government intervention to survive. Don't expect to find that volume in any Army Corps of Engineers vessel plying the Missouri.

In the spirit of Thomas Jefferson's instructions to Lewis and Clark, McFadden has commerce in mind. "This ecosystem has value, but since it's not in the marketplace, it doesn't get valued," he says, referring to priorities along the river.

He is a man who will make his grievances known. When we first met, I recalled to him my first Missouri journey two years earlier, on the towboat full of politicians, farm business leaders, and barge industry representatives. I happened to mention that a peculiar Army green vessel had dogged our journey.

"That was me, in *Tugboat Annie*," he replied. "This river is mine; they can't keep me off of it."

Aboard *MorningStar*, we pass by Liberty Bend, or more properly, the former Liberty Bend, which shows us how Army engineers teamed up with local communities to yank the meandering Missouri into rigid formation.

On April 16, 1949, a Corps survey boat, the *Sgt. Floyd*, ferried civic leaders to this spot for the planting of 1,500 sticks of dynamite. At 11:30 A.M., on a perfect spring morning, *Kansas City Star* president Roy Roberts shouted "Let 'er go" and detonated a blast that was photographed from an airplane by the *St. Louis Post-Dispatch*'s Lloyd Spainhower. Looking at his photo alongside old river maps, I notice that the plume it showed was shaped like the river bend blown to oblivion. The *Post-Dispatch*'s Richard Baumhoff provided the words:

Mud, sticks, debris and doubtless a few catfish soared several hundred feet toward the cloudless sky in a broad column. Then clear water churned up like a giant showerbath and turned the freshly graded ground around the channel into mud. An army launch with news-reel photographers had to duck the debris quickly. With an unexpected rush, the spectators surged past a handful of military police, running like participants in a new gold rush to the brink of the channel.

It was fervor, fueled by the Army Corps of Engineers, to take hold of that accursed stream and whip it like grabbing a snake by the tail and snapping. If there were any sardonic Jeff McFaddens around, they would have joked that the Corps brought so much firepower that it damn near buried its own boat with debris. When the debris had settled, eager Kansas Citians looked out on a ramrod-straight channel in a river that civilization had just shortened by four miles. Gone were two tricky bends through which that promiscuous river no longer could cavort.

McFadden will tell you the attack on the Missouri typifies Kansas City's relationship with the river. He can't understand why the river is still run with barge navigation as its central purpose. He scoffs at farmers like Tom Waters who argue that the river was rightly chopped and sculpted for barge traffic so as to keep the railroad's shipping rates down.

"If we really believe all this free market malarkey, then why are we subsidizing one industry to keep the profits down in another industry?" McFadden demands. "There is nothing more flexible than conservative philosophy," he says of the perceived incongruity.

That 1949 blast was just another skirmish in a long war. In the late 1870s, the Kansas City Commercial Club began campaigning for channelizing the river to spur barge traffic. The railroad was fast supplanting river navigation as the way westward, and Kansas City saw its development dream fading. Robert Kelley Schneiders's *Unruly River* (1999) concludes that Congress never would have provided funds for a project of such dubious value had the Kansas Citians not lobbied persistently.

In 1891, Commercial Club president G. F. Putnam laid the unvarnished hopes of the Kansas City promoters on the table. Opening a convention of the Missouri River Improvement Association, he said: "The Commercial Club does not claim to be above the inspiration of selfish motives. Neither do the people of Kansas City claim to be too magnanimous to be mindful of their own interests."

Money to channelize the river began to flow, but it would be halted by Congress a few years hence amid reservations about what looked to be a boundless pork project. The work might have proceeded more swiftly were it not for a stubborn Army engineer in Kansas City, Lieutenant Colonel Herbert L. Deakyne. Kansas City boosters responded with outrage when Deakyne led a study to the conclusion that barge traffic probably never would be sufficient to merit the government spending that locals wanted on the Missouri. He recommended that the government abandon channelization and instead restrict its work on the river to removing snags.

Deakyne would lose the fight, but he is a hero to McFadden. If one day his business outgrows *MorningStar*, McFadden has a new name in mind for the forty-footer he might build: the *Herbert L. Deakyne*.

MCFADDEN WASN'T BORN with river water for blood. He says you couldn't get his father, Leville Freeman McFadden, a Veterans Administration adjudicator, near water. As a child, young Jeff played in Town Fork of Brush Creek, a body of water that Kansas City could handle and did—filling its banks and bed with concrete until nothing but a trickle remained.

"I could already see that this is dumb, this isn't working. What's wrong with having some life in a creek?" he said.

As a boy, McFadden followed that trickle until it got loose again, broadening with some deep pools before reaching the Blue River and then the Missouri.

In four hours of boating the Missouri with McFadden on Saturday afternoon, we have seen one jet ski and one red canoe with paddlers fore and aft. "We're ten miles from a city of a million people. Where are they?" the captain asks.

He wants to introduce those invisible people to their river, he says, but Kansas City officials offer little assistance because no ramps suitable for boarding his boat exist where he wants to operate. They fear liability, they tell McFadden, who's impatient with their excuses and tells them so.

"If I can get this boat in front of people, I can make a living. I can fill this boat up all day long," McFadden says. "But we don't let people go down to the river; we don't want them there. If Kansas City had a nickel's worth of sense, they could have made something of all this."

MCFADDEN IS AS restless for action as he was in Vietnam on the day he almost died. It was May 1968, near the end of the months-long battle for Dak To. The enemy had his infantry unit pinned down and all but sleepless for days, and Sergeant McFadden had put up with enough. "They keep you up all night for a week. You get tired of them doing that shit to you."

He'd been in 'Nam nearly a year already and been wounded once. He was due to come home in two months, and probably could have laid low—but they kept messing with his head. After wearing you out, they run over you and your buddies, he knew.

McFadden was mad when he stuck his head out, hoping to get a fix on the enemy position and call in an air strike. He stayed out of cover too long, and they got a fix on him. The mortar landed a few feet away, and it was like getting hit in the head with a nine-pound sledgehammer. The shrapnel itself wasn't as bad as the force of the explosion, which left him concussed so badly he threw up for fifteen days straight. When he stopped, he was still a mess and down to 120 pounds, a quarter of his weight gone.

The Army gave him two Purple Hearts and an Army commendation medal with a "V" for valor. But bureaucracy never works out well for McFadden; they lost his papers. After getting blown up in May, he didn't get paid until November. He and his young wife lived off scraps.

Now, McFadden is getting no help from another bureaucracy. Over the two years we spoke, I could see it weighing on him. "I've met nothing but obstacles, and I haven't asked for tax breaks or anything they give the big developers," he said. "Operating in Kansas City was a significant part of my business plan. But they just can't see the value of putting people on the river. I've about decided that they flat don't want me there."

McFadden, who is now divorced ("Try living with a guy with post-traumatic stress disorder," he explains), lives near the town of Richmond, Missouri, on forty acres with five donkeys, two sheep, one goat, three dogs, and roughly ten cats. But he longs to be on the Missouri, and he insists that he'll win out in the end.

When I phoned McFadden a year later, he told me he'd just knocked a hole as big as a bushel basket in his hull when he'd struck a piece of concrete dumped into the Kansas River. It would have meant disaster for most vessels. "They'd have had a good chance of looking at the bottom," he said. But *MorningStar* rides on pontoons, so McFadden and his six-pack of passengers made it back to port, which spoke well of both boat and captain. His vessel would be out of water for repairs, but McFadden was undeterred.

"I plan to make a living doing this. It took me a long time to figure out what I wanted to do when I grew up. Everybody describes the river as ugly and dead and useless and only fit for being a highway, and nobody wants to take a vacation on a highway," he said.

"But I think the river is beautiful. Back in Lewis and Clark's era, this was probably the richest ecosystem on the North American continent. It has this great desire to turn itself back into its glorious self, and no matter what Kansas City does, the Missouri River is doing that every day."

∾ PADDLING ∾

THE ROBBING OF HARDIN CEMETERY

Whole cemeteries have been undermined and swept away by the ghoulish waters of the stream. The Missouri River is a regular body snatcher.
—Stanley Vestal, *The Missouri*

FIGURE 1. At Hardin Cemetery in western Missouri, site of the worst cemetery disaster in recorded American history, recovered headstones were placed side-by-side and remains reinterred after the Missouri River's Great Flood of 1993. (Photo courtesy Bill Lambrecht)

At the east end of the Hardin, Missouri, Cemetery the headstones line up on parched field a pace apart like pieces on a chessboard. Seven rows contain from twelve to twenty-one engraved stones honoring women, men, and children on whom death called in the nineteenth and twentieth centuries.

Ura Pearl Hayes, 1879–1945, holds the corner of the first row.

No bodies lie beneath these memorial stones. At the opposite end of the cemetery, people they honored—and the remains of many more—have been reburied beneath 12-by-18-inch tablets marked *Unknown*.

Hardin Cemetery was reconfigured after the worst cemetery disaster in recorded American history. In 1993, the Missouri River climbed out of its own entombment to blow levees and rampage across the land. The river's distance from the cemetery—eight miles—did not diminish the damage, reminding America's heartland that a mighty force runs through it.

The river washed out 793 of 1,576 graves, sending burial vaults floating on currents across corn and soybean fields, some right out of Ray County. With homes, streets, fields, and churches inundated, the Missourians hadn't immediately noticed the graveyard disaster. Then the stories spread: of a vault crashing into a fishing boat; of an "ice chest" that turned out to be the casket of a child; of a woman's body afloat, her head still resting on a pillow.

The search-and-recovery operation spanned 64,000 acres, retrieving bodies and their parts, as well as tombstones and caskets, from as far as 30 miles away. Along a fence row a half-mile east of the cemetery, a row of skulls collected. Remains of 645 people were recovered in the August heat by volunteers and funeral directors from across the state. One hundred twenty bodies were identified, thanks to relatives who endured visits to a makeshift morgue at a farm, where they examined burial garments.

Bodies or remains of 525 never were identified; for some 148 nothing surfaced that could be identified.

To all of them, a monument has been dedicated.

A decade later, Ray County coroner Dean Snow, who operates the funeral home in Hardin, told me that he hasn't forgotten the disaster—though he wishes he had.

"A lot of the people in the cemetery who became displaced, I buried them in the first place," he said.

Snow, who was born in 1946, has since signed on to the government's Disaster Mortuary Operational Response Team. To help recover and identify human remains, he's worked a train wreck in Illinois, a cemetery flood in Georgia, and air crashes as far away as Guam. He leads his regional team, which is coordinated by the Department of Homeland Security.

But no horror has surpassed his hometown disaster, when the mighty Missouri rose eight miles to carry the dead on its crest.

"It's still going on," Snow said. "People are still calling to say they've found skeletal remains."

4

ROLLING ON THE RIVER

Your true pilot cares nothing about anything on earth but the river, and his pride in his occupation surpasses the pride of kings.

—Mark Twain, *Life on the Mississippi* (1883)

IN WHICH WE RIDE A TOW PAST THE GHOSTS OF
STEAMBOATS, COTTONWOODS, AND SCHEMES
FOR TAMING THIS WILD RIVER

*Big boat is up the river
Lord, stuck on a bank of sand
I'll never see my baby
I'll never make that land.*

LANDING
CLIMBING THE MISSOURI

CAPTAIN HARRIS PATTON GERLACH celebrates his forty-eighth birthday in the wheelhouse of the towboat *Lauren D*, pushing barges laden with fertilizer up the Missouri River toward Kansas City. He is thrilled with the gift that has come his way. "The good Lord is looking out for me. He sent me a little water for my birthday," Gerlach tells me the day my quest washes me up on his tow.

Actually, it was the Army Corps of Engineers that dispatched the birthday gift into the Missouri River. The Corps and the navigation industry always have been buddies; Army engineers were the enablers of the barge industry, pegging down the Lower Missouri into a tight channel. In the modern age, the Corps' bible, the *Master Manual*, anoints navigation as its first priority, saying Congress has ordered it thus.

The captain's suggestion that the extra water was ordained on high is not that far off. The federal government has statutory control over rivers deemed navigable. Its agent is the Corps of Engineers, the Army's $4 billion civil works agency, a department that technically is under executive branch control but has become closer over the years to Congress. But the specific orders enabling the birthday boy's excursion didn't come from the White House or Congress or any historic Washington edifice. They came from a black brick building in suburban Omaha, Nebraska, where the Army Corps of Engineers Reservoir Control Center is situated. Shouts about the Missouri River's petulance have also been known to emanate from that building. These days, decisions about the water's flow are e-mailed upriver to Gavins Point Dam in Yankton, South Dakota.

A number almost always containing five digits shows up on a screen in the Gavins Point control, where it is heeded not by a crew of muscled workers who crank gates open or closed, as I had imagined. A single operator in the control room retypes the number—typically in the vicinity of 33,000 cubic feet per second—and hits the "enter" button on the keyboard. Instantly, 10-foot-high, 4-ton wicket gates inside 54,000-horsepower turbines open ever so slightly, like Venetian blinds, allowing additional water to gush forth from Lewis and Clark Lake.

THE LAST CRUISE

That's what happened a week ago, which is how long it takes water to travel some 700 miles downriver to where the *Lauren D*, a 135-foot-long vessel operated by Blaske Towing of Alton, Illinois, is steaming. Captain Gerlach, who is clad in a garish red St. Louis Cardinals T-shirt, has more than one reason to celebrate: His journey is the first by any sizable barge tow in a month, as Gerlach tells another captain.

"Here we go again. They finally got those birds hatched out and we've got some water," he says eagerly into his VHF radio.

The birds are the piping plover and the least tern, both federally protected species. Some one thousand of each remain in Missouri River environs. The plover skitters about the shoreline; terns swoop like diving swallows. Together, they are confounding a navigation industry operating since the fur trappers plied the Missouri River; they are threatening barge operators with their own extinction.

Six weeks earlier, Army engineers had ordered the flow from Gavins Point Dam dialed back to avoid washing away tern and plover nests. And the water had receded in the latest—but definitely not the last—confrontation between the barge industry and conservationist armies battling to restore the river's wildlife. Now, most chicks have flown from their nests, the water is coursing down the river, and a big boat is hazarding a run up the Missouri. But even on his birthday, Gerlach can't relax: He must keep an eye on the depth finder or risk the fate suffered not just by hundreds of vessels over the years but also by a sister boat a week before.

While heading downriver, the *Omaha*, a smaller Blaske vessel that can operate in shallower water, ran into trouble of the sort no one wants. Smack in the middle of the channel at Mile 60, a rock in unanticipated shallows punched a hole in the flotation tank of one of the barges in her tow. The barge began to sink. The *Omaha* moved the rest of the barges in the tow to safety, then called in a crane to unload 8,000 bushels of soggy, ruined soybeans. It was a costly mess, at least a $50,000 loss for Roger Blaske and his boys.

On his birthday, Gerlach says he is not worried, even though he can envision threats around every bend as he shoves 600 feet of barges in barely navigable waters. In one scenario he especially wishes to avoid, his tow would smack bottom, barges breaking loose from the jarring bounce and floating downstream, out of control.

Sure, the river is under the control of Army engineers. But the fluctuations are ungodly. Gerlach has seen the water rise eight feet in twenty-four hours. This season the depth gauge at St. Charles, Missouri, read 29.4 feet on May 10. On August 20, the same gauge said 11.6 feet. The drop was nearly 18 feet.

These days, it's all about having enough water, which is why Gerlach wishes aloud that the Corps had released even more of it from Gavins Point. Four or five times, the towboat bumps bottom en route to Kansas City, once so forcefully that it frays a cable that tethers the barges to the boat, the kind of development that can trigger trouble. But unlike the *Omaha* last week, *Lauren D* experiences no mini-disaster.

Gerlach, who lives in Holly Grove, Arkansas, has worked on towboats since he signed on Mississippi River vessels at age seventeen. He knows well that in the time it takes a federal judge to say the words "endangered species," barge navigation along the Missouri could go the way of the steamboat industry in the late nineteenth century. Gerlach also lends a sympathetic ear to the talk about restoring the Missouri and its wildlife. He's an outdoors lover, a squirrel hunter who puts down the gun to watch the squirrels cavort.

"I love this river," he says, his eyes riveted on the depth finder, steady as she goes at 17 feet. "But I'd hate to see it shut down."

Except, perhaps, for endangered wildlife and Indian tribes, the navigation industry has the most riding on the Missouri River. The flow alterations being weighed in every branch of government this new century mean two things. First is providing more water in the lower river during spring—a spring rise—to approximate the river's natural snow-fed surge. Second is systematically cutting back the river's flow in summer—as heat and reduced tributary flow would do in the natural order—to keep sandbars exposed and safe for nesting birds and slow the water so the endangered pallid sturgeon and other fish can spawn and their offspring survive. It's that pattern the Fish and Wildlife Service has been pressuring the Army Corps of Engineers to adopt in a war of wills that has continued since the late 1980s. Inability to operate profitably—perhaps at all—is what that pattern means for the barge industry along the Missouri River. Most barges were unable to run the river in the low water of the summer of 2002, and the big boats were forced off the river again a year later, albeit for just three days, after a federal judge ordered the water levels lowered to protect wildlife.

The industry is under assault from the Fish and Wildlife Service, from conservationists, and from recreation interests in upper basin states. The barge companies and their allies counter with many arguments of their own: Barges give farmers shipping options for their grain; they keep down rail rates; they even help to preserve national security. But underlying them all is history. Since recorded history began—on the Missouri, that's

Lewis and Clark—navigation and commerce have flowed along the river. Chris Brescia, a principal strategist for the barge industry as president of MARC 2000, a river industry trade association in St. Louis, knows precedent is on his side.

"Commerce was the primary motivation for the entire Lewis and Clark expedition, and the need to continue that commerce is one of the arguments we will be making," he told me in one of our many conversations.

That commerce once was vibrant, never more so than during the Missouri River steamboat era of the nineteenth century. But always, it seemed cursed.

MISSOURI BREAKS

The barge run foul three several times—on logs, and in one instance it was with much difficulty they could get her off; happily no injury was sustained tho' the barge was several minutes in imminent danger. . . .
—Meriwether Lewis, May 15, 1804

It didn't matter what kind of boat: dugout canoe, pirogue, batteau, mackinaw, keelboat, or bullboats made of willow frames covered with buffalo hides and smeared with grease for water resistance. Always, they were challenged by swift currents, eddies, and those infernal snags— limbs or even whole uprooted trees that assaulted in raging currents or replanted themselves in mounds of shifting bottom sands to snare and puncture passing vessels.

There were expeditions up the Missouri River not nearly as successful as Lewis and Clark's, in handling either the river or the people along its

FIGURE 2. A stranded barge near St. Louis waits for higher water before decisions are made about its future. (Photo courtesy Bill Lambrecht)

banks. The Missouri Company, formerly the Spanish Commercial Exploration Company, learned that pirogues handled the river's currents far better than the frail birchbark canoes. But their boats never reached the Pacific Ocean, as Lewis and Clark did, nor did they learn to protect their cargo. In 1794, a Missouri Company expedition had its goods pillaged by the Sioux; a second expedition en route to resupply them was relieved of all its cargo by Indians.

Even after Lewis and Clark showed that keelboats were the way to go, expeditions encountered disaster. In 1827, a St. Louis entrepreneur began his troubled venture by scouring the city's bars and brothels to assemble the ninety crew members needed for a two-keelboat trading expedition.

One night, a contingent ventured into the camp of Arikaras, who by then had no use for the Euro-Americans trespassing on their river. One of the men didn't return. Inquiring before embarking the next day, traders were told their missing colleague had died the night before. The Indians offered to fetch the corpse, but they noted that it wasn't in very good shape, the eyes having been gouged out and the head cut off. In a fight with the Arikaras soon afterward, another thirteen of the St. Louisans died and ten were wounded.

IN THE STEAMBOAT ERA, captains and pilots who could successfully negotiate the river's perils and protect their crew and cargo were paid handsome sums—$1,000 to $1,500 a month—and treated as folk heroes by writers of that era, among them Joseph Mills Hanson.

"They have looked upon nature in her unconquered strength and majesty; they have grappled with her creatures in equal combat and have come off victors. The continent will not see their likes again," Hanson wrote in his *Conquest of the Missouri*, published in 1909.

Steamboats were distinctly American, embodying the character of the aspiring nation, just as the fur traders who preceded them carried hopes of American entrepreneurs outdoing Britain's Hudson Bay Company traders. William E. Lass, who wrote *A History of Steamboating on the Upper Missouri* River (in 1962), said that people took steamboats, rather than wagons, in part because of the impulse of speed: "Everybody wanted to get there in a hurry." Early as late in the nation's history, people loved a new technology. Steamboating was the latest in propelled locomotion. The early days also featured entrepreneurship of the riskiest sort. Lass found in his research that building a steamboat cost an average $430,000 in today's dollars, but so great were the dangers of river navigation that their average lifespan was just 4.1 years.

The Missouri has been no more generous to treasure hunters seeking to retrieve the bounty it claimed. In 1967, a pair of investors declared that they had discovered the steamboat *Bertrand*, which had sunk on April 1, 1865, twenty miles north of Omaha, after hitting a snag. The men had records showing the old sternwheeler had gone to the bottom with thousands of pounds of pure quicksilver and 5,000 gallons of whiskey.

The treasure hunters imagined sipping whiskey aged for a century as they counted hundreds of thousands of dollars in proceeds from the sale. But after spending more than $50,000 on the operation, the principals— Jack McGuire, a Nebraskan, and Dan Jones, of Iowa—reported an initial discovery short of expectations: five cases of Dr. J. Hostetter's Celebrated Stomach Bitters.

Later, the sailors recouped their investment and their reputations—by finding nine of the mercury containers thirty feet deep in the mud; the rest apparently had been retrieved shortly after the wreck. But the true reward from the operation was the *Bertrand's* cache of some 200,000 Civil War–era relics, from hobnail boots to honey to French champagne, all remarkably preserved in the anerobic muck. The cargo is on permanent display at the Desoto National Wildlife Refuge in Missouri Valley, Iowa.

TAMING THE RIVER

More than half those sunken vessels—240 by former steamboat inspector W. J. McDonald's count—were taken down by snags. Since the 1830s, the Army Corps of Engineers had been combating those damn snags, setting in motion a river control operation that would be comprehensive, expensive, and destructive. Eventually six main dams and countless dikes shaped the channel and stabilized the banks.

As well as the river, railroads—reaching the West in the 1880s—hammered the steamboats. But the river fought the rails as handily as it had attacked the big boats. In the central Missouri town of Harmony, there was no harmony between the railroad and the river. In the late 1920s and early 1930s, the Chicago & Alton Railroad—which ran alongside the river—fought unremittingly to stop the sugary soils from melting away and undermining the tracks.

During one of the skirmishes, a government crew spent ten days weaving together a 200-foot-long willow mat to clamp down the bank. But the wild river rose to set it free, sending the contraption floating down the river, with launches full of pursuing workers flinging lassos in a river rodeo.

All along, politicians played into the hands of the profiteers who dreamed of the Missouri as a highway running through America's breadbasket to the West. So it wasn't only snags that had to go. Competitive commerce required a regulated river. Deep-draft barges could hold their own against the railroads that had pushed steamboats into obsolescence.

As early as the 1870s, Congress listened to schemes seeking a permanent five-foot-deep channel from the mouth of the river to Sioux City. The government wasn't easily persuaded. Not until 1912 did Congress authorize a channel with sufficient depth—six feet—for barges of the day. And they took that channel only from St. Louis to Kansas City. But the feds were eventually won over. By the late 1920s, Congress had become conditioned to spending vast sums to channelize and stabilize the lower river: $12.8 million in 1929; $14 million in 1930; $10.9 million in 1931.

The engineers went about taming that river as if they were fighting a war. By the summer of 1929, twenty-six work crews had been assembled between St. Louis and Kansas City, and one thousand five hundred men were camped at one spot, in Booneville, Missouri. "Missouri River Six-Foot Channel Becoming Reality," a headline in the *St. Louis Post-Dispatch* proclaimed. The story's subhead described another goal: "River to be made to flow in continuous series of gentle curves."

Like the steamboat captains, Missouri River engineers and construction captains were lionized in print. Among them was the football star R. S. Uhl, once a feared running back for the University of Nebraska. A *Post-Dispatch* account of Uhl's labors as superintendent of a ninety-man crew observed: "Almost fifteen years ago, the yell which stirred the blood of young Uhl to greater varsity triumph was: 'Fight the Missouri Tiger.' But now it has changed to an almost nationwide appeal: 'Fight the Missouri River.'"

The siege on the river was so sustained that electricity was strung to some three dozen spots so that the men could work round the clock weaving the thin willows into bank control contraptions and hauling stone into revetments. As a foe, the Missouri River behaved much like the indigenous people in the century before: breaking out of Euro-American boundaries to cause mischief or disaster. Near Kansas City in 1935, the government deployed a massive suction dredge to shove the river back toward Parkville, "whose once busy water front was left high and dry by the stream's meanderings," the *Post-Dispatch* reported.

It was the Great Depression, a time when people needed work. On the river, men could find all they wanted at forty-five cents per hour, and a little less if they stayed in government camps. A *Post-Dispatch* article of 1930 told how the river project was bringing a bonanza of $1,000 a day to the tiny river town of Miami Station where men quarried rock. The rock hauled to the river was dropped on the huge willow mats to prevent the erosion that bedeviled farmers and bargers. At the height of construction, the Corps of Engineers employed more than ten thousand people.

Jobs became another reason to redesign the Missouri as a barge canal. Novice lawmakers learn swiftly that the path to steady pork, whether cut as a school or a new road, begins with breaking ground. By the mid-1930s, so much ground and Missouri riverbank had been broken that congressmen could seek huge appropriations: $40 million in 1935. Half of that amount was planned for the next phase of river control: construction of Fort Peck Dam in eastern Montana.

The Kansas Citians and the pro-navigation forces had the good fortune to be pushing expensive, labor-intensive river development just as President Franklin Roosevelt launched his public works campaign to put the nation back to work. "The only reason [the dams] are there is that Franklin Roosevelt couldn't figure any other way to get people to work," Stephen Ambrose told me. Roosevelt watched as the Germans were building their Autobahn, but highways weren't his thing. "Why in the hell should we be spending money linking cities to rural areas?" Ambrose recalls Roosevelt asking.

River commerce was another thing altogether. National need converged with local want to build the Missouri River's first dam. While it was at it, the federal government dug that river first a six-foot—and ultimately a nine-foot-deep—channel all the way to Sioux City.

THE RIVER BARGES COULDN'T CLIMB

Despite millions of dollars and the best Army engineering, barges couldn't climb that river. At Sioux City, a June day in 1940 presaged the troubled course of barge navigation on the Missouri.

A towboat, the *Kansas City Socony*, pushed two Mobil Oil barges laden with 400,000 gallons of gasoline toward a long-awaited celebration: the arrival of barges nearly to the Dakotas. Several thousand people awaited their arrival, and two radio stations prepared to air the festivities live. But approaching the dock, the tow vessel hung up on a shoal. The party languished while a pair of government vessels fetched the stuck tug and its tow.

In 1946, people again lined the river as the aptly named towboat *Franklin D. Roosevelt* made a trial run from St. Louis to Omaha with barges containing coffee from Brazil and steel from midwestern mills. Federal and state officials speechified at every stop. But north of Nebraska City, the river refused to cooperate; the *Roosevelt* lodged on a sandbar, where it remained for nine hours.

As Army engineers dug their nine-foot channel, barge traffic remained stuck. But the Corps could trumpet increasing annual tonnage, and news accounts routinely interpreted the calculations as a new day dawning for river commerce. Or sometimes an old day resurrected, as when the *Post-Dispatch* declared in 1947 that—once the ice breaks— barges will be running regularly to Sioux City, "the first time since the 1880s that the big shallow-draft vessels have carried freight regularly this far upstream."

Twelve years later, the story line hadn't changed. "Golden Age of River Transport on Missouri May Be Returning," a *Post-Dispatch* headline proclaimed in September 1959. Beneath was the news that river freight that year had reached 586,000 tons, a new record. The story saw only one drawback: "No more will fancily dressed riverboat gamblers teach gullible travelers what a royal flush is."

The barge industry recorded steady increases in traffic, perhaps

3.1

3.2

FIGURE 3. These Corps of Engineers photos show the progression of channelization and bank stabilization at a Nebraska spot in the Missouri that bears little resemblance to its name, Indian Cave Bend. '34–'36 (Photos courtesy Army Corps of Engineers)

3.3

3.4

thanks to shippers' believing all those stories about the return of the good old days. Livestock farmers like Gerald Harrison experimented, in 1964 converting an old automobile barge into a floating animal farm to send one thousand head of cattle up the Missouri to Omaha for slaughter. In Washington during the 1960s, Missouri Senator Edward V. Long, beseeching colleagues for still more money for river improvement, spoke of the "dream of a vast inland waterway system" and the Missouri's rise as "one of the nation's major transportation arteries."

Headlines such as "Heavy Shipping on the Missouri," "Missouri River Shipments Rising," and "Traffic Will Be Getting Heavier on the Missouri River" suggest that newspapers were disciples of the Corps of Engineers. Certainly they were not taking the time to look at what was—and was not—bought by decades of expensive construction. By 1981, when that 732-mile 9-foot St. Louis–to–Sioux City channel finally was finished, traffic on the Missouri already was in decline, which continues to this day. In 1977, barge tonnage on the Missouri reached its zenith of 3.3 million tons, considerably short of the 5 million tons predicted by Army engineers. After 1988, it never exceeded 2 million tons. In this new century, it hovered at a paltry 1.3 million tons annually.

That number reflects failure of no small magnitude given the century spent reengineering the Missouri River in the name of navigation. It looks especially puny set against navigation on the Mississippi River, which averages more than 100 million tons annually. The paucity of Missouri River barge traffic demands an answer to the question begged for a century: Should society continue to subsidize a failing industry by supplying it with scarce water at the expense of the recreation industry, wildlife, and the broader environmental health of the river?

A study in the summer of 2003 pinpointed what's gone wrong. For one thing, it costs more to run barges on the Missouri—55 percent more than on the Mississippi—because of vast distances and fuel consumption of river towboats. Working the fast Missouri always has been a challenge. As early as 1937, Corps officials muddily acknowledged that they might have gone too far in slicing away river bends, thereby increasing the river's slope and speeding its flow: "During the periods of high water, which usually occur in April and June, drafts of eight feet or more are possible, but the increased velocity of the current during these periods renders impracticable depths in excess of five feet for the type of equipment normally used for navigation."

The 2003 study, by C. Phillip Baumel, an Iowa State University economics professor, and Jerry Van Der Kamp, chief executive of AGRI-Industries—a midwestern farmer-owned cooperative—saw little prospect for improvement. Not only is the Missouri difficult to run; farming is running away from the river. Nationwide, exports of grain have declined since the 1980s—and that trend is unlikely to change as Brazil challenges the United States for world soybean hegemony and global markets spin over genetically modified crops. Meanwhile, more farmers are growing their corn for nearby ethanol facilities, and railroads are winning customers for their shipping services by building shuttle-train lines to grain elevators near the river, the study found.

DEFENDING THE STATUS QUO OF FLOW

As turbid as the Missouri's swirling eddies is the politics of managing this river. The status quo flows like downstream water, fast and certain. Change is upstream going against momentum two hundred years strong.

Management of the river is decreed by a document from which the

Army Corps of Engineers does not depart without orders. That document is the *Missouri River Main Stem Reservoir System Reservoir Regulation Manual*. The *Master Manual*, as it's known among friends, conveys a deal of information about the relationship between the Army and the Missouri River. At 1.1 inches thick, it is a fat, homely, beige typewritten document, but the Army Corps of Engineers behaves as if Moses himself had delivered it to that squat black building in Nebraska housing the Reservoir Control Center. It had not changed significantly since 1960, leading up to a bureaucratic struggle that unfolded swiftly during my quest.

Subsection 9-1 of section IX on page IX-1, which has its roots in the 1944 Flood Protection Control Act, spells out Operational Objectives and Requirements of the river: flood control, irrigation, navigation, water supply, power, fish and wildlife, water quality, and recreation.

Those uses and their hierarchy are a monumental snag that have waylaid the courts, the Congress, and the president, who ultimately commands the Army Engineers. Until that wording changes in the *Master Manual*, the Corps will continue to operate the river as though the barge industry's New Day had indeed dawned.

Changing those words has proved, over the three decades, about as controversial as rewriting the Bible.

Allied on the side of flood control, irrigation, navigation, water supply, and power are the Corps, the barge industry, and farmers. Farmers may or may not ship their grain by barge, and they could care less about the low flows that would protect endangered, sand-nesting birds but leave bargers high and dry. But river bottom farmers abhor the spring rise, which is the second part of the strategy for a living river. So the farmers sign on to defend bargers from the low flows while bargers repel the high water from farmers' lands.

Downstream politicians are another allied force with yet another reason for fighting flow changes. Their fear is that changing the status quo might deprive their populous downstream constituencies of the water to stake—and slake the thirst of—future development. So one fight blends into another.

"What we've got here is like an old-fashioned Western water fight," said barge industry executive Don Huffman. Huffman, who has been running barges on the Missouri for more than thirty years, stayed on the job after selling the towing company founded by his father to MEMCO Barge Line Inc. "They want the water up there and we want it down here," he said.

It takes perspective as long as Huffman's to defend the vitality of Missouri barging. *We were headed toward success until the 1980 grain embargo,* the barge industry says. *Managed low flows have destroyed reliability and run off potential customers. We just need another chance.* But they're an industry under siege. Ranked against them on one side, conservationists undermine their standing. Meanwhile, upstream recreationists covet their water and shrinking revenues threaten their future.

Roger Blaske, who put the *Lauren D* on the Missouri, has fought in the courts to protect his family's half-century-old business. But the pressure gets to him. "No matter what happens on this river, they blame us," Blaske, a lanky, genial man, told me in his office in Alton, Illinois. Alton is a river city that, like the barge industry, has seen better times.

A year later, when Blaske and I talked again, he'd decided to keep his vessels in the dock rather than risk the uncertainties of court-imposed low water spoiling his upcoming Canadian fishing trip.

"My boat's tied up, my boys are on unemployment, and I'm sitting here in my office trying to make payroll. It's no fun," he said.

THIRTEEN WAYS TO SINK A STEAMBOAT

In its career of sinking steamboats, the Missouri River has had plenty of human help. Retired steamboats inspector W. J. McDonald catalogued some 441 Missouri River wrecks from the early days of steamboating. He compiled his list in three articles he wrote in 1927 for the *Missouri Historical Review*, all under the headline "The Missouri River and Its Victims." Scholars say that no better published record exists.

Nearly half of the sinkings resulted from snags; but crime, human foibles, and other griefs and misfortunes made the Missouri River a graveyard for steamboats, as you'll see in this catalogue of catastrophe selected (and recategorized) from McDonald's compilation.

TEMPTATION: Too many people knew that the side-wheeler *Boreas* was carrying a large cache of silver bullion in addition to Mexican money. What's more, one fellow had boarded upriver carrying bags of gold dust. His remains were never found after *Boreas* was destroyed by fire, near Hermann, Missouri, in 1846.

CAPTAIN'S CHOICE: In 1852, impetuous Captain Francis Belt had waited for two days for the current to slow so that his steamer, *Saluda*, and its load of Mormons could negotiate a harrowing bend near Rocheport, Missouri. Finally, he stormed into the engine room and demanded more steam. "I will round this bend or blow the boat to hell," he said.

"The steamer swung into the stream," McDonald reported, "and, within a few minutes, the boilers exploded and blew the steamer to pieces." More than two dozen people died, the captain among them, in an explosion so mighty that it propelled the ship's safe 200 feet onto land. Surviving children were adopted by citizens of nearby Lexington.

DOUBLE TROUBLE: Heading back from Montana with a load of furs in 1855, the crew of the *Kate Sweeney* met disaster when a snag brought the huge side-wheeler to the bottom in what is now South Dakota. Losing the vessel was but an inconvenience compared to what happened next: When crew members decided to walk to civilization rather than wait for help, they were killed by Indians.

ENGULFED BY SPIRITS: In 1857, a fire broke out aboard *Chippewa* as passengers, among them European tourists, ate dinner while steaming in Montana. Passengers were saved and the boat exploded. The fire was traced to deckhands with candles who had been tapping a whiskey barrel in the hold.

GOVERNMENT KNOW-HOW: Operators of the U.S. government–owned *J. Don Cameron* decided to dispense with hiring a trained Missouri River pilot and instead used an Army officer when transporting relatives and property of the 5th Infantry. On its first trip in 1877, the vessel hit a snag and sank.

CUSTER'S LAST CRUISE: The famous *Far West*, which had been used by the ill-fated Indian fighter for a war council in 1876, returned the wounded from Little Big Horn. It sank on October 30, 1883, near St. Louis after being pole-axed by a snag.

LONGEST PORTAGE: The stern-wheeler *Messenger Boy* traveled a river of no return in 1881 when the Missouri changed its course in Nebraska, leaving the steamer three quarters of a mile from water.

SAVIN' THE BACON: When the *Minnie Herman* sank on a snag on August 23, 1887, General Charles H. Thompkins happened along in time to rescue crates of bacon bound for the Standing Rock Agency at Fort Yates.

TENDER IGNORANCE: On July 18, 1897, the bridge tender at Sioux City, Iowa, missed the signal. The *Benton*, which had been resurrected from two sinkings already, crashed into pilings, opening a vast hole in the hull, and sank to the bottom never to steam again.

HUNGRY RIVER: Owners of the 160-foot-long *Glenmore* thought their vessel was safe while being repaired on dry land in Kansas City. But in 1897 the Missouri, known for going out to lunch, raged at the shore, undercutting the bank so thoroughly that the swath of earth holding the *Glenmore* sloughed into the river, destroying the boat.

HIGH AND DRY: The opposite fate befell *Little Dick*, a modest-sized center-wheeler that found itself high above water near Rocheport, Missouri, when the river dropped precipitously. As its crew tried to lift and pry the boat to water, it somehow fell in and sank.

ASLEEP ON DECK: Watchmen's duties were second in importance only to captains'. In March 1920, the watchman of the side-wheeler *Dorothy* slept soundly as the water rose higher and higher, finally sinking the vessel and rendering her a total loss. The watchman avoided ignominy by drowning.

TEETOTALER EXPRESS: The *Deapolis* apparently was not blessed sufficiently in a ceremony when E. H. Chapin, a Prohibitionist Party politician, christened her with water and not champagne. *Deapolis*, sunk after becoming engulfed in ice in North Dakota in the winter of 1922–23, was dismantled and abandoned.

5

1944: WHEN HISTORY CHANGES COURSE

It was not conceded that at the hour of creation the Lord had divided and classified natural resources to conform to the organization chart of the federal government.

—Tennessee Valley Authority Board, 1944

IN WHICH WE REVERSE THE FLOW OF TIME TO WATCH RIVER GODS AT WORK

It's a hard, hard lesson
That you're gonna to learn
On the river of no return.

LANDING
ARMY CORPS OF ENGINEERS RESERVOIR CONTROL CENTER, OMAHA

ARMY ENGINEERS IN SUBURBAN OMAHA lord over the life of the Missouri River.

On this Monday, my quest to understand how the Missouri runs and why has led me to the Reservoir Control Center in Omaha for the first of two weekly meetings that will decide how the waters of the Missouri River will flow. Before my curiosity is slaked, I will have had to reverse the flow of time, traveling backward for sixty years.

Guiding this twenty-first century's command meeting on the river and close at hand for easy reference is the Corps' *Master Manual*. Like any book of scriptures, the manual inspires and it incites. It is weighty—more than two pounds—and full of commandments as to where the water flows, when, and for whom. Written in stone long ago, these orders barely have changed over four decades. Recreation, fish, and wildlife come last in the litany "insofar as possible without serious interference" to the river's three articles of faith.

Here in Omaha, the first order of business is taking stock of when it has rained along the river, and when it might, which takes some attention in a basin consisting of 541,000 square miles. To calculate how much water might be entering the Missouri from the 220-plus rivers and streams that feed it, fourteen Army engineers and civilian workers fix their eyes on an oversized computer terminal. As I watch, the corpsmen and women study a series of National Weather Service reports.

A handful of reports forecast rain. This is news for rejoicing among the god of rivers, as the Army Corps of Engineers has been ordained by Congress. The Corps invoke satellites on high to consult readings from eight hundred rain gauges. The calculus of flow decisions also must factor in the volume of water in reservoirs behind the dams and the volume of water needed to generate the electricity that can be sold that day on the spot market.

Rain is forecast south of Sioux City, Iowa, so the team decides to release slightly less water into the lower stretch of river that flows from Sioux City into the Mississippi above St. Louis. The water gods command that the flow of river through Gavins Point be scaled back to 32,500 cubic feet per second from 33,000, as it had been. A flow of 33,000 cubic feet of water amounts to roughly 250,000 gallons, enough to inundate a football field to the depth of one foot.

They e-mail their instructions to Gavins Point Dam, 160 miles north at the South Dakota–Nebraska border, where they arrive on Dennis O'Rourke's computer screen much faster than I can make the trip north to see them executed.

Releasing all this water from Gavins Point is a one-finger job, and I imagine Michelangelo's "Creation of Adam" as O'Rourke stretches out his finger to enter the command.

The new flow draws slightly less from Dakotas' reservoirs, but that fact does not reconcile North and South Dakotans to the "theft" of their water. No happier downstream are barge operators, who have come to accept as birthright all the water they can use.

The Army Corps of Engineers pleases no one in its management of the Missouri, leaving Omaha managers like Larry Cieslik little option but to shift blame.

"All of the people think it's the Corps that determine the purposes we're going to serve," he told me before I left town. "It was Congress that decided that."

IN THE BEGINNING

For more than a half century, the Corps had worked to corral the river, penning it within its banks and slicing away its most heedless stretches. But the mid-twentieth century brought the most sustained assault on the river and its environs: dams.

The Missouri's dams are relics of a massive program of dam building that sprang from a series of events in 1944. What I discovered looking back was the story of a mighty clash of purposes abetted by a failure of leadership.

In this tale of political intrigue I discovered a player I hadn't anticipated: my own newspaper, the St. Louis Post-Dispatch.

In 1944, a nation flush with its power from success in war imagined
new conquests at home. Eric Johnston's America Unlimited was published
that year, and poets were reimagining America's creation myths: Stephen
Vincent Benét was awarded a Pulitzer Prize posthumously for his 1944
epic poem about the American frontier.

After two years of flooding in the heartland, no conquest looked more
challenging than the willful Missouri. Beginning in early April 1943, the
Missouri River had risen to flood stages unseen since 1881. More than
700,000 acres of the river and its tributaries were under water after a
rapid snow melt along the northern Great Plains, where a half-dozen
people perished.

This also was the era of crusading journalism, and few American
newspapers flexed more muscles that year than Joseph Pulitzer's Post-
Dispatch as it campaigned to chart a new course for river management.

On May 14, 1944, three weeks before D-Day, the Post-Dispatch
sounded a call to arms to newspapers along the Missouri. Confessing misguided parochialism as a sin of its past, the paper exhorted newspapers
throughout the basin to take charge of the Missouri's future before the
government arrived with its own heavy-handed, misguided solution.

"It is not one thing in Montana and Wyoming, another thing in the
Dakotas and Iowa, a third thing in Nebraska, Kansas and Colorado, and
a fourth in Missouri," read the Post-Dispatch's 1,500-word editorial. "It is
not primarily an instrument to be used for irrigation, or for navigation, or
for power, nor is it primarily an evil force to be controlled against its repeated and disastrous flooding. It is a synthesis of all of these," the edito-

rial asserted, calling for a holistic approach long before that word grew popular.

In two springs of flooding, high water had triggered "homelessness and paralysis and ruin," the editorial noted. "Whole villages were swallowed up by dark water. Transportation stopped. Food production stopped. Unfattened livestock was evacuated to the cities to glut packing houses."

The *Post-Dispatch* was following tradition in building its case on fear of floods. Always, floods have shaped Missouri River politics. The Great Flood of 1881 triggered the federal bank stabilization program that continues to this day. In the twenty-first century, lower basin politicians fighting against spring pulses of water and other wildlife-friendly changes invoke the Great Flood of 1993. In the middle of the last century, the Great Flood of 1943 unleashed not only water but also a public policy debate that the newspaper longed to shape.

The *Post-Dispatch* proposed an autonomous federal agency equivalent to the eleven-year-old Tennessee Valley Authority (TVA) with a charter to make riverwide decisions and the authority to enforce them.

The Missouri Valley Authority, it would be called, and it would be an entity of the people to carry out the people's business along their longest river. "This can be done; it has been done. There is nothing theoretical or dreamily visionary about a plan that could accomplish all these things and give the valley new wealth and power as well," the editorial exhorted.

The editorial ended with a rallying cry to competitive newspapers to join in the campaign: "In the past, we have splintered our lances against each other's shields; blunted our swords to no purpose; divided ourselves into partisan camps in which the work of one was to nullify the work of the other. There must be men up and down the valley who have a vision that transcends the futile rivalries of the past. The editors from Montana to St. Louis have it within their power to preach the gospel that the Missouri is one big river with one big problem."

Alongside the editorial ran a chart with the names of editors from some fifty newspapers along the river. With its fighting words, the paper hoped to persuade them to counter the determined march by two federal agencies—the Army Corps of Engineers and the Bureau of Reclamation—to reengineer the river and divide up control over its waters. Pulitzer's populist appeal swiftly won friends in Congress and from a few newsrooms.

Did it come too late?

THE MAN WHO WOULD PLAY GOD

Forces in the federal bureaucracy had their own plans for river reengineering, and none was more audacious than Colonel Lewis Pick of the Army Corps of Engineers. Pick, who devised his river control plan when he headed the Omaha District, had been personally insulted by the flood. Along with much of Omaha, including the airport, his office was deluged. In August 1943, Pick fought back with a thirteen-page report to Congress proposing massive river construction. Beyond Fort Peck Dam in Montana, a reengineering feat of the 1930s, Pick wanted five new dams on the Missouri River, a levee system, and a nine-foot-deep navigation channel.

Disaster urged his case as he recounted the flooding of more than 1 million acres along the lower river in 1943. Some of the land was so inundated that returning it to crop production might take three years, he argued. Highways and railroads along the river were crushed, and that year nearly every agricultural levee between Sioux City and St. Louis overtopped or breached.

The plan was bold as Pick—an imperious, tempestuous man who mercilessly drove civilians and corpsmen. He did not abide challenge, and he punctuated his conversations with the words, "See, see," to accentuate his opinion. Rufus Terral, who wrote about the Corps of Engineers for the *St. Louis Post-Dispatch* in the middle of the twentieth century, reported that Pick's first command at the Omaha District was seven-day work weeks. His second was making telephone calls to check who'd left their desks on a Sunday afternoon. Third, he signed orders to transfer slackers, among them an engineer caught taking a Sunday boat trip on the Missouri when he should have been minding it from his office.

Pick later directed Army engineers in Burma. There, he fired a team of surveyors whose demanding engineering slowed down his pet project, a highway that would be christened Pick's Pike. "A technician who is also an astute politician and a far better lobbyist than he is a water engineer," wrote University of Illinois researcher Marian E. Ridgeway in 1955.

Pick was the first of an audacious new breed of Army engineer who would transform the Corps from starch-shorts technicians into public works entrepreneurs with big dreams and a $4 billion budget. Pick saw the future and understood he needed to sell it. The Virginia Polytechnic Institute grad ventured where no West Point Corps general had imagined; he hired a public relations man, a former reporter named William Langdon. Together they set out on a marketing tour.

This was a man who had condensed into a mere thirteen pages a blueprint for massively intrusive engineering that would reorder natural resources along one third of America and force thousands of people from their homes. It would also provide the basis for the *Master Manual* and Corps of Engineers control over the Missouri—if Pick could get it approved. Pick and Langdon knew how to accentuate the positive. "By these improvements," the document read, "not only would large flood damages be prevented along the Missouri River and its tributaries and the Mississippi River, but also floodwaters would be retained for their best use for all purposes including irrigation, navigation, power, domestic and sanitary purposes, wildlife and recreation."

Pick's plan was so big it encompassed the hopes of a river basin. A fellow Army colonel, Delbert Freeman, described it as "a flexible framework into which the plans of all other agencies, federal, state and local, could be fitted." Such enterprising earthscaping has come to be known in the Corps' twenty-first-century sales vernacular as "adaptive management."

The colonel was vague but seductive and his salesmanship masterful. He promised to save people's lives and property while feeding, electrifying, cleansing, and exercising them. Pick's audiences swallowed his plan like sugar. My journalistic predecessor Rufus Terral concluded, "Where he strode through the valley, he left men dazed and dreaming."

"If he succeeds," wrote the editor of the *Bismarck Tribune*, "he will become one of the greatest figures in the history of this state and a hero to every North Dakota school child for generations to come."

It would be his plan or nothing, so when the Bureau of Reclamation proposed a competing plan, Pick fought to kill it.

DREAMING EVEN BIGGER

Glenn Sloan had been five years in writing the Bureau of Reclamation proposal, and by the time he finished in 1944 it was even more drunkenly grandiose than Pick's. Sloan's plan called for ninety dams—nearly four times as many as Pick's, including those on tributaries; it promised to irrigate nearly 5 million acres of the Great Plains. Its price tag, twice the cost of Pick's, startled a pre–decimal point era: $1,200,000,000.

Sloan's pitch began by repeating Pick's, though its writing was less visionary. His goals were "control of the devastating floods along the lower river and the stabilization of agriculture in the Dakotas and eastern Montana." Where Pick promoted navigation, Sloan preferred Plains agriculture and irrigation. Thus upper and lower basin were divided in a competition still bitter today.

Pick regarded his adversary as barely his equal. Pick was a colonel who would retire as a two-star general. Sloan was but an assistant chief in the Bureau of Reclamation's Billings, Montana, outpost dismissed as a player even in his own department's bureaucracy wars. Sloan was easygoing; Pick overweening. A famous photo shows the adversaries. Looking severe, Pick is dressed in uniform, his hands clasped behind his back. Sloan is open-collared and loose. A two-foot space divides the two men.

Sloan wasn't spit-polished, but he was formidable in his own right. Confident, fearless, and certain in his aims, Sloan met Pick's challenge.

While both plans sought control over the willful Missouri, they hopelessly conflicted. The Bureau laughed at the Corps' promise of navigation. The Corps mocked irrigating the northern reaches of the American desert. Neither agency would back down, and each had to prove itself right. The Bureau picked a dry cycle of years to illustrate what minimum rainfall could be; the Corps picked a wet cycle to plead flood control. What mix of flood control, irrigation, and navigation would win out?

"A difference of opinion appears to exist between the Corps of Engineers and the Bureau of Reclamation over the use and control of the waters of the Missouri River," Bureau of the Budget director Harold D. Smith observed in neat understatement.

In fact, control of the Missouri was at stake when the Army Corps of Engineers fought the Bureau of Reclamation in Congress in 1944. Each agency set a powerful lobby to undermine the other's mission. Their simmering feud between the federal government's principal development agencies had come to a showdown, and neither would back down.

BATTLE OF THE TITANS

Of course, the plans were irreconcilable. Not enough water flowed in the Missouri for irrigation, navigation, and everything else the two agencies wanted.

Then the St. Louis Post-Dispatch got wind of Sloan's plan, and another would-be Titan joined the battle. The sixty-six-year-old newspaper published its editorial two days before Sloan's plan hit Congress. Allied with the National Farmers Union, the Post-Dispatch lobbied for a third alternative, its Missouri Valley Authority.

Every good government, New Deal ideal that the liberal Post-Dispatch could want was embodied in the Tennessee Valley Authority. Like the New Deal itself, the TVA put people to work. With that came even bigger ideas. The main goal, as outlined in 1933, was unified development of the Tennessee River for the nation. It also put into practice an emerging conservation ethic based on the conclusion that enlightened self-interest could not, in itself, protect natural resources for the public good. Replanting trees and restoring an exhausted region continued a philosophy of river management pioneered by Theodore Roosevelt and his conservation czar, Gifford Pinchot.

Major newspapers—*The New York Times* and *The Washington Post*—seconded the *Post-Dispatch* plan. The *Chicago Sun* agreed, calling the Missouri Valley Authority "the only real solution to the problems of that valley. Irrigation interests in the West want to control it for their purposes; navigation interests for theirs; food control and power interests for theirs. To complicate the situation, some strong agencies have their own purely negative fish to fry—the railroads don't want improved navigation and private utilities don't want public development of water power."

Next, the *Post-Dispatch* argued its case to the people. In a radio debate, the paper's Jean Lightfoot Coghlan argued that people needed an authority that "doesn't run to Washington and ask, 'What do we do now.' Every decision is made right in the valley, in answer to the big question, 'What's best for the people right here?' "

Interior Secretary Harold L. Ickes, Sloan's boss, declared that the Missouri Valley Authority was a fine idea—as long as it was part of his federal agency. The *Post-Dispatch* reported Ickes's sentiments in a news story under a loaded headline: "Ickes for an MVA—But He Also Wants to Boss It."

The Army Corps of Engineers hated it. Mindful of its future with the war winding down, the Army saw the MVA as a threat. The *Post-Dispatch* plan had to be killed. On that, the Reclamation Bureau agreed. Its states-based lobbying arm, the National Reclamation Association, derided the MVA as "a child of the *St. Louis Post-Dispatch*" and pilloried the paper in its bulletin: "With little information of the major issues involved, with no appreciation of the history and tradition of reclamation of Western lands through irrigation, and with scant knowledge of the appropriation doctrine of western water under state law for beneficial consumptive use, but anxious to be helpful, the *Post-Dispatch* was easily susceptible to the . . . 'one river, one problem' motto."

Lobbying in Congress was ferocious. The *Saturday Evening Post* likened its intensity to the fights over Prohibition and women's suffrage. Alabama Senator Lister Hill described utility opposition to the MVA as a "widespread, vicious and unprincipled lobbying and propaganda."

Then the populist senator asked the question our age now ponders: "Shall the wealth of our many rivers and their watersheds be developed in the public interest for the benefit of the people or shall they be turned over to those who would exploit them for their own profit?"

The *Post-Dispatch* fought hard. Along with the big-city newspapers, organized labor allied with the paper, adding the endorsements of the American Federation of Labor and the Congress of Industrial Organizations. But most papers along the river, among them the cross-state rival, the *Kansas City Star*, condemned the *Post-Dispatch* plan before turning on one another in an editorial river war. Allied with the Corps as it had with Kansas City's Commercial Club decades before, the *Kansas City Star* accused upper basin states of "parasitism."

Upriver, the *Miles City Star* called the Kansas City newsroom "the mouthpiece of these super deluxe, pork-barrel projects." Glossing its insults, the *Star* continued: "We apply the term 'gentry' to the Kansas City pirates who would rob us of the waters of the Missouri River basin with due regard for its meaning, and not that it applies to them in its true sense."

President Franklin Roosevelt—a proponent of the MVA, as was his vice president, Harry S Truman—let the battle wage. Their administration was playing an endgame in World War II and this was an election year, both far more important matters. The conclusion of this congressional war teaches a lesson, still good in our time, of the danger to the homelands when the White House is preoccupied.

In that climate, the *Post-Dispatch's* campaign altered the course of events in a direction its editors could not have foreseen.

Neither the Corps nor the Bureau was willing to risk losing, so they cast their lot together. But the treaty the combatants signed in Omaha, on Corps turf, and after little more than a day of negotiations on October 17, 1944, had little to do with compromise. It combined their proposals in a union summed up famously by National Farmers Union president James Patton as "a shameless, loveless shotgun wedding."

Post-Dispatch reporter Rufus Terral wrote of the Corps and the Bureau: "We will let you build all the projects we consider a waste of public funds if you will let us build all the projects you consider a waste of public funds."

The Reclamation Bureau got nearly all it wished, at least on paper. The Corps got authority over main stem dams, flood control, and navigation. The Pick-Sloan Plan, as the massive Missouri reengineering plan came to be known, brought a hundred projects to congressional districts back home, only a half-dozen or so having been lost in Omaha, so the "compromise" was everything Congress could have wanted. It swiftly passed the Pick-Sloan Plan as part of the Flood Protection Act of 1944.

Just as swiftly, after winning a fourth term, Franklin Roosevelt sign Pick-Sloan into law. But he added a condition of his own: Pick-Sloan was but "a basic engineering plan to be developed and administered by a Missouri Valley Authority," he wrote in a letter to House Speaker Carl Rayburn in November.

Five months later, Roosevelt died, and with him the Missouri Valley Authority. Following the death of the great New Dealer, the river's people would have no say as their watershed was reengineered.

A year after Pick-Sloan, the River and Harbor Act of 1945 authorized the Corps to dredge a nine-foot-deep channel on the 732-mile stretch of Missouri River from St. Louis to Sioux City, Iowa. By the time the channel was finished in 1981, the barges it was designed to accommodate already were growing scarce.

～ PADDLING ～

WILLIAM THE TRAVELER

A river philosopher long ago observed that the problem with taking a trip up the Missouri is that you have to take your boat along. That assessment still holds true, and not just because of the hull-crunching rock dikes built by the Army Corps of Engineers to shove the current into a swift, scouring flow.

In fact, anybody with big river sensibilities who is mostly sober (and unblinkingly attentive) can motor up the Missouri, or down, at least until running into a dam. Unlike the early days on the Missouri's lower third, wicked tree-snags won't savage your hull.

But if it weren't for Matt Cooper, you'd probably run out of gas.

It's eighty miles from the last fueling stop near St. Louis to Cooper's Landing, situated at Nashville, Missouri. And it's that far west after Cooper's to fill up again. Blame the Missouri or the people along its banks, but travel can be inconvenient. Travelers of popular rivers east and west arriving here for a river journey are stunned at the shortage of support services: food and water, camping, and help out of emergencies.

But they're nonetheless lured by the inspiring bluffs that not even the Army could conquer.

Matt Cooper makes such journeys possible, seeing to your vessel's needs and to yours. Should you desire the respite of land, Cooper will rent out his lone camper, a tiny enclosure, for thirty dollars a night.

There's music, art, Thai food, junk food, and community gatherings, assembling mostly around a long table in an erstwhile garage that, over nearly two decades, has collected ten different kinds of chairs for sitting. No hard liquor is allowed on the premises, but there's plenty of beer, except when the authorities yanked Cooper's liquor license over a mix-up related to an indiscretion many years past.

You can get to Cooper's Landing by river, gravel road, or the Katy Trail, a former rail right-of-way. Now a state park transversing the state and often paralleling the river, the trail offers bikers and hikers a splendid route. All roads lead to Matt Cooper's place, sometimes delivering flotsam like William the Traveler, who arrived by canoe at sunset one recent fall evening.

William threw me a line as he negotiated the current, and I pulled him to a floating dock. He'd been on the water for 119 days since embarking near the end of June on the Yellowstone River in Mile City, Montana. He was hungry.

William, twenty-eight, is broad-backed and burnt umber. With his hair and beard like matted straw, he looks to be the twenty-first-century version of the old river rats I'd been hearing about, like the frontiersmen of the Corps of Discovery or "Liver Eatin'" Johnson, who, according to legend, earned his nickname for eating the livers of Indians vanquished in battle.

After I fetch William two cans of beer, he tells me about surviving along the modern Missouri and about the pistol he carries. It's less for creatures, he says, than for human predators: property rights nuts; menacing drunks; or homeless thieves like those he met in Kansas City, living in wooden crates on the river's edge.

"You know, when you start hearin' stuff outside your tent in the night, you don't know what to think," he says.

William is no student gathering material for a thesis; no writer in search of his muse. Eating Thai noodles from a paper plate, he tells me that he is a traveler who has nothing to anchor him down. Before this journey, he'd spent a year on the beaches of Micronesia. When he'd finished the Missouri in a few days, he intended to keep moving in whatever direction struck him.

He has no particular longing for what he refers to as "creature comforts"; he'd slept in a real bed just three nights in three months. It's dark by the time we get to the subject of food, and I'm startled at what he tells me he eats when there's no one in sight.

He'd left Montana with a single box of flour, two pounds of granola, and some edible odds and ends. He dragged a fishing line with enough luck to lay out a few suppers. With that little .25-caliber pistol of his, he'd nailed a few sitting rabbits. During his forty-five days in South Dakota, he says he also enjoyed an abundant supply of fried eggs along the river.

They were tiny but filling, he says. I'm having trouble imagining chickens along the forsaken reaches of the Dakotas, when I realize what he's talking about: William had been raiding the nests of two rare shorebirds, the endangered least tern and the piping plover, which the federal government categorizes as threatened.

I will be learning much more in my travels about these protected birds and their struggles to survive. Now, I know enough to be alarmed, and I tell him he has been violating the Endangered Species Act.

William has no interest in listening to people like me telling him about right and wrong. That is why he travels and why he's spent three months alone on the Missouri River, which, despite its troubles, still offers people as much freedom as they can endure.

"I've got nothing against those birds," he says, shaking his head. "But if they left their eggs up in trees, like normal birds, they wouldn't have to deal with people like me. I gotta survive, too."

6

SPECIES ON THE BRINK

I went with ten men to a Creek Damed by the Beavers . . .
with Some Small willow & Bark we mad a Drag . . . and
Cought 318 fish of different kind [:] Peke, Bass, Salmon,
perch, red horse, Small Cat, & a kind of Perch Called Silver-
fish, on the Ohio.

—William Clark, August 15, 1804

IN WHICH WE SHARE THE SHOCKING REALITY
OF FISH AND AN ANGRY SCIENTIST

You take my shrimp, baby
You know you take me down
I couldn't do nothin'
Til I get myself unwound.

LANDING
ON THE MISSOURI RIVER SOUTH OF OMAHA

ELECTRODES DANGLING FROM LARRY Hesse's broad-hull johnboat deliver 600-volt pulses, sending fish rolling and skittering
across the surface. A 27-inch-long grass carp twists through the air, landing with a sloppy thud on the laces of my boots. In this landing of my
quest to know occupied Big Muddy and its creatures, I have been
"carped," a word coined, as best as I can tell, nearby on the Mississippi
River. It describes being struck by one of these airborne Asian invaders.

It doesn't take Hesse's electrofishing charges to rile these carp into flight; the vibrations from outboard motors are sufficient. Big river fishers compare notes about flying fish and carp-upside-the-head. In a bait shop, I met a carped woman wearing her broken nose like a badge of honor. A Japanese film crew traveled to the Mississippi River in hopes of recording such an incident for themselves; they nailed the story when a camera-man had the good fortune of tasting scales and slime.

In midwestern rivers now there are bighead carp, silver carp, and grass carp. Behind certain dams, these interlopers "stack up like cord-wood," an Iowa state conservation official told me. They are unwanted intruders, brought to the United States to devour weeds in catfish-farm ponds. But they escaped from their impoundments in Arkansas and probably elsewhere during floods and bred in the wild. And bred and bred. Now they are muscling native fish out of food and disrupting the lower third of the Missouri River's already out-of-balance ecology. The black carp, a behemoth that grows four feet long, is yet another worry on the horizon. Imported by fish farmers to control system-clogging mollusks, these carp are equally fond of native river mollusks and clams, some rare and nearing extinction. Fisheries experts want the government to ban their use.

One Monday morning in 2000, reporters in my *St. Louis Post-Dispatch* Washington bureau met to plan coverage of the final days of a hair-splitting presidential election and various geopolitical doings. A political reporter by trade, I malingered, excusing myself to work on a story about a giant flying carp that should join the walking catfish, the mongoose, and the India wild dog as federally designated "injurious species." I could tell from the glances of my esteemed colleagues that

FIGURE 4. Larry Hesse, a biologist from Nebraska and a member of the National Academy of Sciences, deploys electrofishing to count species in groundbreaking research that proved decline in the Missouri's aquatic life.

(Photo courtesy Bill Lambrecht)

they feared I had gone mad out in the Missouri River badlands. Perhaps they were right.

If they'd seen these flying fish, perhaps even been carped themselves, they'd understand my fascination with creatures of this river.

SHOCKING FISH

Hesse, his assistant Ryan Stalleum, and I are working a stretch of the brown Missouri south of Omaha, Nebraska. Here and now, alien carp are being spooked not just by vibration; they have the extra provocation of thirty pulses of electricity per second from Hesse's on-board generator. Lying at my feet is the sucker-lipped grass carp, a particularly voracious species, and Hesse rushes forward from the helm. With ferocity I hadn't expected from a member of the National Academy of Sciences, he beats the fish dead with a rock, tossing it onto a jetty where it will be enjoyed by raccoons. What I have seen is barely a sliver of Larry Hesse's determination.

For nearly twenty-five years, Hesse was the large-river ecologist for the state of Nebraska. In 1992, his unremitting willingness to get wet and dirty and his tenacious research earned him a nomination to the prestigious National Research Council.

But in his state job, he failed to advance as he believed he deserved, and he went on his own in 1995. He was angry, too, for his own Nebraska Game and Fish Commission ignored his research. "It was like, 'You can gather data till the cows come home, but just stay out of our hair,'" he said.

Hesse bludgeons no more fish this day. When he pulls up a net of stunned specimens (gathered over 700 yards of poky motoring upriver about 12 feet in from the shore), he handles them gently, almost lovingly. He picks up each one, calls out its species to his assistant Stalleum, then measures and weighs it. From some he scrapes scales that he shakes into a plastic bag. Then back in the river they go with no-look tosses made like a point guard in basketball. After drifting for a moment in the current, the fish give a flip and disappear.

Hesse calls his work "biomonitoring." Supported by modest state and federal grants, he's been biomonitoring most weeks from April into November since the mid-1990s. Fish-shocking is only a portion of his research on the Missouri River, which he's studied for nearly thirty years. You don't get more expert than he about what swims, or swam, here. Along the Missouri, the tally of decline and extinction has only recently been taken, and Hesse is chief among the witnesses.

After several loads from the left bank (in river navigation, that's the bank on your left when you're heading downstream), Hesse is troubled at what he's seeing. There have been quite a few catfish: brown-gray turbidity-loving flatheads, channel catfish, and the blue cats that William Clark called in his journal white catfish; also smallmouth buffalo; a blue sucker (which looks to me like any old carp); freshwater drum; and a few white crappie. But on each pass, nearly three fourths of the fish are carp, giving the plastic tub on the deck the look of a koi pond.

In more than three hours, we have raised nary a sauger, plains minnow, chub, burbot, or any of the species that belong in the Missouri River. We've certainly spied no pallid sturgeon, the species whose troubles in the Missouri have generated ripples all the way to the White House. This is my first meeting with Hesse, and it must have sounded like I have the brains of one of the species flopping in the tub when, eliciting quotes for a newspaper story, I ask why the sturgeon and the other species of fish swim hereabouts no more.

"We took away just so much of this river; where it used to flow, what you see now is corn. It doesn't take a rocket scientist to know what happened," says Hesse.

What happened, of course, was destruction of an ecosystem through the massive reengineering of a river at a time when conservation values in this country were tested seldom in the political arena and more rarely still in the courts.

Just look around, he instructs. The river here is a ditch now, even narrower than the channelized portions downstream in Missouri. It's fast: the elevation drops about one foot per mile, and the channel has been pinched to the center with dikes. From Kansas City to Sioux City, Iowa, the mighty Missouri is barely two football fields wide, less than a quarter of its former reach into the floodplain. The cottonwoods, together with much of the natural bounty Lewis laboriously catalogued—239 specimens in his herbarium alone—have disappeared.

On the stretch of river between St. Louis and Sioux City, Army engineers sacrificed 100,000 acres of water, 114,000 acres of wetlands, and 65,000 acres of sandbars and islands. Even commercial catfishing in what Lewis and Clark called "the catfish river" was banned in the mid-1990s in five states. The prohibition was largely due to the research by Hesse, and because of the ruckus that he set reverberating, he now totes not one but two pistols to work on the river.

TOWARD "IRREVERSIBLE EXTINCTION"

In Washington, some folks were shootin' mad in December 2002, when the National Research Council—that august body of scientists of whom Hesse is one—finally put out its much-anticipated report on the prospects for Missouri River's recovery.

By now, the ingredients for a brave new river policy had reached a simmer. No kidding this time, the Army Corps of Engineers said, it was really just about to rewrite its *Master Manual* anew. The U.S. Fish and Wildlife Service was standing up to its threat, vowing to accuse the Corps once more of violating the Endangered Species Act of 1973 unless it substantially altered the lower river's ebb and flow for the sake of protected species. Indeed, it looked like the tail out in the heartland was beginning to wag the big dogs in Washington, where the White House and Congress prepared for a new environmental fight.

The fight was simmering, but sure not yet at a full, rolling boil. Then Hesse's National Research Council turned up the temperature.

Damage to the Missouri River and its surroundings "is clear and continuing," the scientists wrote, and deterioration would continue unless the river's natural flow was significantly restored. The verdict was in; the 2,200-some river studies already done were plenty, and what was happening was plain, scientifically, to see.

"On the eve of the 200th anniversary of the Lewis and Clark expedition, a critical crossroads regarding the Missouri River ecosystem's future is approaching," the report noted, looking ahead to the 2004–06 celebration.

"The ecosystem also faces the prospect of irreversible extinction of species," the study said. Now was the time for action.

At a news conference at the academy offices across the street from the State Department in Washington's Foggy Bottom, I have tired of listening to speakers and I page through the appendix. Eighty-two species of fish, plants, reptiles, birds, mammals, insects, and mussels in the river or along its banks now are rare, threatened, or endangered. Of sixty-seven native fish species, fifty-one are rare.

I run through lists to see if I recognize any of the species extinct or headed that way. Two of the plants—Small White Lady's Slipper and

Spring Ladies Tresses—recall to me the days of cultured St. Louis women heading upriver on steamboats for adventure, perhaps of the scandalous variety. I struggle to picture the rare Dakota Skipper Butterfly and the Tawny Crescent Butterfly. Then there's the Six-banded Longhorn Beetle. That's surely a well-armed little fellow ready to stand and fight, unlike its timid cousin, the American Burying Beetle.

Seeing the Yellow Mud Turtle, I wonder which was yellow: the mud or the turtle. I'm not certain what business the Texas Horned Lizard had so far north to begin with. And, truth be told, I may be glad that the alligator snapping turtles aren't as prolific as they once were.

But ah, fish are close to my heart. I long to meet just one paddlefish and to see if the black-nosed shiner and the flathead chub live up to their names. I can imagine the mooneye and know immediately that the high-fin carpsucker is a lowlife in the Missouri. But I have not a clue as to the appearance of a northern redbelly dace; nor can I figure whether the brassy minnow got its name from its color or the impudence of its movement. For a fish we may never again see, the ghost shiner is named just fine.

The scientists write about saugers, which once made up as much as 65 percent of the fish population in the main channel. I get confused. From the photos I've seen, saugers look nearly identical to walleyes, those tasty fighters that have become a mainstay of river impoundments to the north. Both have sharp teeth that can rip flesh of prey (and fingers), and neither open their mouths willingly out of water. They have the same spiny dorsal fin that sticks straight up, like the spike hair of 1970s-vintage punk rockers. The scaly body of each is rough to the touch. A key difference is the sauger's ability to exist in a muddy, turbid river like the Missouri, once the king of the muddy rivers. (Like newspaper editors, walleyes need to have things presented to them very clearly.) Saugers are all but gone now, having declined by as much as 98 percent after the river's reengineering. I fished expressly for them once for three days and caught nary a one (although my fishing friends would say that proves nothing).

The report describes how Plains minnows swam abundantly in the turbid Missouri, playing out their supporting role in the river's web of life. They, too, have been hit hard by damming and channelization. Minnows recovered a bit in the mid-1990s after the river leapt out of its bounds in the Flood of '93. But when "normal" times returned and the river was again locked away from its floodplain, as the engineers wanted, the minnow all but disappeared.

The resilience of the Plains minnows is a ray of hope for conservationists amid 147 pages of bad news. This river ain't dead yet.

CATFISH WHOPPERS

As they made their way up the Missouri, Lewis and Clark marveled at the huge, whiskered specimens lurking in the Missouri's muddy waters. They made mention of catching their first catfish near the mouth of the Platte River in Nebraska, and they marveled at the loglike specimens that lay in deep waters. Sergeant Patrick Gass noted "nine that would together weigh 300 pounds."

Throughout the nineteenth century, catfish sustained many westward travelers, as well assuring homesteaders something to eat—and often to talk about. Captain William "Steamboat Bill" Heckman wrote of a blue catfish that must have resembled a submersible: a 315-pound specimen hauled up by a boy named Struttman at McGirk's Island near Morrison,

Missouri, in 1866. There was a 242-pounder weighed in at Hermann, Missouri, in 1868. Heckman also recalled a fish caught along the Columbia Bottoms near the mouth of the Missouri that was so large that no scale in the vicinity could handle it. The head alone weighed thirty-eight pounds, Heckman wrote, reminding me of the joke about the fish so big that its photograph, depending on who's telling the story, weighed three, five, or eleven pounds.

Well into the twentieth century, opportunity swam in these waters. Heckman recounted the good fortune of the Thompson brothers, young Missouri fellows of the World War I era who possessed a little fishing knowledge, a rowboat, a bit of net, and get-ahead spirit. In a month's time, selling catfish in Jefferson City and shipping upriver to Kansas City, they turned $28 into a business with $1,200 in assets, a load of gear, and what was described back then as a gasboat with cabin.

That was then. In our times, catfish did not grow so big—and everybody knew it. Larry Hesse was the first to document what was happening to the Missouri's catfish. The Corps of Engineers' tinkering and shape-shifting had sucked away the river's life. Gone with the snags that bedeviled nineteenth-century navigation was the muddy habitat where these horned cats could grow into lurking giants. At the same time, commercial fishermen were fast overharvesting Missouri cats. As a result, catfish were harvested younger and smaller, averaging a puny twelve to fourteen inches.

Threatening to close any fishery is like flipping a stick of dynamite in a whirlpool: You can't tell where in the swirl the explosion will sound or what the damage will be, but you damn sure know there'll be a bang. Commercial fishermen, like many of their prey, are fighting species who view new regulations like treble hooks they're being forced to swallow.

Whether they go after fish, oysters, or crabs, fishermen have long since learned to school for safety. They organize, hire lobbyists, and select well-presented spokespeople from among their ranks to tell the story of how government is about to ravage their livelihoods and families. That's what happened in Nebraska when Larry Hesse started his campaign to close the commercial catfishery.

By then, Hesse's data told an irrefutable tale of woe. By 1978, only 4 percent of the flathead catfish he shocked and netted measured longer than the legal commercial limit of thirteen inches. In 1990, fish were even smaller; just 2.3 percent of Hesse's electrofishing take were above the limit. In other words, more than 97 percent of the flatheads in the river weren't worth fooling with.

The pioneer ethic of catch-as-catch-can was, he concluded, "an unacceptable management ethic for the times."

"The Missouri River catfish is a durable species, but its worth today should not be defined by the taste of its flesh but rather by the mystique of one-time behemoths," he wrote in one of his papers.

Even so, the best Hesse could achieve against the well-organized fishing lobby in Lincoln was persuading the Nebraska Game and Fish Commission to increase the minimum length for the most valued species of catfish: for channel cats, from thirteen to fifteen inches; and for flatheads, from fifteen to eighteen. If there was a problem—and the commercial fishermen didn't admit there was—that new minimum size should take care of it.

"It didn't do a thing; not a thing," said Hesse of the new regulation's success. "They were taking whatever they could sell, and it was obvious that they sell fish beneath the [legal] fifteen inches."

In 1989, Hesse fired an even broader salvo in the Missouri River catfish wars. Under the title "The Catfish and Big Muddy," he wrote in a state conservation magazine that catfish might need to be stricken from the list of approved species for commercial harvest. By then, Hesse knew the problem was bigger than his native Nebraska. So he packed up his research and traveled the lower third of the river, visiting the capitals of each of the five river states.

Hesse was surprised at his own persuasiveness. All of the surrounding states—Missouri, Kansas, Iowa, and South Dakota—said yes, it's this bad; we need to close this fishery down. Everybody agreed with Hesse except one state: his own. Nebraska's recalcitrance sticks in his craw to this day.

In 1990 Hesse was, as he recalls, "beat bloody" in public hearings over his proposal in his own state. Upwards of one hundred fishermen, mostly commercial, showed up for every gathering. The sportsfishermen who could have balanced the testimony hung him out to dry. "I would talk to these guys days and weeks ahead of time and say, 'You know damn well that this needs to be closed because we can't catch a fish worth a shit on rod and reel.'" But Hesse could rely only on Jim Mason, an ex-commercial fisherman out of Brownsville. Mason had become a rod-and-reel guide fond of going after the remaining lunkers in the river—sixty- and eighty-pounders—using five-pound carp as bait.

Finally, the Nebraska Game and Fish Commission saw the handwriting on the wall and followed the example of its neighbors. But for Hesse the damage was done. "I had worked awful hard for twenty years and my commission was not supporting me in the final analysis. There was an awful lot of damage that got done to me personally," Hesse told me.

So bitter was the strike that Hesse's life was threatened. A decade later, meeting pickups along the Missouri's backroads, Hesse still might see a hard-bitten man thrust a middle finger in his direction. He keeps one pistol in his truck and another on his boat, both in grabbing distance. He handles a weapon as deftly as he does fish, if it comes to that. As he maneuvers his research boat on this unpredictable river and counts fish, it's another kind of confrontation that gives him pause.

"What worries me is getting blown out of my boat by some shithead on the bank that I didn't see," he says.

~ 7 ~

IN A WICKED STICKY DILEMMA

Fish are like humans; if you want to have healthy babies, you need to build a nursery.

—Ted "the Catfish Man" Hirtes

IN WHICH WE VISIT WINNERS, PREHISTORIC FRY, AND THE SCIENTIST WITH A POPULIST PLAN

I wish I was a catfish, swimming in the deep blue sea.
I'd have all the pretty women fishing after me.

LANDING
WEIGH-IN UNDER THE WAVERLY BRIDGE

I'M PROWLING FOR A GOOD-NEWS story. I admit that. I've heard far too many tales about what swam in the Missouri River, not what swims. I'm also understanding better the human disconnection with the river. With the river's beauty robbed, its creatures going or gone, and its waters fast and dangerous, why should people care? How do you drum up the political will for restoring a dead river?

I'm thinking nothing but negative when I spot the truck of a fellow named Ted Hirtes, who also knows something about what swims in the Missouri.

They call Ted Hirtes "the Catfish Man" for good reason. Just about everybody who fishes the Nebraska stretch of the Missouri River saw his photo in the newspaper with a sixty-pounder that he had horsed into his boat. Hirtes is a pro, a fishing guide with a sponsor, a bait company called Junnie's Cat Tracker.

Along the river at Bellevue, just south of Omaha, Hirtes tells me that fishing has been "pretty good"—which right away makes me suspicious. In the lexicon of fishing guides and charterboat captains everywhere, the spectrum of descriptions of fishing runs from "unbelievable" to "fantastic" to "great" to "good." To hear that it is just "pretty good" hereabouts is not the happy ending I had hoped for in this fish story. Hirtes allows that he hasn't hauled up any more of those sixty-pounders. But he says he's yanked in a few in the twenty- to forty-pound range. He catches and releases them, a conservation-minded fishing policy that Lewis and Clark could not have foreseen as they labored to provide protein for the hungry men of the Corps of Discovery. In Lewis and Clark's journals, the first mention of fishing comes north of here in this stretch of river we're on.

Had Corps of Discovery members been sporting, they still couldn't have followed Hirtes's catch-and-release method: "Weigh it. Photograph the hell out of it. Throw it back in."

Hirtes, who was born in 1950, remembers the fishing in the days before the Army Corps of Engineers finished resculpting the Missouri into a speedy ditch. "Before it got all channelized, it was like going out and picking apples off the trees," he tells me. Like many outdoorsmen, he speaks disdainfully of both the Corps and the barge industry. He tells me that it's time to halt the pathetic amount of barge traffic that remains and let the river run naturally again. More naturally, he means.

I'd rather talk fish than politics, having never before been in the company of someone who caught a sixty-pound catfish, least of all someone sponsored by Junnie's Cat Tracker. Junnie's, a beacon in the world of cat-fishing, is situated in Dubuque, Iowa, where it was established in 1988 by Junnie Mihalakis, who claims that he has fished for every fish in the western hemisphere. In the world of baits, he is an innovator who creates his own plastic worms and experiments with various dip bait concoctions. Mihalakis doesn't care for the term "stink bait," a common reference to what Missouri River anglers and catfishers everywhere glob on to treble hooks. That wasn't always the case; Junnie did well when he sold a product he labeled his Sewer Baits. There's also Junnie's Blood Bait, the Almost Illegal Shrimp Bait, and, my favorite, Jojo's Pole-Snatcher Catfish Bait. Mihalakis likes to point out that what he sells comes not from some unthinkable stink trench but from cheese made from the wholesome milk of cows. He has recently sent Hirtes something new to try, a rank, catfish-just-gotta-have-it goop called Wicked Sticky.

Hirtes is eager to put some Wicked Sticky to work. Before he goes fishing, he utters a sliver of common sense that ends up beneath a photo of his tanned, bearded face on the front page of the *St. Louis Post-Dispatch*:

"Fish are like humans; if you want to have healthy babies, you need to build a nursery."

WEIGHING THE CATCH

It would be another year before I could measure the dividends of Larry Hesse's campaign to build that nursery. In the waning hours of an August afternoon, the digital thermometer outside the bank in Waverly, Missouri, reads 103°. Down a dog-leg off the highway under one of the many

FIGURE 5. Ted "Catfish Man" Hirtes and Richard Losee display a prize-winning whiskered bottom-dweller. (Photo courtesy Bill Lambrecht)

bridges that are the closest most Missourians get to their river—until it sweeps them out of their graves—a horn sounds. With it, entrants in the Waverly Cats Catfish Tournament have ten minutes to deliver their flags to a picnic shelter in the community park. They can then return to their boats and fetch their catch from their liveboxes.

One by one, the twenty-eight two-man teams haul up plastic tubs of their catch to be weighed, gawked at, and returned to the river. After a day in this heat, some of the competitors look as though their method is leaping in to wrestle behemoths from the old days. In that competition, they've clearly lost. In this one, too, some lose out. I see from the scoreboard that four of the teams have registered zero poundage; either they quit, their boats conked out, or they got skunked. Then the crowd sounds a collective "Wow."

A dirt-streaked twentysomething fellow built like he hoists motors out of cars sans block-and-tackle has shaken his catfish into the hanging scale with wet muffled thuds. Four of his catch are unspectacular. But the fifth, which he gingerly lays across the scale pan, is another matter. It is a flathead catfish resembling a young hog, and when the weight is announced—14.9 pounds—cheers sound. Together, his fish weigh twenty-six pounds. Looks like a winner.

This is one of two tournaments that Jim "Doc" Yowell puts on every year. A month before, when the heat was less smothering, Doc's competition had drawn thirty-nine boats and one of them returned to port with a 28.3-pound cat. Doc's a big-time catfisherman himself, and he has reeled in an even bigger hog than "Catfish Man" Hirtes—a seventy-pound blue cat. He tells me that the angling has been up and down the last couple of years, and I can see that the fishing business is tricky indeed. Biologists say that the endangered pallid sturgeon, among other species, need low waters in the summer for fingerling fish after high flows have recreated backwaters for spawning. But Yowell tells me high water is all the better to bring in from the Upper Mississippi those big blue cats that make a man's reputation.

Yowell squeezes the last blast from an air horn, which means that if you haven't delivered your flag to the picnic table within minutes, it won't matter even if your catfish is bigger than your boat. I'm staring at a bulletin board, dumb from the heat, before it dawns on me that a photo I'm seeing is none other than Ted Hirtes and that sixty-pounder that made him famous. Then, as if by magic, I see the Catfish Man himself, double-timing up the rise toward tourney central, gripping his half of a plastic tub. When he and his partner, Richard Losee, begin sliding fish on the scale, it looks as though we have a competition. But when Ted and Richard's big-fella cat is weighed, it comes in at 14.2 pounds, the second largest of the day.

I follow as they hurry their catch back to the river. "Good try," I say.

Ted doesn't look upset. The reason, I learn, is that the big prize goes to total weight. Each team gets to bring back ten fish, which requires strategy; the two-pounder you hook in the morning might no longer be among the ten biggest by the end of the day. What's more, you can weigh in just one dead fish, which are given away to catfish-eating spectators.

Doc Yowell needs a calculator to tally up what these hot fishermen have brought him. I do some figuring myself, and the day's catch comes to 235.9 pounds. Of that, Ted Hirtes and his partner brought in 27.1 pounds, which captures first place by 1.1 pounds.

Ted is looking satisfied, as well he should. Doc is about to hand him a check for $1,000, first-prize money. Ted is lighting a cigarette and still sweating when I ask him about his day. He tells me that he and Richard caught more than fifty catfish. The fishing was "pretty good," he says, and I understand now that he wasn't low-balling me when we'd met up in Nebraska.

I remember to ask Ted what bait he used to snag all those fish.

Wicked Sticky, he says.

GOOD NEWS: UGLY BABIES

The internal memorandum written by biologist Jim Milligan of the U.S. Fish and Wildlife Service in the first week of the new century brimmed with excitement. Milligan's office in Columbia, Missouri, finally had gotten back the desired conclusion from the Larval Fish Laboratory at Colorado State University. "Good news," he began.

One confirmed and two probably post-larval pallid sturgeon specimens collected from the Lower Missouri River in mid-August, from the large sandbar complex at the lower end of Lisbon Chute on the Lisbon Bottoms Unit of the Big Muddy National Fish and Wildlife Refuge at river mile 214. We believe that this is the first confirmed reproduction of pallid sturgeon in the lower Missouri for many years. It provides compelling evidence that there is at least some suitable spawning habitat available between Gavins Point Dam and RM 214 under certain conditions. It also provides at least anecdotal support to the "build it and they will come" philosophy of big river habitat restoration.

It took a month for the policy whizzes and wordsmiths in Washington to convert Milligan's memo for public consumption.

The first known reproduction of the pallid sturgeon in the Lower Missouri River in at least the last fifty years has been confirmed by U.S. Fish and Wildlife Service biologists, who point to the startling discovery as evidence that the fish, whose ancestors date to the days of the dinosaurs, may have a better chance at recovery than previously believed.

The release quoted then-Interior Secretary Bruce Babbitt:

This remarkable news is more than just a testimony to the need to conserve habitat in order to pull an endangered species back from the brink of extinction. It speaks eloquently for the need to restore some natural flows to rivers so they're more than just dammed and channelized flood control projects sluicing fresh water toward the sea. When the Edwards Dam was removed from the Kennebec River in Maine, Atlantic salmon were seen back in that stretch of river almost immediately. When we let the Big Muddy be the Big Muddy, suddenly one of America's historic and most endangered game fish is spotted spawning in nature once again.

The discovery had proved to be a marvelous propaganda tool to go with the halting process of river restoration. The work at Lisbon Bottoms, in Missouri, was part of a modest effort reconnecting the river with its floodplain by digging the sort of channel that had been blocked in taming the great Missouri. The news also highlighted the significance of the sturgeon as an endangered species, one of the three protected creatures that had generated tortured negotiations between the Fish and Wildlife Service and the Army Corps of Engineers.

The pallid sturgeon thrived in Big Muddy's sediment-rich waters when the river lived up to its name. But pallids began to disappear after the river was clamped into a channel and disabused of its lust for surrounding soils. Biologists believe that the number of pallids living in the Missouri dropped to as little as a few thousand; in 1990, the government formally designated them as endangered. The pallid sturgeon have been on this earth for 70 million years, since the Cretaceous period, and they exist nowhere on earth but in the Missouri and the Lower Mississippi. Fish and Wildlife Service biologists warned early in the new century that the disaster of their extinction could befall the Missouri in a decade.

Government biologists are breeding pallids at the Gavins Point National Fish Hatchery in South Dakota, where I visited. I returned, perhaps because I couldn't believe what I had seen.

With their flat, shovel-like snouts and reptilian tails, pallids look like a genetic concoction of dinosaur, shark, and alligator. They are unprepossessing in looks; damn ugly, most people would say. Even the Fish and Wildlife Service's cyberspace bulletins label them one of America's ugliest fishes. A Missouri River advocate remarked, only half in jest, that if the pallid sturgeon had the classic looks of a coho salmon, the Missouri River might snag some of that federal bounty awarded the Columbia River for fish restoration.

I think people are being a tad harsh, and I come to that conclusion while stroking the bony plates of a juvenile pallid's back. Herbert Bollig agrees. "They're so ugly, they're beautiful," says Bollig, the project manager at Gavins Point.

Bollig, a stocky, genial man who relishes his job, has overseen the sturgeon hatching almost since it began, in 1990. Ever since, he and his colleagues have been writing the book on rearing these homely, rare creatures. Each chapter has been a breakthrough. First, they had to find and catch them; initial stock came from near the confluence of the Missouri and Yellowstone rivers. Then it was like bringing the baby home from the hospital. Bollig and the hatchery crew had to figure out exactly what to feed them. For a while, the pallids ate tadpoles. Now they're consuming a diet of herring meal and anchovy revved up with nutrients. And growing two inches a month.

The baby always gets sick, and the parents frantic, which is what happened when a virus struck the population in the mid-1990s. Illness, too, was conquered, and spawning techniques perfected, and since 1995, ten thousand pallid sturgeon have been stocked into the Missouri River. "You screw up and fall back and re-gather yourself and learn," Bollig says.

Uncertainties still nag. "Here is a fish that lived for eons in a huge river and then you put them in a six-feet by twenty-feet tank. What does that do them?" Bollig worries.

I wonder that, too, watching thirty-five-pounders circling the perimeter of their tank like tigers in a zoo. It is an appealing dream to think of even larger ones—eighty-pounders that are six feet long—fought and caught by sportfishers in a restored Missouri River. Of course, there's no proof of a political will in society to head in that direction, another reason for Bollig to remain diligent in his task.

"It's very gratifying to be able to work with a species that would disappear from the face of the earth if there wasn't somebody here to help them," he says.

"THIS RIVER BELONGS TO YOU AND ME"

Larry Hesse, the electrofishing research pioneer, makes his headquarters in the countryside of northern Nebraska, near Crofton, near an east-west artery known as the Outlaw Trail Byway. Some of the people he has irritated over the years with his outspokenness probably think he's well situated.

He lives close to his family home. When he was no more than three, his father would haul him to the duck blind, where he'd sit all day, too shy to get up and pee. Finally, they'd be loading up, and he'd pull it out but he'd be so cold he couldn't go so he'd have to wait until he got warm back home. He fished with his father and his grandfather and just never left northern Nebraska except to go to school up at the University of South Dakota, at Sioux Falls, and later with the Army to Vietnam as a medic.

His office is a stripped-down house devoted to his research. For his daughter, who works for the Santee Tribe, he's building a house next door, which he framed himself. He's a carpenter on top of being a scientist, and he'd love to build houses for a living to get away from the maddening sense of shouting in the wilderness without being heard. But they probably wouldn't sell out in rural Nebraska, where towns aren't rising well to globalization.

Rifles lean in a corner of his office, and four trays of .257 and .300 shells are waiting for Hesse, a hunter, to fill them. He's armed well enough to fend off at least a platoon of commercial catfisher assassins. Two walls of shelves hold stacks of research papers dealing with fish: burbot, gar, shad, drum, suckers, and, of course, catfish. Nearly all the studies bear his name, singularly or with research partners.

Hesse is dressed in his summer attire: a camouflage cap and a faded green T-shirt, sleeveless. He looks ready to go to war, and sounds it, too, at my mention of the Army Corps of Engineers.

"The Corps has been saying for years that there's not enough data. But they have thumbed their nose at my data and never explained why they wouldn't use it. And here it sits, as good as anything that there's ever been or probably ever will be. Tell me why that is. I don't get it," he says.

Under the gun of a federal court, the Corps had declared that it intends to begin a round of river monitoring that will include research similar to what Hesse has done. Hesse sees it as a stall, and a wasteful one, and the more he thinks about it, the madder he gets.

"I think it's scandalous. Shame on them for that bullshit. Who the hell do they think they are kidding? What a bunch of horseshit. This is all about keeping government scientists busy," he tells me.

When I remark to Hesse that he's viewed in some quarters as an advocate, he says, yes, he's an advocate for fixing the river. But never at the expense of science or his principles.

Most of all, Hesse is tired of being ignored. So he's spending his own money to assemble all the scientific research related to the Missouri River. The database he's building at the University of Nebraska will bring together some 1 million fish records and 2 million insect records, along with vast amounts of data about water quality and chemistry. He says nothing like it has been done for any body of water anywhere in the world. When Hesse finishes, he expects to have assembled evidence incontrovertible in any court of the river's demise. He's looking forward to waving his proof in the faces of all the naysayers, especially the Army Corps of Engineers.

"I intend that sometime, the Corps won't just be able to say, 'Here's another study by another dumb fish guy. Who cares?'"

Hesse is no politician. If he were, he'd have been bounced out of office long ago for irascibility. He is, on the other hand, a planner. His plan for the river is built around a deliberative body he calls the Missouri River Adaptive Management Council. He's written its constitution, a dense, eleven-page summation of the damage to the river which amounts to a manifesto demanding that control of the river be yanked from the Army. Congress should give people of the Missouri basin an "equal role" in future management with government agencies, it says.

Under the word "Vision," Hesse defines his: "That the citizens of the Missouri River basin, through collaboration, cooperation, and compromise, will find common ground for the recovery and preservation of ecological, economic, and social resilience. Success means the Missouri

River will regain the capacity for self-renewal at the ecosystem level, which includes native flora and fauna, as well as humans."

He tells me in plainer language what he has in mind. "Screw the Corps. They will become just another stakeholder. They will have no more power than Farmer John out here. The time is past for the Corps of Engineers to stop acting like God and saying what the river's priorities are.

"What's wrong with good old-fashioned democracy? Everybody has a right to have some expectations for this river. This river belongs to everybody in the country."

⟡ PADDLING ⟡

BLACKBIRD'S SKULL

The sign at the entrance of the park overlooking the Missouri at Macy, Nebraska, advises against smoking and assorted forms of disrespect. Apparently, authorities have decided there's been enough bad behavior hereabouts, considering the reputation of the man who is buried here. Or mostly buried.

The memorial doesn't begin to tell the story of Omaha chief Blackbird, as it has been passed down over two centuries. Blackbird, who died in 1800, built the Omahas into a power of the Eastern Plains. Along the way, he earned a reputation for uncanny power and ruthlessness, for he ruled by potent medicine and his ability to predict the future.

Untimately, his methods would be exposed: Blackbird's medicine was arsenic, procured from traders, and he would secretly administer the poison to his rivals along with public predictions that they would soon succumb to his powers.

Blackbird was also labeled a narcissist for his obsession with his dress and his looks. His fascination with his image reflected in mirrors, novelties delivered to him by fur traders, continued even after he had swelled to such grotesque proportions that it took several braves to move him about on his blanket.

Smallpox was also delivered by the Euro-invaders. Infected, Blackbird foresaw his own death, as he had seen the deaths by pox of hundreds of his people. So the vainglorious chief ordered a burial befitting his life. Legend has it that his body was clothed in headdress and battle buckskins and draped with his collection of scalps. Then the massive corpse was roped onto a live stallion, lowered into a grave along the Missouri, and buried to his neck. He wanted his head facing the river so he could remain watchful.

I don't know, even after consulting historians, how much these legends were embellished over the years. Lewis and Clark wrote in their journals that they knew of Blackbird's Machiavellian reputation and visited his grave four year after his death. They came on a rainy day with a harsh wind blowing and planted a white flag, which the Omahas took as intention to lay claim to their land.

Like most Indians in the Missouri basin, today's Omahas are dismayed about the destruction to their river at the hands of the Army engineers who followed Lewis and Clark to tribal land. Antione Provost, the Omahas' environmental chief, told me that his tribe fears the turbid waters of the channelized river. I first met Provost shortly after a tribal police officer had died rescuing two of his children in the river's savage currents.

"About the only recreation we get from the river is sitting along the bank and watching the barges go by. And there aren't many of them," he said. Provost was heartened when the Army Corps of Engineers agreed to reconnect the Missouri with a long-dried lake destroyed in the river's reengineering.

Their ancestral river is not all the Omahas have lost to the followers of Lewis and Clark. In a last twist to the Blackbird saga, George Catlin, the portraitist, traveler, and ally of tribes, visited Blackbird's grave in 1832. An early souvenir hunter, he dug around, found the skull, and returned east with it among his possessions. Blackbird's skull is said to have found its resting place in the Smithsonian Institution in Washington, D.C.

Omaha historian Dennis Hastings is more interested in the fate of Blackbird's remains than debunking alleged transgressions of the old chief.

"We've been looking for that head for a long time," he told me. "You say you're from Washington? If you could get it for us, we'd be much appreciative."

Back in Washington, I was dead-ended in the Smithsonian phone system eight or nine times before I caught the attention of a young curator at Smithsonian's Museum of Natural History. I told her I was looking for an Indian skull dropped off by an artist 170 years ago.

"We have 125 million items in our collection," she said.

"Could you take a look around?" I asked, making certain she had my phone numbers.

Like the Omahas, I never heard back.

8

BIRDS VERSUS BARGES

It is the policy of Congress that all federal departments and agencies shall seek to conserve endangered species and threatened species.

—Endangered Species Act, 1973

IN WHICH FEDERAL AGENCIES WAR OVER WHICH DIRECTION THE MISSOURI SHOULD FLOW

*I give up. I've had enough. Followed my blues on down to the gulf.
She loves you Big River more than me.*

LANDING
ON A PAPER TRAIL

THE INTERIOR LEAST tern chicks from nest No. 959028 never struggled to find food in the vanishing habitat of the Missouri River.

On June 12, 1995, the nest, with its three eggs, was discovered flooded at river mile 807.7, near Gavins Point Dam, lost to rising water loosed from an Army Corps of Engineers dam.

Nearby, piping plover nest No. 959029 was also found flooded, its four eggs lost. That July was a bad month in one of the worst years for these federally protected birds, according to remarkably detailed records the Corps of Engineers has never made public.

From 1986 through 2003, 414 least tern nests and 368 piping plover nests—all told, 782 nests and 1,937 eggs—were lost to Corps dam operations, according to the Historical Mortality Report compiled by the Corps as it revised its bible of river flows, the *Master Manual*.

That number is likely low. Way low, according to the U.S. Fish and Wildlife Service, the Corps' rival power along the Missouri River. An internal Fish and Wildlife Service memo calculates that at worst case, more than 3,600 nests—not 782—were lost over the eighteen years.

The two sets of figures are unreconcilable, as are two agencies tugging the waters of the Missouri in opposition directions. The struggle between the Corps and the Fish and Wildlife Service is far bigger than the Missouri River. But the degree to which one agency or the other prevails in the American heartland will influence decisions on the Everglades, on the Columbia and Snake rivers in the Northwest, and all across the country where the survival of species collides with commerce and property rights.

The Corps and the federal government's wildlife agency report to one boss, the president, but their missions are much different. Commerce and engineering drive the Corps, while the Service exists as the protector of wildlife and, in its modern role, as Endangered Species Act enforcer.

As the Army's civil works branch, the Corps of Engineers has the power to direct projects to locales along all the navigable rivers it controls. Its huge dams and engineering feats in the mid-twentieth century poured hundreds of millions of dollars into Missouri River communities. All those projects need constant maintenance, levee work, and occasional dredging, and still more vast projects are proposed continuously to reengineer inlets and river systems as expansive as the Everglades. The Corps has evolved into a powerful development force with a $4 billion budget and 35,000 employees.

With all those works in progress, affinity has evolved among Army engineers desirous of protecting and expanding their domain: farmers, barge operators, and developers seeking favors along the river; and members of Congress hunting job-creating projects to prove their own political worth.

Indeed, the Corps thrives on a unique symbiosis with Congress. The Corps' intimacy has always excluded other federal agencies—until the Endangered Species Act came along. In 1973, Congress declared "that species of fish wildlife and plants have been so depleted in number that they are in danger of or threatened with extinction."

Already, the act noted, various species "have been rendered extinct as a consequence of economic growth and development untempered by adequate concern and conservation."

The federal government is uniquely responsible for species under the act, and must not only abide by the law but set the standard. Federal agencies are forbidden from harming protected species and from damaging their habitat.

The act deputized the Fish and Wildlife Service as a police force preserving the survival of the rarest fish, birds, and plants.

And it turned the Corps into lawbreakers.

A STRUGGLE BEGINS

By 1985, the law put the Corps of Engineers and the Fish and Wildlife Service at war on the Missouri. That's the year the government's wildlife agency added the least tern to its endangered species list and designated the piping plover as threatened.

One of the now-protected birds had inspired Meriwether Lewis—who apparently suffered from writer's block as well as that ailment's intestinal opposite on his travels up the Missouri—to a burst of more than a thousand words. The young explorer and biologist had better than an amateur's eye. Male and female terns are all but indistinguishable, but Lewis reported weighing and measuring a male, one of two of the species he killed. For that killing, he could have been arrested today and fined $25,000—ten times what Congress originally authorized for his voyage of discovery.

Lewis wrote, correctly, that terns exist on small fish, worms, and bugs that they take from the water's surface, and seldom do they alight on either trees or water. "I believe them to be a native of this country and probably a constant resident," Lewis wrote of North America's smallest tern.

The probability that terns would no longer be residents of the Missouri River prompted their 1985 "endangered" designation. Another rare bird, the piping plover, was listed in 1986 as "threatened." Terns and plovers often share nesting colonies on islands in the river and shorelines of the largest reservoirs. Unlike plover chicks, which forage for food soon after hatching, the terns remain in their nests to be fed, vulnerable to the rising waters from Corps-operated dams and vulnerable as well to predators.

Nell McPhillips, a former biologist in the Fish and Wildlife Service office in Pierre, South Dakota, watched the birds struggle over the years: terns fighting vainly to pull minnows from the swift, channelized river; inundated nests of plover and tern chicks, and eggs.

"The birds were squeezed down to almost nothing as far as habitat," she told me.

The Corps wasn't exactly gunning down endangered species or even bringing in its heavy equipment to dig up habitat. A few birds were drowning, the Corps acknowledged in 1986, when it submitted to Fish and Wildlife's authority on endangered species. But drowning the birds was unavoidable if that 1944 Flood Control Act prescribing navigation as a priority was to be followed.

In 1987, the Corps acknowledged, for the first time, that following one law meant sidestepping the new law protecting endangered species. Yes, the engineers admitted in a newly required biological assessment of the Corps' Missouri River management, the ebb and flow of dam management could harm protected birds. Then, for more than two years, the Corps evaded Fish and Wildlife Service requests for more information.

The tortured negotiations, mistrust, and outright hostilities between the two ever since offer a textbood example of how federal agencies function and fail.

WHAT'S A FEW BIRDS HERE AND THERE?

In 1990, when the Corps began its first significant revision since 1960 of its thirty-year-old guidebook for river operations, the *Master Manual*, the Fish and Wildlife Service officials had the authority to do more than observe. And much of what they saw, they didn't like. More alarming was what they didn't see. Admonishing the Corps fell to John Spinks, a Fish and Wildlife staff member in the Denver office. His 1990 letter was the first of dozens of Fish and Wildlife Service communiqués reminding the Army Engineers that they weren't living up to the law.

"Limited consideration has been given to fish and wildlife resources and their habitat," Spinks wrote, in bureaucratic understatement. "Recreational uses and related economic values have been included; however, no attempt has been made to correlate habitat conditions with the various alternatives and to relate changes in habitats to fish and wildlife and recreational sites." In other words, the Corps was up to business as usual, managing the Missouri for barge commerce.

Part of the problem, Spinks wrote, was the Corps' attitude. "The Service is concerned about the Corps' references to the Endangered Species Act as 'constraints' on operations," he noted in a feat of textual analysis literary scholars might envy.

"In passing the Endangered Species Act, Congress declared that, 'It is the policy of Congress that all federal departments and agencies shall seek to conserve endangered species and threatened species and shall utilize their authorities in furtherance of the purposes of the Endangered Species Act.'"

Thus, the Corps was violating not only the spirit of the law but also its letter. Spinks picked up on the evidence, as would one angry judge thirteen years later. The Corps now acknowledged that it frequently inundated tern and plover nests, which meant that it was killing protected species. In a memo to Fish and Wildlife, more than a decade before compiling its historical mortality report, the Corps admitted causing the destruction of 118 piping plover nests and 56 least tern nests. The birds were, to the Corps way of thinking, "incidental take in the operation of the Missouri River."

A dead tern here and a drowned plover there don't add up to criminality, the Corps responded in 1990, when chief engineer Colonel John Schaufelberger wrote the Fish and Wildlife Service that "The Corps of Engineers has ensured, and will continue to ensure, that our actions do not jeopardize the continued existence of these two species."

In November 1990, the Fish and Wildlife Service again faced off against the Corps. "It is our biological opinion," wrote the Service in a decision that survived a decade as the controlling scientific opinion on river species, "that the operations of the system are likely to jeopardize the continued existence of the endangered interior least tern and the threatened piping plover because operations eliminate essential nesting habitat."

Every year, the Corps might be erasing as much as 12 percent of the least tern population on the river and 22 percent of the plovers, a Fish and Wildlife memorandum concluded.

Yet months went by and the charge was ignored. In the administration of President George Herbert Walker Bush, the Endangered Species Act didn't carry much weight. Indeed, the Fish and Wildlife Service was so far out of the loop in 1991 that biologists didn't receive a copy of the Corps' newest annual operating plan.

"Coordination and measurable progress in *Master Manual* planning activities between our two agencies has been limited," Roger Collins, a Fish and Wildlife Service biologist in North Dakota, observed in an internal memo.

A "TOWER OF BABEL"

Back in 1991, early in the standoff between the two agencies, Nell McPhillips took stock of all manner of creatures. From her South Dakota office McPhillips had written most of the 1990 landmark biological opinion identifying what ails birds and fish. Now, she pinpointed what she believed was the Army Corps of Engineers' main affliction. She boiled it down to what she called the engineers' "knowledge gap" about the Endangered Species Act.

"Corps staff commonly tells the states and the public that 'Fish and Wildlife made us do it' rather than [that] the action is a requirement of the Act," she wrote in an internal memo.

> The Corps staff's lack of understanding severely impairs the ability of the Corps and the Service to communicate effectively. This problem permeates every program with which our agencies work together.
> For years, we have been talking terns and plovers to the Corps at all levels. Unfortunately, we have never been talking the same language. It's like the people that were building the Tower of Babel. The building was going well because everyone was communicating in the same language. Once God changed everyone's language, the cooperation stopped and the tower failed because no one was talking the same language. We all need to recognize each other's responsibilities and learn to talk the same language.

The biologist's solution was training workshops for the Army Corps of Engineers. The prospect of bearded biologists in faded jeans administering quizzes about the mating habits of shorebirds to spit-shined Army officers might have been tantalizing to the Fish and Wildlife Service and their allies in the environmental community. But the training never materialized. In 1994, it looked for a spell like it wouldn't be needed.

A MISSOURI MISS

That historic year, the Corps agreed to propose a spring rise in the river to begin recreating the conditions that had once nourished wildlife.

Before the Missouri was reengineered, the river was flooded twice annually by pulses of water. The first flowed in late March or April from the melting of snow on the Great Plains. The second came down in June, when the runoff from the Rocky Mountain snowpack finally made it downstream. As a partial solution to the species problem—and in hopes of avoiding the dreaded jeopardy finding from Fish and Wildlife—the Corps proposed raising water levels by increasing flows from Gavins Point Dam by 25,000 cubic feet per second over the full-service navigation flow of 31,000.

To say that the Corps' timing was off would be an understatement. A year before, the middle of America had endured one of the three worst Missouri River floods in a century. The prospect of unleashing more water in springtime, no matter what the rationale, struck most level-headed folks as heresy.

Having endured a decade of bickering and loss, environmentalists today would gladly receive such a plan. But in 1994, American Rivers and Environmental Defense—the two principal advocacy groups working on Missouri River issues—rejected the Corps' offer as insufficient. So did the Fish and Wildlife Service, demanding not just the spring rise but a summer drawdown of water to open sandbars, protect nesting birds, and give newborn fish slow-water habitat to thrive.

Corps officials needed only to step out of their black brick building in Omaha to hear cries of opposition up and down the river. Upstream states saw nothing in the plan for their reservoirs. Downstream states recoiled at the prospect of more water released into the river. The Corps' so-called preferred alternative was preferred by no one. So the Army backed off.

DÉJÀ VU ALL OVER AGAIN

Meanwhile, frustration was growing at the Fish and Wildlife Service. In August 1995, deputy regional director Terry Terrell wrote that the impasse had become what she referred to as a major social, political, and environmental controversy.

"The Corps currently is not in compliance with the Endangered Species Act. Consequently, these resources, at least species of the native river fish and the Missouri River ecosystem, continue to degrade," Terrell wrote in an internal memo.

Chicks of protected terns and plovers weren't just degrading; they were dying on the rare stretches of river where they could still breed. When the Corps released water to keep barges floating in the low waters of late summer, nests full of chicks would be swept away. The Corps had a solution to save the hatches that could be rescued: captive rearing. Raising wild creatures in captivity is abhorrent to most wildlife biologists, but the Fish and Wildlife Service had consented to the plan in the mid-1990s high-water years.

For rearing chicks and hatching eggs collected along the river, a captive rearing facility was built by prison inmates outside the Corps office in Yankton, South Dakota. In addition, some birds were fostered out to zoos. The Corps sent fifteen piping plover eggs to the Milwaukee County Zoo and another fifteen to the Lincoln Park Zoo in Chicago. But the biologists were not about to allow the Corps to let trial captivity become a permanent management tool, according to notes from a 1995 conference call.

Nell McPhillips explained the Fish and Wildlife Service position:

Starting a captive breeding program for endangered species was premature until habitat and other management alternatives to save them had been exhausted. The Corps grudgingly accepted this line of thinking.

By the mid-1990s, correspondence between the two agencies resembled conversations among old men who know each other's jokes; rather than repeating them, they recount them by number. Responding to the Corps' continued refusal to make environmentally friendly flow changes in the river, a Fish and Wildlife Service analysis noted that the draft 1997–98 plan was similar to the 1996–97 which, in turn, was similar to the 1995–96 plans. Therefore, the Service told the Corps, what we said in the past applies.

Fruitless meeting followed fruitless meeting. Business as usual was summed up in a memo of May 1997 by Allyn Sapa, who headed the Fish and Wildlife Service's North Dakota field office: "In general, the meeting was not very productive and raises questions about the Corps' commitment to take proactive action for threatened and endangered species."

Visiting Al Sapa in North Dakota after he retired in 2002, I asked him what had gone wrong. Sapa, a brawny, bearded fellow, surprised me by laying the mistakes of his Fish and Wildlife Service on the table. He wondered about the wisdom of assigning field biologists like himself the responsibilities of negotiating with Army engineers. The biologists are, by nature, less formal, less strategic; they didn't always do a thorough job of recording what Corps officials said in meetings, of writing down instances in which Army engineers had agreed with the biologists' scientific conclusions. "The Service puts a lot of faith in low-ranking bureaucrats," he said.

Power and the perceptions that surround it also got in the way of agreement, Sapa said. He recalled an occasion when the atmospherics of a gathering changed mightily with the arrival of a Corps general in a helicopter. Corps officials "are very level-conscious, aware of who's got the power and who doesn't. In dealing with us, they're aware that we're not at the same decision-making level. You wonder whether, if you suddenly say, 'Colonel, you're wrong,' if somebody he brings along is going to whack you over the head," Sapa said.

The Corps' regimentation girds it against change, Sapa believed. He recalled that on several occasions, agreements evaporated when decisions were kicked up the chain of command. "There's an institutional resistance to change that is so strong they can't do it short of a general ordering it, and we couldn't get a general long enough to see it through to the end. They have institutionalized the status quo. For fifty years they have been building this river, and they're not about to change," he said.

AN "IRON TRIANGLE"

Not only biologists were battling the Army Corps of Engineers. The debate over the Missouri River coincided with a siege by Congress, where the Corps had been accustomed to unfailing support. The early days of the new century challenged the way the Corps of Engineers operates on every big water project across the country.

The sheer breadth of the changes wrought by the Corps on the American landscape is staggering: more than 500 dams; 8,500 miles of levees and flood walls; 11,000 miles of inland waterways; more than 140 ports deepened.

Pushing the change was mounting evidence that the "Iron Triangle" of the Corps, Congress, and special interests produced water projects that were not only environmentally destructive but also wasteful and un-necessary.

This was hardly news. In 1836, in an early demand for change, a House Ways and Means Committee complained of some two dozen over-budget projects and requested "actual reform in the further prosecution of public works."

In 1902, Congress set up a review board to investigate the necessity of Corps projects; later the board was abolished.

Harold Ickes, Franklin Roosevelt's interior secretary, was one of many in the executive branch dismayed over the years at the willfulness of an agency ostensibly under executive control. Writing in 1950, Ickes, a Bull Moose Republican turned New Dealer and a determined conservationist, described Corps officers as "our highest ruling class. They are not only the political elite of the army, they are the perfect flower of bureaucracy. At least that is the reflection that the mirror discloses to them."

Ickes, who served longer (thirteen years) than any other American cabinet secretary, defined the Corps modus operandi as "Operation Santa Claus."

"The harder the people scratch to pay their taxes, the more money there will be for the Corps to scratch out of the Treasury with the aid of Congress in order to maintain control of [Congress] by building, or promising to build, more or less justifiable or downright unjustifiable projects for which senators and representatives may claim credit during the next election campaign."

Ickes was just warming up. "It is to be doubted whether a federal agency in the history of this country has so wantonly wasted money on worthless projects as has the Corps of Engineers. . . . No more lawless or irresponsible federal group than the Corps of Engineers has ever attempted to operate in the United States," he wrote.

In this new century, it wasn't just liberals and advocacy groups squawking. Budget hawks and Republicans with environmental sensibilities began pressuring the Corps, among them Congressman Wayne Gilchrest, a GOP ex-Marine from Maryland, who helped devise a coalition to limit Corps operations and require outside audits of studies the Corps conducts to justify large water construction projects.

When I tracked him down, Gilchrest explained the sentiments behind the drive to rein in a wayward federal agency. "The Corps of Engineers has been overused by Congress. They've dredged, they've channelized, they've leveed, and in the process, they've degraded the environment of the United States more than they have needed to," he said.

Reformers backed their charges with proof. Independent experts at Virginia Tech concluded that the Corps had overestimated by $181 million the benefits of a huge Mississippi project called Yazoo Pumps, which would drain 200,000 acres of Mississippi River wetlands to make new farmlands. Ex-Interior Secretary Bruce Babbitt called the Yazoo Pumps plan, "A cockamamie godawful project."

Twice in a two-year period the National Academy of Sciences took the Corps to task, saying that its methods and planning models fail to balance economic and environmental benefits. In 2000, reporter Michael Grunwald wrote a series of stories in *The Washington Post* based on more than a thousand interviews and tens of thousands of pages of documents. The Corps was parlaying its congressional relationships into billions of dollars' worth of water projects, he concluded, and many of them charged heavy environmental costs for dubious economic value.

The Corps sometimes invites scrutiny with its blunders, too, as with the episode on Chesapeake Bay in the summer of 2004 that came to be known as the Corps' Cow-Nosed Ray Feeding Project. In the drive to rescue the Chesapeake's native Virginia oyster, besieged by disease and pollution, Army engineers were put in charge of a multimillion-dollar reseeding plan. The first strike: "carpet-bombing" 1 million baby oysters onto a reef in the Great Wicomico River near the Maryland-Virginia border.

The overall fate of the Chesapeake's oyster recovery remains uncertain, but a species of stingray could be heard applauding with its fleshy water wings the Corps' involvement. In one day, a herd of the kite-shaped cow-nosed rays devoured every last one of a million oyster fry. The Corps didn't do a thing to stifle the giggling of watermen accustomed to the shellfish-loving rays when word of the $78,000 oyster buffet leaked out in the *Virginian-Pilot*.

"We didn't really know anything about the cow-nosed ray," Corps project manager Doug Martin told the newspaper. "It kind of surprised us."

The Corps bridles at scrutiny. "We don't go dream these things up all by ourselves," Paul Johnston, a Corps veteran in the Omaha District, told me. "The Corps is characterized as having battalions of bulldozers poised and ready to go out and rape and pillage. But all these authorizations are supported by a majority of representatives of the people of the United States. That sounds pretty grandiose, but that's the way it is. We are responding to problems that fit into certain sets of priorities. That's what happened along the Missouri River, and over time, those priorities for some people have shifted. In 1944, there wasn't much interest in things environmental."

MISSISSIPPI MUDDIES THE WATERS

Then scandal along the neighboring Mississippi River proved Corps detractors right.

On Sunday, February 13, 2000, a story under my byline on the front page of the *St. Louis Post-Dispatch* reported news that also broke in *The Washington Post* and other newspapers that day. "High-ranking officers of the Army Corps of Engineers rejected the conclusions of the agency's economists in order to strengthen the case for a massive expansion of Mississippi River locks," my opening paragraph read.

The stories reported the conclusion of the Corps' own economists that a $1.5 billion project to double the size of locks at Mississippi River dams was not worth spending taxpayers' money. Corps officers had prolonged what was then an eight-year, $50-plus-million study to justify the massive construction project. Environmental advocates, of course, welcomed the disclosures as obstacles to still more damaging construction on a river already overdeveloped.

The stories rose from veteran Corps economist Donald Sweeney's decision to go public with irregularities he regarded as wrongdoing. Sweeney had detailed his charges in a forty-four-page, sworn affidavit to the Office of Special Counsel in Washington and shared them with a few reporters. He explained to me his sense of what was happening. "There's a lot of money and a lot of work for a lot of people. The industry wants these projects. The Corps of Engineers wants these projects. Congress wants these projects. Everybody is in bed together."

Colonel James V. Mudd, commander of the Rock Island District and overseer of the study, assured me over the phone that the Corps had done nothing amiss; indeed, it had tried to balance the needs of the economy and the environment. But a memo he had sent to an economist, one of Sweeney's documents, suggested a different reality. It read: "You will develop the economic component of the case for a recommendation that includes near-term improvements, recognizing that the nation is better served by improvements that err on the large-scale side than by actions that err on the underdeveloped side."

Sweeney, a Ph.D. economist, had been regarded highly enough within the Corps to have been put in charge of the economics side of one its most sensitive studies. When I visited him at his suburban St. Louis home after he had gone public with his allegations, he told me of a recent assignment that conveyed significantly less trust: He was ordered to cross the Mississippi River to copy down addresses in the floodplain of derelict East St. Louis.

"The real problem is the system," he told me. "It's like asking my ten-year-old son, Cameron, 'What are the options as far as how much ice cream we should eat tonight?' I know what he will say. The whole system is set up so that the taxpayers, who have to pay, are not at the table, and the economists can't stand up and tell the truth."

Sweeney tasted vindication ten months later when the Pentagon released the results of its investigation. The report implicated three Corps officers in altering data to justify construction. This conclusion went well beyond the Mississippi, documenting what was described as "a widespread perception of bias" within the Corps in favor of large-scale construction. The Corps' zeal to please Congress and its allies, investigators found, helped to "create an atmosphere where objectivity in its analyses was placed in jeopardy." The scorching report concluded that Corps of Engineers commanders acted as advocates for waterway interests, departing from the agency's traditional role as "honest broker" for the public.

The report quoted the agency's former chief economist in Washington as calling some Corps of Engineers officials corrupt and questioning whether they still worked for the people.

"Although this investigation focused on only one study, the testimony and evidence presented strong indications that institutional bias might extend throughout the Corps," wrote the inspector general, Lieutenant General Michael Ackerman.

The National Academy of Sciences delivered more damning conclusions. There is no more authoritative body of scientific experts than the academy, a private organization sustained by government cash in its wide-ranging inquiries. Saying it was wading into "a clash of powerful forces and changing values," the academy's National Research Council recommended bluntly that the billion-dollar lock construction be put on hold.

In still more criticism, the scientists said the Corps didn't fathom the environmental destruction caused by its projects and recommended that outside experts be called in to oversee studies.

"What an incredible document. I couldn't have written it better," Sweeney said of the report.

The new head of the Army Corps, Lieutenant General Robert Flowers, summed up the perceptions in testimony in front of a Senate subcommittee. "The Army Corps of Engineers is charged in the press as a rogue agency, out of control, too cozy with Congress and living by its own rules," he said. People in the rear of the hearing room were nodding, and Flowers must have seen the assent, too. "Those allegations are absolutely false," he hastened to add.

NEW CENTURY, NEW CORPS?

In 2000, with the Corps now under fire on many fronts, I visited Flowers in his office near the new MCI basketball and hockey arena in downtown Washington.

The Corps' general grew up in rural Pennsylvania as the son of a soldier. Flowers had a hankering for civilian life, but the military had a hold on him. He'd trained as a civil engineer and had written his master's thesis on preventing pollution in tanneries. Even inside the military, early on, he contemplated working for a big chemical company.

But he'd gotten hooked on soldiering and its interactions. By reputation, he was known to order lower-ranking soldiers to drop down and do push-ups. He had summed up what it took to succeed in life, and it was his duty to set the standard. He had his philosophy printed on a card he handed to Corps officers and civilians alike: "Know your job. Be healthy. Treat people with dignity and respect. Don't complain. Be situationally aware."

Flowers had taken the control of a Corps besieged by Congress, environmental groups, and taxpayer advocates. "Pork soldiers," his troops were being called in some quarters. It was his job to simultaneously shape up and defend his Army engineers.

And that was a challenge; even, perhaps, an opportunity. In Washington, President George W. Bush's new administration had still to define a policy for America's big rivers. In Flowers, the Corps seemed to have a leader who could challenge habit with values.

"The greatness of the Corps is being able to say no when no is the right thing to be said," he told me. "There are times when an interest wants you to do something, and the science and engineering tells you that's not the thing to do, and you've got to look them in the eye and tell them, 'No, can't do that,'" he said.

Perhaps, like the lion and the lamb, birds and barges might find a millennial peaceable kingdom. Perhaps in the twenty-first century, the Corps and the Service might negotiate a peace.

In 2003, the discussions that began way back in the 1980s resumed between the Fish and Wildlife Service and the Army Engineers under Flowers's command. They didn't get far. The Bush administration had taken its stand; in pursuit of the health of the Missouri River and its wildlife, science scored less than the highest priority.

When Fish and Wildlife biologists along the Missouri River pushed for more studies regarding questionable scientific findings by a new group of biologists brought in by the Bush administration at the eleventh hour, the administration slapped a gag order on them. "There will be no peer review that delays this schedule," Craig Manson, the assistant interior secretary, wrote in an internal e-mail, of a White House plan to speed the matter to resolution.

The Army Corps of Engineer's *Master Manual* remained focused on status quo management and unrevised. For now, barges had beaten birds.

9

BIG MUDDY POLITICS

*If the purpose of this process was to engender division, mistrust
and contempt for the Endangered Species Act and the people
who administer it, then success is at hand.*

—Senator Christopher Bond, 2000

IN WHICH WE SLIDE FROM THE CLOAKROOM OF
THE U.S. SENATE DOWN A ROUGH BANK
ONTO THE MISSOURI

*Reeling and rocking to them low-down blues
They live in ease and comfort down there
I do declare.*

LANDING
IN TURBID POLITICAL WATERS

WHEN MISSOURI SENATOR CHRISTOPHER BOND was growing
up on a farm forty miles north of the Missouri River, the sporting
boys harpooned giant catfish patrolling the bank, then hung on behind
for a hell of a ride.

"We called that central Missouri water-skiing. You're okay unless that
catfish heads for deep water," recalled Bond.

Bond, who was born in 1939, used to fish for those catfish, too. By the
time he'd turned politician, Missourians had lost touch with their name-

sake river, forsaking enjoyment of its waters for well-channelized and dammed security from its treacheries.

Bond, a Republican who goes by the nickname of Kit, never strayed far from the Missouri River during his front-running political career, first as a two-term governor elected at age thirty-three, then as a senator sent to Washington in 1987. His strengths are his reputation as a moderate (although environmentalists—who refer to him as "Senator Smog" and worse—would challenge that characterization), his magic ballot name, and his attention to the contentment of his rural political base. In the 1990s, he emerged as Congress' key operator on Missouri River matters, and in this century he persuaded the Bush administration that water is a winning issue in the swing state of Missouri.

Floods like the lollapalooza of 1993 can swiftly transform water into a bigger summer story than even the Cardinals in baseball-smitten St. Louis, Missouri's biggest metropolitan area. When the Corps and those headstrong government biologists lock horns, not a single Missouri politician utters a friendly word about endangered species if that means raising waters in spring. The other business of a summer drawdown played into Missourians' decades-old worries about those sneaky Dakotans plotting to suck the Missouri River dry long before it arrived above St. Louis to rendezvous with the Mississippi.

Republican or Democratic, these were politicians barely a generation removed from the boom era of river development. Un-developing it was unnatural, especially when political donors continued to build in the floodplain. And Missouri environmentalists had other fish to fry: factory-farm livestock feeding operations stinking up the countryside, some of the worst lead mining pollution in America, and Clean Air Act transgressions aplenty. The battle for restoration of the Missouri was fought not by local conservationists but usually by advocacy groups headquartered in Washington—American Rivers; and New York—Environmental Defense.

For all those reasons, restoring the natural environment of the Missouri River had little to offer a Missouri politician.

Kit Bond, a quick study who can work magic when he warms to an issue, has come to care deeply about Missouri River flows. Decades of winning have made Bond irascible, if not demagogic, when challenged. The Fish and Wildlife Service irked him, and he said so plainly. In rising spring waters, he saw the prospect of floods—worse, government-caused floods—despite Corps assurances that no creature-friendly spring pulses would flow in high-water years.

"Floods are deadly, floods are devastating. I've witnessed too many floods. I've seen the families who have lost a child in the floods," Bond said on the Senate floor in the summer of 2000.

I once asked the senator about the value of letting the river run partly free. He allowed that some tinkering could be done and, indeed, he had sponsored restoration projects. Then he straightened out my newspaper and anybody else who would free broad stretches of Missouri to run wide and wild. "You've got people living along the river, people depending on the river. There was one professor who wanted a ten-million-acre wetland reserve. That would be good for fish and birds and snakes and mosquitoes. But there are far too many people living along that river. If we want to go back in time, the first thing I would recommend we do is tear down the five hundred–year flood wall that protects the St. Louis Post-Dispatch. If editorial writers want to go back to the way it was, it's very simple."

Writing to Brigadier General Carl Strock, the commander of the

Army Corps of Engineers Northwest Division who would go on to head the entire Corps, Bond showed an angry pen, too. Bond expressed outrage at the effrontery of the Fish and Wildlife Service, to whose restorative flow schedule the Corps had hinted it might finally submit. "If the purpose of this process was to engender division, mistrust and contempt for the Endangered Species Act and the people who administer it, then success is at hand," Bond wrote.

In defense of lower basin states, Bond took over from Nebraska representative Doug Bereuter the perennial task of appending legislation to prevent the Corps from changing its *Master Manual*. His rider forbade the Corps from spending money on revising its bible of operations. Bond got away with that maneuver until near the end of President Bill Clinton's second term. Then, because of Bond's wording, Clinton threatened to veto the $22.5 billion legislation for water development and radioactive waste cleanup.

"We must modernize the management of the Missouri River," said Clinton—who had not gotten around to doing so himself despite nearly two terms in office.

PRESIDENTS ON THE MISSOURI

Since Thomas Jefferson, presidents have had business with the Missouri River. In the 1880s, Chester Arthur bought into the taxing new enterprise of Missouri River improvement, triggering what would become, with brief lapses, an appropriation in perpetuity. In the early 1930s, Franklin Roosevelt made the fateful decision to build Fort Peck Dam in Montana to put people to work. In 1980, commercial boosters along the river were giddy at the defeat of Jimmy Carter, who was a president like no other in the modern era: He professed his love for free-flowing rivers. Every major and many minor water projects had to survive review to avoid his hit list. So the irrigators and river developers were shocked when David Stockman, President Ronald Reagan's budget czar, threatened to shut off the federal spigot by forcing water projects to submit to more rational economic standards. The Corps' many friends in Congress blunted Stockman's threat. But along the Upper Missouri, reformers succeeded in scaling back one of history's most bloated irrigation projects, North Dakota's Garrison Diversion.

Clinton's White House had tightened the reins on the willful Army Corps of Engineers, going so far after the Mississippi River scandal as forbidding its officials to operate independently on Capitol Hill. On his way out of office, Clinton was determined to keep Congress out of the way and let the face-off between the Corps and the Fish and Wildlife Service take its course, probably with endangered species winning in the end. White House chief of staff John Podesta wrote to Congress to say that Bond's amendment "would prevent the Corps from carrying out a necessary element . . . to avoid jeopardizing the continued existence of the endangered least tern and pallid sturgeon and the threatened piping plover."

The joke that season was that the cast on Bond's right wrist resulted from all the arms he'd twisted in the Senate cloakroom to win passage of the rider Clinton hated. In truth, he was on the mend from an arthritic condition exacerbated by too much tree planting on his Missouri farm. But Bond reveled in both the fight and the friends it bought him back home, and he vowed to make the river an issue in the presidential campaign.

"If the president vetoes this bill, I guarantee you it will have huge political ramifications all over Missouri. And I'm going to ramificate throughout the state," said Bond, sounding more like a Missouri farmer than a University of Virginia Law School graduate.

Clinton acted on his veto threat, forcing Bond to drop his wording so Senate business could continue. Bond, in turn, ramificated.

George W. Bush had a soft spot for ex-governors, like Bond, and packed his administration with men and women who had run state-houses around the country. So Bond's political counsel—and contacts—had extra currency. "You can tell with this president when you touch a hot button, be it baseball or bass fishing," Bond told me once.

Bush and Bond had another connection, one that played a vital role in the Texas governor's political calculations: Like Bush, Bond had re-lied in earlier election campaigns on Karl Rove for political strategy. So it was no surprise when Bush proved true to his roots. Campaigning in the Midwest in 2000, he landed squarely on the side of the Army Corps of Engineers. "I stand with Missouri farmers. I believe we can save species without affecting the farmers' way of life," candidate Bush said, answering reporters' questions on a stop at a regional airport near Marion, Illinois.

In November 2000, Missourians shifted their votes the way a river changes its course. One election after the Clinton-Gore ticket had won the Show Me state by a landslide, Bush captured Missouri by a relatively easy 52 to 48 percent margin in a year that Missourians elected a dead Democrat—Mel Carnahan, who had died in a plane crash—to the U.S. Senate while rejecting soon-to-be Attorney General John Ashcroft.

Even with punditry and all the tools of political science, you never truly know why large blocs of votes shift. The 2000 election was all the more inscrutable with the collapse of exit polling by Voter News Service, the media alliance formed to sort out voter attitudes. But strategists for

Bond argued that the Missouri River had a lot to do with the over-whelming GOP victory in bellwether Missouri. I, too, think it was a win-ning issue for Bush. Homegrown advocates for change hadn't convinced voters in a land of flooding of the intrinsic worth of rivers running free.

In the economic reckoning, the potential loss of a navigation indus-try rich in history was worth more than the recreation industry that might rise along a healthy river and the abstraction of endangered species. And the Fish and Wildlife Service never has succeeded in mak-ing the connection that a healthy river that supports the rarest of species also supports diversified local economies and the people living along its banks.

But with deadlines imposed by the Endangered Species Act looming, both sides watched to see where the new president would lead.

BRINK OF CHANGE

During the 2000 presidential election recount, the Fish and Wildlife Ser-vice issued another "biological opinion," a document reprising its 1990 and 1994 conclusions. Yet again the 2000 opinion accused the Corps of Engineers of breaking the law. This time, impatient wildlife biologists wrote a prescription for flow changes that would rescue creatures and avoid a formal finding of jeopardy against the Corps under Section 7 of the Endangered Species Act.

Then came a surprise: After years of indecision, the Army Corps of Engineers declared its support for the spring rise. The question was how big, when, and where, said Brigadier General Carl Strock, the Northwest Division commander.

"I think we see that as we've changed the natural flow of this river, it has changed the fish and wildlife along this river. What we need to do is try to introduce some of these natural components and at the same time try to uphold some of the other project components," such as barge traffic, Strock said in a 95-minute conference call with reporters.

All that remained were the details, and they were promised by February 2001. But February melted into March, with its most significant development the emergence of a new organization. In a story I filed from Washington, I noted that the name of the group suggested that environmentalists had finally come together along the Missouri River: The Coalition to Preserve the Missouri River, the group called itself.

In fact, the coalition was the Missouri-based political arm of farm and barge interests, who had put together financing and a strategy for derailing the flow alterations the Corps had promised. "We think we are the environmentalists," I quoted a Missouri Farm Bureau executive, Dan Cassidy, as saying. "There are some groups who call themselves environmentalists who don't work for balance on the river. We call them obstructionists."

The coalition's first official action: filing a notice of intent to sue the federal government over the Fish and Wildlife Service's 2000 biological opinion.

Pressure was on for the new administration to back up the president's campaign promise. In their courtesy calls to Bond's office, new Bush appointees would hear about the Missouri in what Bond aides called "the lecture." Bond also lectured the president, writing that "it is imperative that the White House direct the Corps of Engineers to stop all activity immediately until your new team is in place and has an opportunity to review this matter in full."

In March 2001, the Corps revised its timetable, declaring it would be

May before it could sift through public comments to complete its flow plans. A Corps spokesman, Paul Johnston, said he knew of no delaying orders from the White House. Bond said, "This is what we've asked for. Don't go rushing pell-mell into flooding us in the spring."

The environmental lobby countered with a surprise of its own. Every spring, the advocacy group American Rivers gets wide attention when it releases its "Most Endangered Rivers" list. The rankings had achieved a public relations clout not imagined when the list was conceived in 1990 to publicize river problems. By hustling stories to news outlets around the country and orchestrating a standing-room-only news conference in Washington, the press-savvy organization assures itself of coverage in every part of America with a river in trouble. That is across the land.

In 1997, American Rivers had designated the Missouri River the nation's most endangered—the first of three times it would win that dubious distinction—and recruited the television personality Charles Kuralt, a board member, to make the case for restoration.

American Rivers' focus on the Missouri River might have had something to do with the childhood deprivation of its president, Rebecca Wodder. Growing up in Omaha, one of the major cities along the Missouri, Wodder thought it peculiar that the great Missouri should be all but off-limits. Rather than frolicking in their backyard river, Wodder's family would head to the Platte River, twenty miles south. "By the time I was old enough to be outdoors in any significant way, the Missouri already was getting inaccessible: narrow, deep and flat," said Wodder, who was born in 1952.

In April 2001, when the Missouri River's future twisted in the political wind, American Rivers again accorded it the most-threatened distinction. Historian Stephen Ambrose appeared at the National Press

Club in Washington to bear witness. "The river has been damaged—not beyond repair—for the last fifty years because the Corps of Engineers has operated under the dictum of Congress that they make the river a barge canal. It's a great big ditch. We have sacrificed this priceless heritage for the extraordinarily few numbers of people who use barges on the Missouri River," Ambrose said, after reading from *Undaunted Courage*, his account of Lewis and Clark's explorations.

I stopped writing about Corps delays because the news was always the same. But winds of change were blowing from a new direction. Now pro-industry House members had joined the fray, fighting on their side to keep Bond's amendment in legislation. Missouri congressman Kenny Hulshof told me that he was enlisting help from his counterparts whose borders touched not just the Missouri but also the Mississippi River. "This is one of the battles where a regional alliance is needed to carry the day," he said.

Soon afterward, I published a scoop. Despite political pressures, the Corps was sticking to the flow changes that General Strock had endorsed. Not that the Army Engineers were buying into everything that the Fish and Wildlife Service wanted. The government biologists had recommended to the Corps that the average flow of 32,000 cubic feet per second from Gavins Point be ratcheted up by 17,500 cubic feet per second, the midpoint in an acceptable rise range of 15,000–20,000. The Corps plan would begin at 15,000 and gradually increase the volume. "We want to minimize the risk of flooding," a Corps official told me. His agency also had finally agreed to lower summer flows as prescribed by the wildlife agency to open sandbars for endangered birds and slow the water for pallid sturgeon.

Everybody I talked to in both Corps and Fish and Wildlife Service was relieved that more than a decade of deliberations was about to end. Both agencies could finally get on to other matters. But in my page-one Sunday story, I wrote in caution. Rather than saying that announcement of the agreement was imminent, as I had been told, I wrote in the first paragraph that the Corps was "leaning toward" monumental changes in river management. Down in the story, I noted that the Corps could still change its mind. I'm glad I inserted those words.

In a matter of days—in a decision reflecting the pressure on the White House—the Army ordered the Corps to scrap its preferred alternative. Instead, the Corps was told to present only a list of alternatives for managing the river. In a story I wrote based on sources who couldn't be identified, I noted that even the Corps was surprised at the turn of events, which gave a victory to the downriver interests at a critical time in the deliberations. I quoted an unnamed aide to Bond calling the Corps shift an important development. "Like the river, things appear to be moving along nicely," the aide said.

It was yet another setback to environmental advocates and to the Fish and Wildlife Service, and the earliest indication of how the new Republican administration would approach the long-running fracas along the Missouri.

The government biologists were crestfallen. "If the Army decides to go this route, we could be back to square one in a lot of respects after twelve years of work," said the Fish and Wildlife Service's Mike Olson, who carried the title Missouri River Coordinator. Under its new orders, the Corps would offer only a series of options for saving endangered species, options that include conservation initiatives and various combinations of spring and summer flow changes.

Jay Carson, spokesman for Senator Tom Daschle, who was then still

Senate majority leader, spoke presciently. "If the Corps tries to duck that responsibility, it's not going to be a good situation, and that's what appears to be happening now," he told me.

Chad Smith, Midwest representative of American Rivers, accused the Corps of breaking a promise. "If they do not come out with a preferred alternative, what they have been saying all along has been hot air."

BACK FROM THE BRINK

The about-face on the Missouri River fell in line with the George W. Bush administration's determined retraction of conservation and environmental protection. When historians look back on the forty-third president, they may first take Bush's measure from his initiatives on foreign soil. When they look at home, they will see an unexpectedly activist president who altered the course of governing by scaling back regulations and spurning new government interference with industry—like barging and farming along the Missouri River.

As with his bold foreign policy initiatives, Bush's approach to public lands in the West was transformational. He was intent on reversing federal policy that had preserved vast swathes of territory, in his quest to explore wherever oil and gas might be found, including Alaska's Arctic National Wildlife Refuge and the pristine areas of the Rocky Mountain West.

Similarly, the administration maintained its resolve to open up protected forests for logging and to relax roadless rules to give governors the authority to open wilderness lands for development.

The principal shifts often occurred by manipulating obscure rules rather than taking public, saber-rattling stands. In one of those obscure rulings, the Bush White House dropped a regulation that forced hundreds of the dirtiest power plants and refineries to install pollution control equipment when facilities were upgraded. In an action-by-doing-nothing that was all but ignored by the general public, Bush ruled that carbon dioxide—a component of global warming—shouldn't be regulated. Thus vanished new pollution controls on cars and plants.

That Section 7 consultation under the Endangered Species Act was just the sort of low-profile, red-tape business the new administration loved to review. The Bush White House view toward the Endangered Species Act was hostile, but no move was made to repeal it. Conservation interests pressing the White House learned early in the administration of George W. Bush to frame issues in economic terms rather than invoking the authority of the Endangered Species Act. By early 2003, advocacy groups working the Missouri River believed they had exhausted all their economic arguments about the foolhardiness of running a river for a handful of barge operators. They had lost the negotiations with the Corps of Engineers, and they lacked clout in the Republican-run Congress. So they sued—shifting the Missouri River's future course from the status quo supported by politicians to uncertain direction.

The suit melded the interests of two prominent and well-financed advocacy groups. Both American Rivers and Environmental Defense had worked on Missouri River issues for more than a decade. Also signing on as plaintiffs were the National Wildlife Federation; the Izaak Walton League of America; the South Dakota Wildlife Federation; the Nebraska Wildlife Federation; and the Iowa Wildlife Federation.

Stephen Ambrose's death in October 2002 had diminished American Rivers' Missouri River efforts, for Ambrose had pledged $1.25 million from *Undaunted Courage* royalties—$250,000 annually for five years. The omission of the Missouri from American Rivers' 2003 Most Endangered Rivers list signaled that the nation's preeminent river advocacy organization had other priorities. But one more stone remained to be turned. The Endangered Species Act governs not only ranchers, sportsmen, developers, and miscreants with rifles; it also applies to the United States government. The courts had never reviewed the Corps' operation of Missouri River dams for compliance with the 1973 law.

Distracted by the savor of victory, downstream states, the farm-and-barge alliance, and their allies in Washington seemed to have the president on their side, for the Bush White House had ordered the Corps and the Fish and Wildlife Service to let river flows be. A pair of federal court rulings in the Midwest seemingly had affirmed the Corps' authority to operate dams for barges. So the midwesterners—even the savvy Bond—weren't paying much mind to what might go on in a courtroom eight hundred miles away.

Meanwhile, conservationists quietly persisted. There was no question that the Army Corps of Engineers could be violating the Endangered Species Act by allowing the river to run high for the remainder of the summer, they argued in the Washington, D.C., courtroom of U.S. District Judge Gladys Kessler. That's what the government's own biologists in the Fish and Wildlife Service had been saying all along. Now they were being forced to capitulate to a river-operating plan that likely would endanger terns and plovers by washing away their nests and chicks. "Incidental take," it was called.

Those were the facts as I'd reported them in a newspaper story about that decision: "A Missouri River operating agreement reached Tuesday is designed to keep barges running this summer at the possible expense of more than 100 federally protected birds."

But the president's advisers had other things on their minds: the re-election campaign. At a fund-raising dinner in St. Louis for Senator Bond, President Bush noted his agreement with Missouri's senior senator on what he called common-sense environmental policy.

James Connaughton, the president's principal environmental adviser, made a football analogy when I asked him if electoral politics played a role in the White House decisions. No, he said, it was like offsetting penalties in football. No matter what the president did, he would upset either the upper basin states or states downstream.

"This is good government trying to marry economic needs," he told me while plugging the administration's plan, just then taking shape, to spend money to restore wildlife habitat rather than altering the river's flows in a way to avoid breaking the law.

HAIL TO THE (WHITE) CHIEF

Had President Thomas Jefferson imagined what would befall the indigenous people of the land when he dispatched the Army captains westward along the Missouri? I made my way to Monticello on January 18, 2003, two hundred years to the day after Jefferson sent his secret message to Congress seeking the wherewithal to explore the Missouri.

But I did not find the third president at home. Nor did I find him in Washington, where I overlooked the White House every workday for twenty years.

But everywhere I followed the Corps of Discovery, from Charlottesville, Virginia, to St. Louis, Missouri, to Bismarck, North Dakota, there was Thomas Jefferson, in breeches, vest, and sometimes powdered wig. These Bicentennial days, scholar Clay S. Jenkinson stands in for Jefferson. Jenkinson, who has written two books on Jefferson and portrays the third president in the Public Broadcasting System's *Thomas Jefferson Hour*, had borrowed the appearance and burrowed into the mind of the man who directed the Corps of Discovery into the Indian west.

On a September day in 2003, I questioned Thomas Jefferson about the Missouri River Indians, who have their own Big Muddy stories to tell.

You knew something about Indians, did you not, Mr. President?
I have had a lifelong fascination with Indians, and I believe that Indians have a great deal to teach us because they are children of nature. Because they were isolated from the European culture, they are in a position of their development that is several hundred years behind their European

counterparts. You can look on that as primitive if you wish, but it's more useful to look on that as an earlier phase of culture. So I believe that they will teach us about natural law and how people live according to the dictates of nature. So I look forward to this data; it's not just arcane to me. It's sociological lenses that can help us see who we were and ways that we can resimplify our ways.

What were your specific instructions with regard to the Missouri River tribes, Mr. President?
Take down graphic data. Take down their vocabularies. Encourage Indians to send some of their children to be brought up by us and to send delegations to the White House. Treat the Indians with as much conciliation as their own behavior will admit. Bend over backwards to be gentle and generous; don't pick fights. Don't get angry easily. Take the extra step to preserve peace and maintain harmony. I also want Indians, and this is very important, to stop waging war against each other. Warfare is endemic in the Indian world. And I'm against war altogether; I'm a pacifist or a near pacifist. Promote peace by saying that if tribes will agree to live in peace with each other, we would provide a security umbrella to maintain that peace. Bring back the artifacts, but that is less important than promoting Enlightenment values.

Wasn't it your goal, Mr. President, to dominate and colonize tribes?
When it's said by some people that we had imperial designs, that's only true with respect to other Europeans. We wanted the British to withdraw from this continent as quickly as possible. We wanted the Spanish to stay in the Southwest and eventually depart. The French, we assumed, had now forgone any further presence in North America. My geopolitical concern is preemption, to keep the Europeans away from this continent as much as possible. That is more important to me than any geopolitical relations with natives.

But Mr. President, by most accounts, the expedition you conceived set in motion the destruction of those Missouri River Indian tribes.

Here's what I couldn't have known. I couldn't have known that the industrial revolution would so thoroughly transform America. I was in love with gadgets and industrial technology and inventiveness. But I could not have anticipated that the country would be transformed so many times and so thoroughly. So that worsened the differential between the two cultures and greatly increased the power and capacity for domination amongst whites and greatly reduced Indians' ability to exist. In essence, the weaponry gap grew much wider than anybody could have anticipated in my time.

Secondly, we did not realize in my day that the country could be peopled so quickly. If it had taken two hundred years rather than one hundred years to people the West, this would have given Indians much more time to catch up and to adapt and have a smooth transition. That is what is happening today: an Indian Renaissance, with education and legal capacity, of economics, of cultural traditions, of confidence, of health. These things are happening in your time. And if penetration of the West by white Americans had been slower, theoretically, some of that self-reliance and that capacity to live in an industrial world would have come with less damage.

Also, I couldn't have anticipated that my successors like Andrew Jackson would be men of ruthlessness. Jackson believed that Indians should essentially get out of the way or be exterminated. I don't hold that view. I hold a more benign view. It may not seem much more benign, but it is. It's a more cooperative model of exchanges between us. I didn't see Indians as vermin. And in fact I prize them in some regards as ideal citizens.

Along the Missouri River, many Indians blame Lewis and Clark for what happened to them. Is that fair?

When people in your day say that Lewis and Clark were the harbingers of a cataclysm that was coming to the Great Plains, I disagree. Lewis and Clark were harbingers of a new order, no question, and a new sovereign, and it was clear that Indians were going to have to adjust because there's no way that white Europeans were not going to penetrate this continent. I'm not sympathetic to Indian arguments that they should have never been encountered. I am for benign exchange rather than no encounter. And no president of the United States would have the ability or the right to prevent white people from spreading across the continent. My duty was to my own constituents and to the Constitution. The president of the United States does not answer to Indian tribes of the West. The president answers to the people of the social compact that elected him. And my duty is to promote their interest as intelligently as possible but not to thwart their interests. Otherwise I don't deserve to be their president. They would have found another one to do their bidding, as they always do.

~10~

BROKEN TRUST I: THE FLOOD

The Four Bears never saw a White Man hungry, but what he gave him to eat, and Drink, and a buffaloe skin to sleep on, in time of need. I was always ready to die for them. . . . I have done everything that a red Skin could do for them, and how have they repaid it! With ingratitude. I have Never called a White Man a Dog, but to day, I do Pronounce them to be a set of Black hearted Dogs.

—Mandan chief Four Bears, as he
approached death from smallpox,
Fort Mandan, 1837

IN WHICH WE TRESPASS ON SACRED SHORES
AFTER THE DELUGE

There are no trees lining the river any more, any plums turning ripe in July.

—Elizabeth Cook-Lynn,
"The Clearest Blue Day"

LANDING
THE DAKOTAS

I MADE MY WAY to Indian country to discover the consequences on the Missouri of Lewis and Clark, who opened the way to all that has followed. Change is a human measure, and so much that has happened in two hundred years Indians have borne on their backs.

As I went investigating toxic dumping on tribal lands in the final years of the last century, I consulted Hopi spiritual leader Thomas Banyacya in the Arizona desert. Banyacya was the last of four messengers named by Hopi elders in 1948 to warn the world of impending doom, and before he died in 1999, at age eighty-nine, he became a prophet for global peace and for balance in the environment. He told me he was thinking of taking some of the hazardous waste showing up on reservations and spreading it on the White House lawn. Nature, said the elder in his long braid, is difficult to understand because it doesn't talk to us, and neither do the plants and animals we threaten with extinction. We're just as alien to cultures we don't understand. Making his point, he recalled the response of an old Indian told that white people were taking away his land. "Where are they taking it to?" the old man asked.

Now, as I seek to understand what I am seeing along the Missouri River, I have returned to tribal land.

SCAVENGING

I am a black-hearted dog.

The contempt American Indians feel toward me at this moment might even rival the store they reserve for the Army Corps of Engineers.

I am crawling along the shoreline of the Missouri River, pawing through the detritus of civilizations. In my pocket I have slid fingernail-sized pieces of ceramic pottery and a triangular bit of stone that I call an arrowhead but is rightly known as a bird point. I also have collected a thin, featherweight piece of something that I later learn is an awl, a tool carved from buffalo bone more than a century ago for punching holes in buffalo skins. Just where along the Missouri River I scavenge I will not say.

I am walking on higher ground now, in a weedy stretch that was submerged for years until the drought of the new century. Sumped into the water here is a chunk of earth the size of a Volkswagen Bug. The powdery loess soils hereabouts are no match for pounding waves and the artificial ebb and flow of water running through the Corps-operated dam upstream.

Even in sunglasses, I know the nature of the smooth white curved surface reflecting at my feet. It is bone. A human bone.

I am uneasy, to say the least, because I am trespassing. And that is not the half of it. If I persist in what I am doing, I might well violate the Archeological Resources Protection Act, the National Historic Preservation Act, the Native American Graves Protection Act, and probably something more. Regardless of my excuses—writing a story, conducting research, or whatever line I can manage if apprehended—I have no business being here. I was so reminded earlier along a native shoreline where I encountered a confab of rattlesnakes the color of parched grass standing guard in the tall weeds of a known archeological site. When I told them I just wanted to look around, they seemed to listen and scattered in the four directions, like celebrants at a Native American ritual. Except for one unremittingly noisy sentinel, she of eight rattlers.

Where I am now is no certified archeological site, despite the relics it gives up. Nonetheless, having seen one human bone and then another, I know it is time to leave, indeed to flee. In my getaway, I sink calf-deep in silt and fairly dive into my canoe. I push off from a brittle cottonwood limb so hard that it snaps with a crack that echoes off the bank, and I'm certain someone has shot at me. I float sideways downstream, breathing fast and thinking about the human remains I have just seen and the artifacts in my pocket. I decide I must go back.

Just like when I was sixteen and my friend, David, and I swiped a chrome oil cap from under the hood of a hot-rod Malibu on a car lot and then miles away, he tells me to turn around. "I can't do this; I'll have to confess it," he said. I paddle back upstream against the current. It is farther than I recalled, and in the afternoon heat I am dizzy. I worry that I am being seen from the hillocks of the western shore through the binoculars of the sole Army Corps of Engineers ranger assigned some four hundred miles of shoreline hereabouts. Perhaps he, tribal police, or a Bureau of Indian Affairs cop will be waiting where I put in. I am sweating, not sure of where I had been. I reach into my pocket and, without disembarking, fling the contents toward the shore. Floating again, I tell myself that—except for disturbing the order in which the relics lay strewn and having trod on the bones of a long-dead Indian—I have done nothing wrong.

But I am deceiving myself, like all the deception that has accompanied the treatment of Indian tribes with the damming of the Missouri River. For later, in my motel room, in my pocket I find that tiny perfect spear point.

SACRED SHORES

In my pilgrimage to Indian country, I am not alone. Many thousands of history tourists are converging on the Dakotas, Montana, and Nebraska, following a trail that runs along reservation "hard roads," past Indian casinos that now stand as the centers of civilization in remote tribal lands. Most arrivals come by highway, but some via the Missouri River to, like me, sneak about on the fringes of the rez.

People are arriving in this first decade of the new century to commemorate an event that Indians and European-Americans view much differently: the Bicentennial of the exploration of Meriwether Lewis and William Clark. That pair were the most purposeful white people Indians had ever seen, and their journey was even more fateful for America's natives than for the nation they opened to the far ocean.

After the Corps of Discovery came traders, painters, trappers, pioneers, settlers. Now, tribal land is being invaded by a new breed of twenty-first-century explorers, hero worshippers, re-enactors, roots seekers, drunken day trippers, walleye slayers, and, of dubious value to tribes, journalists. The newcomers are trampling inadvertently on sacred Indian sites, of which there are some five thousand along the Missouri River, according to the best guess of the Army engineers who control shorelines along the river that used to belong to tribes. For other visitors, these sacred sites are destinations. This is the breed of intruder that Indians despise: looters, vacation archeologists, and die-hard collectors, exploiters one and all, scooping up the sorts of relics that I have just seen, then digging into the banks for more.

Despite all that has happened to Indians, there are more of them in the river basin than most people know: twenty-seven tribes, and those are just the ones recognized by the federal government. Tribes have lived along the river throughout history and recent prehistory, long before Europeans arrived. The Missouri River was a magnet for human settlements dating back as far as 9500 B.C. There's evidence of their presence then, and there's reason to believe that tribes were here long before that.

So tens of thousands of American Indians lived and died along the river, and the remains of many are buried in the Missouri River banks. If they and their ancestors are lucky.

All too often, bones wash from the banks; skeletons suddenly jut from the earth as banks wash away, as do funereal objects and other relics of earlier civilizations. They are washed from their graves by the flow of water in the Missouri River and America's newest great lakes: Fort Peck, Oahe, Francis Case, Sharpe, and Sakakawea—impoundments that turned tribes into dammed Indians.

For American Indian tribes, among the earth's greatest respecters of the dead, that has meant learning of skulls of ancestors carved into ashtrays by modern-day grave robbers and bloodstained buckskin shirts bringing steep prices in clandestine transactions.

Seeing their dead dislodged from the earth is just one more indignity, but one that cuts deeply.

FLOODS OF DESPAIR

After Lewis and Clark, American Indian tribes endured more disease—like the smallpox epidemic that came by steamboat in 1837 and reduced Four Bears's village from 1,600 Mandans to 130—and then massacres, deceit, and forced relocations. Indians were confined to some of the poorest, most unforgiving land. Until the 1930s, the official announced aim of the government's assimilation policies was to destroy tribes. After that came the termination policy, and until the 1960s, the government sought to dissolve tribes' legal and cultural identities.

In recent decades, western tribes may have lost as much as $10 billion in royalties from gas and oil in a government-mismanaged trust fund.

Over two years in the early 1990s, I documented in many newspaper stories tribes' exploitation by waste brokers who came negotiating to turn reservations into dumps for chemicals, hospital waste, and even radioactive wastes from across the nation. Not only the environment and public health hung in the balance; the desecration of sacred lands further threatened these fragile cultures.

Amid all that damage, the flooding of tribal lands along the Missouri River in the middle of the twentieth century ranks among the most profound, systematic, and least remembered violations of indigenous people.

In building the Missouri River dams during the 1950s, the Army inundated over 200,000 acres of Sioux land, forcibly dislodging 580 families. That was just in South Dakota during construction of the Fort Randall and Big Bend dams. In North Dakota, Garrison Dam took 156,000 acres from the Mandans, the Hidatsas, and the Arikaras, also known as the Three Affiliated Tribes, on the Fort Berthold Reservation. The flooding uprooted 349 families from some of the most felicitous bottomlands in the Dakotas.

The dislocation of Indian tribes is a sad, familiar tale, notorious from the forced relocation of Cherokees from Georgia to Oklahoma in the 1830s in the march that became known as the "Trail of Tears." The flooding of tribes during the dam building days of the mid-twentieth century became a modern chapter in that tale.

Throughout Indian Country, tribes say they have not yet recovered. The specter of waters engulfing forever their finest ancestral lands continues to haunt the tribes, who insist that they never have been compensated—neither in money nor in public acknowledgment of the enormity of the insult.

MICE BEANS AND A BELLIGERENT BRAVE

Indians still speak poignantly of tribal losses. Ladonna Brave Bull Allard is one of several women from whom I gather details of The Flood and the disconnection after the waters were made to rise.

"We gathered up the kids and sat up on the hill. We had no time to get our chickens and no time to get our horses out of the corral. The water came in and smacked against the corral and broke the horses' legs. They drowned, and the chickens drowned. We sat on the hill and we cried. These are the stories we tell about the river," said Brave Bull Allard. The granddaughter of Chief Brave Bull, she told her story at a Missouri River symposium in Bismarck, North Dakota, in the fall of 2003.

Before The Flood, her Standing Rock Sioux Tribe lived in a Garden of Eden, where nature provided all their needs. "In the summer we would plant huge gardens because the land was fertile," she recalled. "We had all our potatoes and squash. We canned all the berries that grew along the river. Now we don't have the plants and the medicine they used to make."

Her tribe's customs stretched back centuries; their ways were already old when Lewis and Clark documented them in the winter of 1804–05. Among those old ways was the winter hunt for mice beans. "We would go down to the river and dig there to find mouse holes, where the mice had gathered the sweetest beans," Allard recalled of the then-unbroken continuity of culture. "Of course, we would put corn and beans in the holes because we wouldn't take the beans without leaving something."

The Flood washed that culture away. "Now, we have no more mice," Allard continued. "We have no more beans. I always thought, 'Who gave them the right to kill all the mice?' They fed our people. And huge cottonwoods stood on the shore. There is not one tree left. I tell the Corps of Engineers, 'You owe us two million trees.' We miss our trees. How much our lives have changed since we lost the river."

More than a lament, Allard has a vision for the future. "I keep thinking, do something, do something," she exhorted. "Save this river because it is our lives. It is everybody's responsibility to save the river. It has a life of its own. Maybe one day, it will take revenge on us for what we have done to it. Nature is stronger than us, greater than us, and we can never control it."

Tribes have pushed, with a smattering of success, to be part of negotiations about the river's environment and flow. In Nebraska, Omaha Indians won the promise from the Army Engineers to reconnect the river to a lake dried long ago when the river was reengineered for barges. Until then, the Omahas' only river recreation was going to the banks to watch the barges float by, and they didn't come very often, Antione Provost, the Omaha Tribe's environmental director, told me.

Indians are overwhelmed by frustration. Allard's Standing Rock Tribe lost more acreage to The Flood than did the Three Affiliated Tribes of North Dakota. But the impact on the Three Affiliated Tribes may have been more devastating. The Sioux had been largely nomadic tribes who came to farming and grazing later in their histories. But the Mandan, Hidatsa, and Arikara—formally, since the mid-nineteenth century, Three Affiliated Tribes—had settled much earlier into farming. They were descendants of village tribes living in cultural systems that had centuries-deep roots in place and time. They are the same peaceful, trade-loving Mandans who welcomed Lewis and Clark, providing them space, food, and friendship in the frigid first winter of their expedition.

My quest to understand the Three Tribes' loss took me to rural reaches of the Fort Berthold Indian Reservation in North Dakota. Here The Flood is remembered in biblical terms as the divide between past harmony and present travail.

Celina Mossett—in her eighth decade when I awaken her at her double-wide mobile home—is still in her nightgown. But after having coffee and giving me some, she is ready to talk.

"Let me tell you a little story," she begins. "First came the cavalry and they took our land. Then they changed their name to the Corps of Engineers, and they still take and they keep taking till this day. And now we have nothing and have lost our way of life."

She and her late husband, Cliff, had their log home in a cottonwood grove along the Missouri. They raised horses and cattle alongside grapevines and orchards with plums and cherries, the remains of which lie at the bottom of the impoundment. Now Mossett lives 110 miles by auto from tribal headquarters and 14 miles from water. Now she must pay to have her water hauled to her by drum in trucks.

"We had everything; we didn't need anything. They took everything we had, and they just keep taking and they always will. I want my children and I want the children in our future generations to know this," she tells me.

Betrayal hangs in the air and wafts over the 178-mile-long, aquamarine blue lake that supplanted the muddy river. The government has since provided reparations, principally a $150 million lump sum that contributes about $9 million interest every year to the tribal budget. But tribal members have received considerably less than the value of land they lost to the lake, which amounted to one quarter of the reservation. They are still waiting for the free electricity they were promised. Nor have they yet succeeded in building the clinic to replace the hospital they lost.

Insult is compounded by the name the Army Engineers gave the betraying lake: Sakakawea, a form of Sacagawea, the young Shoshone who was the only woman on the explorers' journey. The lady of this lake the Corps pictures on its brochure is white, blond, and holding a walleye, a fish imported to these waters.

The enmity has deeper roots. In the stories the Mandans, Hidatsas, and Arikaras tell, their betrayer has a face and a name: Lieutenant General Lewis Pick, that ubiquitous figure in the transformation of Big Muddy.

After engineering the Pick-Sloan Plan, Pick rose to head the Army Corps of Engineers. In 1946, he traveled to North Dakota to meet with the three Tribes, who hoped for a settlement. Pick's attitude spoiled during that meeting, which took place in a reservation classroom, when he was confronted by a traditional Mandan chief, Drags Wolf, in painted face and war bonnet.

"You'll never take me from this land alive," Drags Wolf shouted at Pick.

To Pick, the display was a grievous insult. Labeling the tribes "belligerently uncooperative," he charged forward with a bullying plan that ignored their pleas.

Like other grandmothers, Celina Mossett recalls Lewis Pick, and his memory triggers her last flood of words. "They lie, they steal," she said. "They have never done right by my people. The things they have done to me and my people, I'll take to my grave with me. It has always been like this since Columbus set foot here. But I don't want to talk about this anymore because it makes my blood pressure go up."

Providing drinking water to the reservation would cost some $80 million, I'm told. In 2000, as part of the so-called Dakota Water Resources Act, Congress authorized nearly that much—$70 million—for just such a distribution system. There were celebrations and fulsome praise in editorials for the politicians. Yet the Three Affiliated Tribes remain thirsty—though Indians now know the difference between an authorization and the actual appropriation.

EVERYTHING IS UNDER WATER

Along the Missouri River, The Flood always will be part of the story North Dakota Indians tell. I make that discovery again as I read an obscure Fort Berthold Indian Reservation report entitled *Rural Water Supply System Phase II Planning. Volume I: Needs Assessment.*

"Before the Garrison Reservoir, ninety percent of the population of the reservation lived within the Missouri valley," according to the 1997 planning guide, which is also a history of the reservation. "Consequently, relocation required that ninety percent of the total population move their permanent residence to new homes on the highlands. Families were uprooted, shuffled and mixed. Every semblance of organization was destroyed and would have to be reorganized with an entirely different group of members. Relocation changed all aspects of life."

The spiral-bound assessment painstakingly detailed the changes. School ties ended: "Elbowoods was the agency headquarters and the location of a boarding high school, grade school, and a day school. When Elbowoods disappeared under the Garrison Reservoir, every school child on the reservation had to change schools."

Roads were flooded, and people herded in a roadless wilderness:

"Eighty percent of the road system was within the Missouri valley and the area taken for the reservoir. The people relocated into areas of the reservation that were virtually roadless. To replace the inundated highway system it was necessary to build a system of 230 miles of new highways."

Snatched from a subsistence economy and dropped in a market economy, the relocated Indians found themselves destitute:

> The people of Fort Berthold had lived by a somewhat natural economy in the Missouri valley. There were numerous springs and creeks in the valley for water supply and the Indian people used river water to a considerable extent. Coal beds were available for fuel supply and plenty of wood for the same purpose. The timber in the river bottoms also provided logs for their houses, fence posts for their farms, and a natural cover for wintering their livestock. There were wild fruits and abundant wild game to supplement the food supply.
>
> The people relocated from the Missouri River valley to a residual highland area of the reservation where, instead of a natural economy, they faced a cash economy. They could no longer go down to the timber to cut logs for houses or fence posts because the inundated timber was lost. The wild fruit was practically all gone and game driven out because it no longer had cover. The livestock required corrals, feed lots, and barns to replace the natural cover of timber. Water must come from wells and fuel has to be bought.

Losses have been so many that tribespeople sometimes don't know where to begin. Many times, they start with The Flood itself, and often the stories have tears in them.

In New Town, North Dakota, Beverly Wilkerson tells me that she was just eleven in 1953, but her father had her drive the truck loaded with the family cattle up from the river bottoms. Afterward, the women in the family gathered at the edge of the rising water and, like the Sioux in the stories of Ladonna Brave Bull Allard, wept.

New Town, which sprang up after The Flood, is home to the Three Affiliated Tribes casino. Named after the great Mandan chief Four Bears, who died in the apocalyptic smallpox epidemic in the 1830s, the casino is also the tribal cultural center. There I meet Edward Hall, who was a teenager in the year of The Flood, working on a crew digging up graves and moving long-buried ancestors to high ground.

"Where they moved us there were no trees, no roads, no electricity, no telephone. It was an economic and social disaster," Hall tells me. He left the reservation for a successful engineering career across the country, and he had recently retired back to tribal land because, he says, this is where he belongs.

At a tribal council meeting at Four Bears Casino, other business is put aside to help me connect the past and present. Councilman Malcolm Wolfe tells me that he was told long ago by an elder to take care of that river or someday he might be paying for what flows there. "Now I'm driving up to the convenience story to buy bottles of water," he says. "Our culture, our belief systems, everything is under water."

Tribal chairman Tex Hall, the pony-tailed leader who soon would have to fend off Wolfe's election challenge, continues the story. "We were fully self-sufficient tribes, with no welfare and no unemployment. But the dam devastated us. There is not enough money to compensate us for the damage that has been done because we haven't yet been made whole. To me, it's a human rights issue and a discrimination issue," he says.

Later, I would meet up with Hall in Washington, where he reminds

FIGURE 6. George Gillette, chairman of the Mandan-Hidatsa-Arikara tribal business council at Fort Berthold, weeps in 1948 as Secretary of the Interior J. A. Krug signs a contract that calls for the tribe to turn over 155,000 acres of its finest riverbottoms for the construction of Garrison Dam. (Photo courtesy AP/Wide World Photos)

U.S. senators during a congressional inquiry into dam management that tribal members had called the Missouri River "grandfather" because it enabled them to survive for many generations.

I would also visit him again in North Dakota, where he tells me of Indians' desire to play a larger role in brokering the modern negotiations between upstream and downstream states over river management.

"We need to get everyone in the room, lock the door, and not come out until we balance the interests of the upstream states, the downstream states, and Mother Earth," he says of modern river politics.

On Hall's office wall in New Town is a photograph taken on May 20,

1948, the day the papers were signed in Washington turning over land for the new lake. The signatories strike a stiff and formal pose except for one—tribal chairman George Gillette, who covers his eyes as he weeps.

"Right now, the future does not look good to us," Chief Gillette said that day.

~ PADDLING ~

THE FOOL SOLDIERS

A photo of dead Indians, their legs stiff and frozen arms pointed skyward, hangs in a pictorial display at the Army Corps of Engineers headquarters at Fort Randall Dam, in South Dakota. The bodies are being gathered by soldiers after the massacre at Wounded Knee. In the Corps display, a bone lies on a table. The young woman managing the office doesn't know what kind of bone.

Here, at the site of the first permanent fortification in the Upper Missouri, photos and artifacts give a troublingly realistic lesson in history. Alongside dead Indians, white settlers like Gustav Reider are recalled for their prowess in fighting the menacing tribes. Visitors learn that Reider once rode into the fort with an arrow dangling from his thigh, blood flowing down to his feet.

Along the Missouri River, many tales are told of heroes conquering savages. But in Mobridge, South Dakota, I heard a story of a different kind of encounter between Indians and Euro-Americans. More than a century after, it's turning into a tale of reconciliation.

The story of the Fool Soldiers begins far away from the Missouri River along Lake Shetek in Minnesota. In August 1862, the Dakota Tribe's resentment over years of mistreatment boiled over on a fire stoked by late annuity payments. The white families of Lake Shetek paid anger's price.

The settlers were ordered off tribal land. Fourteen settlers claiming Indian land were killed in a running firefight that also took the life of the Indian chief, Lean Bear. Two women, Julia Wright and Laura Duley, and six children between five and eight years of age were taken captive. Among them was six-year-old Lillian Everett, who had been beaten nearly to death by Lean Bear's vengeful wife.

Led by Chief White Lodge, the Indian band headed west, moving through the fall with the women and children in tow. Not for three months would the fate of the captives become known. While the Indians were botching an ambush of a mackinaw boat ferrying miners down the Missouri River from Fort Benton, one of the captured women ran to the bank, yelling for help.

When the miners reached Fort Randall and reported what they had seen, Colonel John Pattee formed a rescue party. Word of the army expedition reached Fort Pierre, where ten Teton Lakotas had formed an alliance to promote harmony among tribes and among tribes and whites. They were called the Fool Soldiers Band by their own people because of the risks they took in the name of peace.

Now the Fool Soldiers took their biggest risk. They rode out in search of White Lodge's camp, hoping to beat the army to the rebellious Dakotas and prevent bloodshed.

A brave named Martin Charger led the Fool Soldiers. With him were Kills Game and Comes Back; Four Bear; Mad Bear; Pretty Bear; One Rib; Strikes Fire; Red Dog; Charging Dog; and Swift Bird. After traveling about one hundred miles, they came on the Minnesota renegades near the Missouri River at Mobridge. Negotiations with the skittish and dangerous Chief White Lodge were tense, but they purchased the freedom of the captives with horses, guns, and blankets.

Traveling back to Fort Pierre, the party was hit by a blizzard. Five of the children were loaded on a travois pulled by the only horse the Fool Soldiers hadn't traded. The women took turns riding the horse, and Pretty Bear carried the sixth child. All the settlers survived.

The Fool Soldiers got no credit for their exploit. They were neither rewarded nor recompensed for the goods they traded. Indeed, they were outcast by their tribe and dismissed by their white fathers.

That's how the story would have ended, were it not for Paul Carpenter, a white man with a long memory. The Minnesota cardiologist and history buff is a descendant of Lillian Everett, the rescued child who survived a Dakota widow's wrath. He tracked down Harry Charger, great-grandson of the Fool Soldiers' head fool Martin Charger, and invited him to his home. The year was 1991, 131 years after the rescue, and they smoked a peace pipe in the beginning of a campaign that Carpenter describes as his attempt at reconciliation.

In 1996, some 180 descendants of the Fool Soldiers and 60 relatives of the captives sat down for a banquet in Eagle Butte, South Dakota, on the Standing Rock Sioux Reservation. Blankets and other gifts were exchanged. "We didn't have horses and guns," Carpenter told me. But he commissioned a painting by native artist Del Iron Cloud called *Going Home*, depicting the return of the captives. A series of prints are on sale, with proceeds funding scholarships for the Fool Soldiers' descendants. The young Lakotas seeking financial help must reconstruct the past in their application by explaining why they believe the Fool Soldiers were not honored by whites and were regarded as traitors by Indians.

Carpenter told me that the prospect of a reconciliation hadn't occurred to him when he learned from a historian in the early 1980s that descendants of the Fool Soldiers might be located. But the more he thought about the treatment of American Indians, not just the Fool Soldiers, the more clearly he felt compelled to do something.

"There was a great injustice done to the whole Sioux Nation, but we have a personal debt to pay to the Fool Soldiers for what they did," Paul Carpenter said.

~11~

BROKEN TRUST II:
THE SKULLS OF WHITE SWAN

The Chiefs . . . wer happy to find that they had fathers which might be depended on Etc. We gave them a Cannister of Powder and a Bottle of whiskey and delivered a few presents.

—William Clark in Council with the
Ottoes and Missouris, August 3, 1804

IN WHICH GRAVES AND OLD WOUNDS ARE OPENED

*There's a destruction in the land
Can't you see, can't you see
Men and women are passing away . . .*

LANDING
THE DAKOTAS

M Y QUEST HAS cycled back to South Dakota, where I am standing along the Missouri River with Faith Spotted Eagle of the Yankton Sioux. I have come along as she and some "grandsons"—teen-aged boys of the tribe that she looks out for—weed and water a garden near the river on her family's ancestral land. The boys have leaped into the river to swim, and in my rental car, Faith and I have scraped and clanged over a rutted meadow to a place that exists no more.

As Lewis and Clark traveled up the river, they worried about the ferocity of the Sioux tribes and, indeed, ran into some trouble. But the Yanktons were an exceedingly friendly lot, and on an August morning after a feast of fat dog, the traveling captains bestowed medals and wardrobe trappings that left the Indians bewildered. As well as handing out disappointing presents, the voyagers committed a political faux pas by elevating one of the five chiefs who came to call over the others. Thus opened a tenuous relationship between the Yankton Sioux and the Army that would become complicated by the construction of Fort Randall Dam and Lake Francis Case and the loss of tribal land. The Standing Rock and Cheyenne River Sioux reservations were reduced by construction of Lake Oahe. The Crow Creek and the Lower Brule Sioux suffered from both the Fort Randall and Big Bend projects.

Land along the river that once was theirs now is owned by the federal government and controlled by the Army Corps of Engineers, including the strip of shoreline along Lake Francis Case where Spotted Eagle and I now stand, 1,200 acres that she is angling to recover for the tribe. Across the river, on the western shore, lies another ninety-mile stretch to which she wants unrestricted access for her tribe. She tells me her goal is a place for the boys to hunt and camp as they approach manhood, carrying out vision quests, their search for guardian spirits to lend purpose and strength to their lives.

"The loss of the river keeps us from communicating with the spirit world. What we have lost is our holiness," Faith Spotted Eagle says.

Spotted Eagle was born in 1948. She was a little girl when the waters that inundated part of the Yankton Sioux Reservation began to rise. But she recalls a scene of people carrying beds, as well as the urgency that permeated the reservation. "I could feel the sadness," she tells me.

Indians' loss of their river and their land is at the root of the disorder that Spotted Eagle, who is an anger management counselor, calls "red rage." She also is a founder of the Braveheart Women's Society, a community seeking ways to reconnect young Sioux with the culture and language of their past. The name comes from battle days, when Sioux women had the job of bringing home the dead. Sometimes the corpses had lain in the sun for many days, and it took women with brave hearts to retrieve them, she tells me. To Spotted Eagle, it is the heart that matters, I conclude; her acre-sized garden of cucumbers, melons, and tomatoes is the Good Heart garden. One day, she hopes, it will help stock a Good Heart Grocery for her community.

On her reservation, hearts are still breaking.

In December 2000, a few hundred yards from where we stand, a sudden drop in the waters of Lake Francis Case exposed graves—and opened a Pandora's box of grievances. Army engineers operating out of the Omaha District office had dropped the lake by some eighteen feet to take water from two dams upriver, Big Bend and Oahe. On December 10, a Corps ranger made a macabre discovery. He reported his find and, finally, three days later, the phone rang at Yankton Sioux tribal headquarters in Marty, South Dakota.

Along the shoreline of the community of White Swan, tribal leaders learned, some thirty graves had been washed out. For more than a half century, the graves and their human remains had remained submerged. Now drought and Missouri River hydropower production had plunged the lake to the lowest level in its history, and there were consequences.

Todd Kapler—an archeologist from Sioux City, Iowa, hired by the tribe—braved 50-mile-per-hour winds on his visit to the shoreline to catalogue what lay there. He described to me what he had seen: "There was casket hardware; lead handles. There was exposed human remains.

The skeletons were disarticulated; they were scattered. I think there was one partial skeleton.

"We didn't touch the human bones," he added. "There were tribal members there, and we are very aware of the sensibilities. One thing we don't do is wantonly handle remains. If at all possible, we don't touch them at all."

Tribal officials counted seven or eight skulls and the remains of some thirty people. The sacrilege sent Sioux leaders into crisis mode. Reburying the dead and preventing similar exhumations became the tribe's most compelling business during an emergency meeting at the Fort Randall casino three days before Christmas.

Striking insensitivity by the Army Corps of Engineers didn't help. While expressing regret at the uncovered skeletons, the Corps declared its intention to raise the lake level by ten feet—which would cover the graves and the bones—to create backup electricity in case Y2K fears of power disruptions proved founded. The Western Area Power Association—its acronym, WAPA, sounds like an Indian word—warned that lost hydroelectric revenues along the river would amount to nearly $4 million if the water in Lake Francis Case remained low.

Spotted Eagle, who represented the tribe in negotiations with the Corps, was quoted in a news article as saying: "The Corps of Engineers believes that if people are poor enough and have no political leverage, it's okay to destroy the remains of their relatives." She was among those who kept vigil over the bones at an encampment where Yankton Sioux and American flags flew side by side near tipis and a sweat lodge.

Bones lay bleaching in the sun as mediators failed to reconcile the Indians to the Corps and the exigencies of Missouri River hydropower production. Earlier transgressions also were unearthed.

In 1949, when the Corps was condemning land along the river to build the Fort Randall Dam, the engineers promised to reinter 438 graves at the White Swan Cemetery, where the Sioux had buried their dead since 1838. Chief White Swan, for whom the village was named, had been placed on his burial scaffold and his bones later buried here.

In a report dated June 10, 1949, the Corps of Engineers said it "accepts responsibility for the disinterment, removal, and reinterment of the burials that will be inundated, including the acquisition of new cemetery sites." The Corps contracted an Oklahoma funeral home to exhume and rebury the remains. More than fifty years later, it is impossible to know whether the work was done.

The twenty-first-century tribe has acquired the legal savvy to sue the Corps. At White Swan, they sought a court order, preventing the Corps from raising the water for thirty days and arguing that the Corps was violating the Native American Graves Protection and Repatriation Act and possibly other federal laws. "This is to notify you," a 2000 letter to the Corps read, "that the Yankton Sioux Tribe considers your agency out of compliance with Sections 106 and 110 of the National Historic Preservation Act with regard to the conscious fluctuations of water levels in the Missouri River while knowing of the White Swan Burial Grounds."

In court, the tribe prevailed; for more than a month, a federal judge in Pierre, South Dakota, prevented the Corps from raising the water. Finally, still in deep Dakota winter, the order ended. Slightly more than two months after the discovery of the bones, on the afternoon of February 17, a burial procession departed Fort Randall Casino at two o'clock for the journey to White Swan. Most of the remains were deposited in four wooden caskets and placed on a scaffold, in the mid-Missouri tradition Captain William Clark had described in 1804: "The Mandans and the nations above them Scaffold their dead and pay great Devotion to them after Death, frequently Sacrifice to them."

For his part, Father Conrad Ciesel of the local Episcopal church prayed. "We raise our hearts in fervent prayer that God will bring comfort to all the families of our faithfully departed at White Swan and to show our deepest respect for all those who have been buried there."

Yankton Sioux spiritual leader Galen Drappeau offered a pipe to the sky during a traditional ceremony of drumming and singing. Afterward, he spoke the feelings of many river tribes: "If the dam hadn't been built, the ancestors would still be down there."

STANDING ON THE DEAD

In Pierre, South Dakota, my next Missouri River landing, Pemina Yellow Bird's voice is rising. I worry for the safety of the Army Corps of Engineers. Perhaps for the entire town. When she gets wound up, I look for the sign that reads RUNAWAY TRUCK RAMP. Yellow Bird is a force of nature, and were it not for her, people would not be gathered to make history.

My quest has brought me to witness the first ever negotiation toward a formal agreement between the U.S. Army and Indian tribes along the Missouri for protecting the graves and cultural sites sacred to Native Americans. About half of the tribes have sent representatives, as have several states and federal agencies, to sit across from these Army engineers. I am the only journalist. Had Yellow Bird not alerted me to this gathering, there would be no one to report it.

Yellow Bird is an Arikara from the Mandan-Hidatsa-Arikara Nation of Fort Berthold Indian Reservation in North Dakota. In 1803, the

FIGURE 7. Faith Spotted Eagle, of the Yankton Sioux tribe in South Dakota, says that alteration of the river "keeps us from communicating with the spirit world. What we have lost is our holiness." (Photo courtesy Bill Lambrecht)

Arikara were a people in their own right, separate from their northern neighbors, the Mandan and Hidatsa, but already much reduced by smallpox introduced by early fur traders. Still, they greeted the Corps of Discovery with hospitality. "These people gave us to eate bread made of Corn & Beens, also Corn & Beans boild . . . all Tranquility," wrote Clark on October 11.

The three distinct tribes affiliated in 1845, when war and disease had made them too weak to stand on their own. A century and a half later, Yellow Bird rejects the official title of Three Affiliated Tribes as an affront to the tribes' heritage. Thus, so do I, herein and in newspaper stories that I write.

Yellow Bird has the knack of swaying people to her way of thinking.

She is a striking woman who alternates between charm and tenacity in reminding non-Indians of their sins.

On the morning of the second day of this negotiation, which meets in a second-floor conference room at the King's Inn, a few blocks from the Missouri River, proceedings are delayed. Glancing around the room, I see why: Yellow Bird hasn't yet arrived. Finally, the double doors open. She has entered and business can begin. She's a tad late, she says, because she was watching a gardening show on the television in her room down the hall. It's the charming Pemina Yellow Bird, and no one admits their irritation. But soon, it is she who is irritated when the Corps' lead negotiator, Larry Janis, a lanky man who sports a thin black mustache, challenges her.

The issue on the floor is not future protection but past sins, particularly a slice of eroded riverbank in South Dakota that the government did not shore up in time.

"That chunk of shoreline contained the bodies of my ancestors," Yellow Bird says. "That never should have happened. In a very short time, that was going to end up in the water and tourists were going to be picking through the bones of our dead to take what they wanted."

Janis does his best to hold up under fire. "I know Pemina is very passionate about this issue," he says.

I have met no one more passionate than Yellow Bird about protecting graves and cultural sites. Respect for the dead is just part of it, I have come to understand. When those relics and worse, human remains, show up on shorelines like the one I prowled, the painful history of Indians' disconnection with the Missouri River is laid bare. A preamble submitted for inclusion in the contractual agreement—a passage written by Yellow Bird—captures the tribes' sentiments about that history.

When the Army Corps built six mainstem dams on the Missouri River, life for the indigenous peoples who called the river home changed immediately and dramatically. Gone are our ancient river-bottom homes, our medicines, our sacred places, the earth lodge and tipi village and hunting camp sites created by our beloved ancestors. Gone are the places intrinsic to our origin stories and to events in our oral histories that are alive in our people's minds and hearts that are still related today.

The loss of our river homes affected every aspect of the quality of our lives: spiritual, mental, physical, emotional, and socio-economic lifeways, all of which make up our very identity as native peoples. Altering the flow of the river altered the face of our Mother Earth, and we are still reeling from and dealing with the consequences of the changes brought by the dams.

The tribes are speaking today, but in the broader debate over restoring the Missouri River they have been all but ignored. Corps decisions are driven by other politics in Washington and downstream, the vote-rich region of the basin. Indians' voicelessness in how the river runs and how its resources are divided is rooted partly in tribes' historic independence, which translates into political disorganization. I know from past interviews with members of dozens of tribes on environmental matters that animosities remain among tribes. For most of the twentieth century, so did the conviction of many tribal leaders that it is wrong to intrude into the affairs of other tribes.

But finally, the Missouri River and this outrage—the matter of long-dead Indians turning up on the shoreline where looters and relic hunters kick through the remains—have brought Indians together. Yellow Bird is their undeclared leader on this wrenching issue. There is irony in their alliance, and in Yellow Bird's plaintive cry. When she speaks of the bones of her ancestors in South Dakota, I know that she is referring to the time when Arikaras were farmers and hunters who lived far south of their present North Dakota homeland—before they were slaughtered, and their survivors driven away, by the Sioux.

Today the tribes stand together, and I watch Pemina conferring especially closely with Tim Mentz of the Standing Rock Sioux Tribe, whose ancestors might have attacked Yellow Bird's. Mentz, who is his tribe's cultural affairs officer, also is angry about the Corps' inability to protect land along the Missouri. "It's been ten years now. You have had ten years to do this and you didn't do it," he tells Larry Janis.

"FATHERS WHICH MIGHT BE DEPENDED ON"

The stretch of Missouri shoreline that tribes worry about especially is roughly the middle third, the Dakotas, which archeologists refer to as the Missouri Trench, and it is one of the richest archeological regions in North America. The Missouri River's Indian heritage is subtle, not visually engrossing like, say, the pueblos of Chaco Canyon in New Mexico. But the Missouri's archeological wealth is profound. For in much of South Dakota and the High Plains, land away from the river was too barren and unforgiving to support settlement. Always the tribes came to the water and the bottomlands, and so did the animals they hunted. Much of the Missouri River banks remains undeveloped, so many caches of relics have been undisturbed—until losing their hold to waves, wind, and indifference.

The designation is official: In 2002, the National Trust for Historic Preservation added the Missouri River to its short list—just eleven at the time—of America's Most Endangered Historic Places. Besides archeology troves, cultural sites beg for monitoring and law enforcement protection: prehistoric villages and campsites; battlefields; parcels where the tribes killed and processed game; and places of religious ritual. It is up to the Army Engineers to protect these lands; it is a matter of the trust between the government and tribes.

But here the tribes see another broken trust. The Corps itself had identified a huge backlog of $77 million in bank stabilization and other spending needed to protect the Missouri River shoreline. In 2002, a report by the Advisory Council on Historic Preservation, a federal agency, scolded the Corps of Engineers, saying there was "no workable framework" for identifying and evaluating the cultural sites—let alone protecting them.

Beginning in the late 1700s, the U.S. government promised in treaties to watch over Indians. Following Jefferson's orders, Clark pledged himself, Lewis, and the nation behind them as "fathers which might be depended on." By the 1830s, the Supreme Court had decided that the government had a trust responsibility with tribes. By 1871, more than six hundred treaties reflecting that arrangement had been signed. In modern times, that duty has been expanded by Congress and court rulings affirming that the government is the trustee over Indian land.

The tribes want rip-rapped banks that do not erode when the water rises and falls in the river. That's a pricey proposition requiring the hauling of barge loads of rock on waters often perilously low from drought; but this price is nowhere near as high as what the Corps spent to bring in rock to stabilize banks on the Lower Missouri. In 2003, the Army allocated $3 million for a program to protect cultural resources; when I asked how many bank stabilizations had been completed, I was told three. The

Indian leaders also want more surveillance. They especially want a voice in decisions about land that once was theirs. In this negotiation, the tribes demanded "co-management" of their cultural sites. The Army says no.

Just as Corps of Engineers' failures endanger places held sacred for centuries, so does news of the failures. Many non-Indians are eager to prowl tribal lands in search of artifacts for sport, profit, or lust to hold history as their own. The impending arrival of what I've heard referred to by Indians as "the Lewis-and-Clark hoards" had tipped the balance in favor of demanding protections, loudly if necessary. But an uneasiness remained, which you can hear in the words of Jim Peacock, historical officer for the Cheyenne River Sioux Tribe at the negotiations.

"We don't want to draw people a road map and tell them what's on the shelf," he said.

Gregg Bourland, who was chairman of the Cheyenne River Sioux Tribe for twelve years and who was chosen facilitator in this negotiation, struggled to understand what drives those who plunder Indian heritage.

"A tourist would never think of going to the Roman Coliseum and grabbing a chunk of it for a memento. But nobody has a problem going to Native American sites and taking a stone ax. Native Americans have not been showed respect," he says. "And unfortunately, American society has encouraged these activities."

TRACKING GRAVE ROBBERS

On Crow Creek Sioux land along the river, the three Oklahomans had a fishy explanation when Corps of Engineers ranger Mike Key asked why they were prowling.

They were fascinated by the area, they said. Apparently, they wanted to hold onto that fascination; in their pickup, Key found arrowheads, pottery shards, scrapers that long ago had cleaned buffalo hides, and other forbidden items.

Along the Missouri River's Lake Oahe impoundment, my quest has turned up Mike Key, the Corps' sole ranger dedicated to tracking down these looters. Without a firearm or the power of arrest, he is left to match wits with the invaders.

"I live and breathe figuring out how to combat this problem," Key, a divorced father of three, tells me in the summer of 2003. "When I get out there, I want to know what really went down. How did they do this?"

Sometimes grave robbers succeed in this escape by maneuvering their boats between cottonwood stumps that remain standing a half century after the bottomlands were flooded. Sometimes they tear away in four-wheelers over the parched hills that slope down to the water. The real professionals work after dark, avoiding Key's low-budget night-vision gear.

I've seen the bounty. One private "collector" who insisted that he had broken no laws showed me a glass-mounted case in his riverfront home with hundreds of fine pieces: awls, fishhooks, spear points, bird points, ceremonial double arrowheads and serrated arrowheads, a drill fashioned from buffalo bone for carving holes in clam shells for necklaces, and thumb-scrapers for preparing buffalo hides.

In South Dakota, locals told me of a "collector" who made regular runs to California to sell his finds. There's also Indian-on-Indian crime: a tribal politician, also in South Dakota, recalled to me the case of two young men dispatched to tidy up a newly eroded burial site. They sold a necklace and other nice stuff, as he put it, to non-Indians.

Plundered goods routinely turn up on the Internet, which has made Key's job even harder. "We could have done without that," said Key, whose policing dates back to pre-Web days.

With a sheriff's deputy's help, Key had recently pinched a scavenger in a well-known archaeological site in North Dakota. Besides arrowheads and scrapers, he had a flint knife and pottery shards. The looter's violation of the Archaeological Resources Protection Act cost him $500, which may have been just a cost of doing his business, considering that I'd seen Plains Indian knives selling for nearly that much.

Sometimes guilt works to Key's benefit. Outside his office, he has found paper bags containing human skulls. Usually they are dropped off after news of other people's troubles with the law. Key knows that tribes scoff at the paucity of money and manpower the Army devotes to catching the plunderers. He understands.

"If somebody was in the cemetery stealing bones and jewelry from my relatives, I'd be just as upset as they are," he says.

A LOST WAY OF LIFE

Circling back on Lakota land, I find more trouble; another reinterment. This morning, the Yankton Sioux have broken their protest camp after standing guard near a pile of earth dug up along the river. More human remains had been discovered when state bulldozers were carving out new campsites at the North Point land that once belonged to the tribe.

Tribal lawyers won another injunction from federal court to delay work until the soil was returned. It is spread neatly in its former place, but bitterness rankles, as I see when the tribe gathers for an old ritual.

At the invitation of Faith Spotted Eagle, I am the only non-Indian at a secret ceremony for teen-aged girls who are entering womanhood. I am told by celebrants preparing the three-day ritual that some in her tribe think that Spotted Eagle is wrong for bringing outsiders so close to sacred matters.

No one asks me to leave, and I remain to witness. We are at a Lakota Sun Dance field, in a remote section of the reservation. In the center is a buried cottonwood tree trunk from which hang the tethers that pierce the chests of the men who take part in the time-honored Sun Dance ritual.

But this is not a ritual of self-sacrifice; these ten girls, ages twelve to seventeen, will spend the days with grandmothers of the tribe, elders who will counsel them on their responsibilities in becoming women. One of the older girls already has spent time in prison. In their lessons about sex and childbirth, these young women will be told why having babies at age thirteen is unwise. First comes drumming and singing and sweet grass smoke. Four of the girls chosen for special duty are blessed by feather plumes carefully removed from a blue cloth. After a prayer, they dance in each of the cardinal directions.

Later, when the girls are putting up their tipi, I take the moment to speak with the grandmothers. They tell me that this riverfront oasis of their ceremonies is fast disappearing. They show me chunks of earth sloughing into the river.

Faith Spotted Eagle joins the conversation. "What you have is the story of emotional attachment to dominance and power. What you have is the story of America," she says, reflecting on what has happened to the river and the tribes along its banks. Her words echo in my mind as I follow America's river west.

∽12∾

WATER WARS

In rivers and bad governments, the lightest things swim to the top.

—Benjamin Franklin, 1754

IN WHICH WE VISIT THE BATTLEFIELDS OF SCARCE WATER

Citizens around Lula was doin' very well
Now they're in hard luck 'cause rain don't pour nowhere.

LANDING
POINT OF VIEW LODGE · POLLOCK, SOUTH DAKOTA

THIS IS A FIGHT about water, I am reminded in South Dakota. Not birds or prehistoric fish or a pretty environment. It's about water, dammit, and about the perfidious Army Corps of Engineers. And about those greedy barge operators downstream that suck us dry, abetted by their pals in Congress. It's about fairness, a virtue folks in the Dakotas and Montana haven't seen since they got turned into water colonies.

Outrage at having been cheated wafts along the shoreline of Lake Oahe, biggest of the impoundments created by the Missouri River dams. *I'm gettin' screwed* is a view especially prevalent at the Point of View Lodge, in Pollock, South Dakota, where the proprietor, Robert Shadwell, will tell his grievance to anybody—even the president of the United States.

> September 11, 2002
>
> Dear President Bush:
>
> I am writing this letter today on the anniversary of the World Trade Center attack. We feel like here in South Dakota we're under attack by bureaucracy and plain bad politics. We know of your promise to Missouri farmers during your campaign. Did you not know that South Dakota, North Dakota and Montana are part of the Union?
>
> It's time to make changes in this system of GOOD OLD BOY POLITICS!!!! Start looking at the big picture. These states have as much right to Missouri River water as Missouri does. Remember what Mark Twain said: "Men will vote over whisky and go to war over water."

When I first visited Bob Shadwell, in the summer 2002, he was e-mailing his Monday morning messages to the White House with an alluring offer: free lodging at Point of View Resort and a guided fishing trip for lunker walleyes. He hadn't heard back, and that's probably just as well. The president professes to be a sporting man, but sport is hard to find along Lake Oahe. Touring Shadwell's sixty-acre property along Ritter Bay, I noted that the water was so low and had receded so far from land that the cove in front of Point of View was roughly a half-mile from water.

That in itself might not be a trip-buster if boat ramps were nearby. But with the lake twenty feet down, ramps—tucked back on bays protected from Oahe's tumultuous winds—resembled high-dives. It takes a muscle-bound truck like Shadwell's double-axle F-350 to conquer the steep inclines and, with a fishing vessel in tow, reach the sole usable ramp, two miles down the road from Point of View. This was no way to run a fishing lodge, I could see right away, especially a fragile, year-old business in the hands of a family chasing a dream.

There were plenty of Bob Shadwells in the Dakotas, people whose Missouri River recreation businesses desperately needed water from federally managed dams. The drought that engulfed the region in the first years of the new century was the immediate cause for distress. In August 1999, the elevation on Lake Oahe calculated in feet above sea level was 1,617. When I visited there in August 2002, it had dropped by 29 feet to 1,588. Water was also low at Fort Peck and Garrison. Together with Oahe, lakes at those dams hold 85 percent of the storage in the Missouri River system.

This was a punishing drought. But rain or not, the problem along the Missouri River is chronic. Routinely, there is insufficient water in a system that gives priority to navigation. The Army Corps of Engineers interprets its *Master Manual* to say there must be sufficient water in the 732-mile stretch of lower river to maintain a nine-foot channel for navigation. Congress and the courts have refused to stipulate otherwise, so somebody has to suffer. Right now, that somebody is Bob Shadwell.

I talked to Shadwell many times over the next two years, as the water continued to drop. He felt more desperate all the time, like a fish flopping in a boat and gasping for air, and I could see that his dream was on life support. Abandonment can take over in a hurry in a remote land. The Point of View is situated near South Dakota's border with North Dakota, where the earth is an exotic blend of camelbacks, swales, and hillocks, some perfectly round, that fellows hereabouts have named after parts of the female anatomy. Otherwise, you see nothing but a few cows on the five-mile gravel road back to Shadwell's lodge.

"It seems like the country really doesn't know our plight out here. It seems that regardless of the situation, downstream barge traffic takes precedence," Shadwell says over beers at his empty bar.

"It baffles me. The Corps says, 'We feel for you, but there's nothing we can do to help.' That *Master Manual* they follow? I think it's a Big Chief Notebook written with a bunch of crayons. The government sits by doing nothing and my business has shut off like a spigot because they have all the water down there. We can't get enough to let us keep going, and no matter what happens to us up here, downstream barge traffic always takes precedence. And the worst part is, you never know if there's going to be light at the end of the tunnel. You'd think people down there would want to slow the flow and improve recreation and the fishery. But they just want to continue stealing the water."

Corps officials receive Shadwell's e-mails, too, and they talk to him on the phone. They say that yes, they are required to keep those barges running, but no, barges aren't the whole problem; it just hasn't rained. Paul Johnston, the Corps' longtime spokesman in the Omaha District, is among many who have spoken to Shadwell. "There are a number of folks I've talked to who think that if navigation were halted, God would return to her heaven and all would be right with the world," says Johnston.

What seems to trouble Shadwell more than the paucity of water or even his diminishing business is the violation of his dream. Shadwell, who was born in 1957, is a burly fellow with a shaved head and a wheeze that, I suspect, is the result of a combination of cigarettes and the hazards of his former job running a body shop in Denver. He was hell on wheels growing up, earning monster fines for tearing around in his Camaro, with 396 cubes and two four-barrels. He was clever enough and competent enough to make a career working around cars every day. In his early forties, he was pursued by a new calling: Not only did he love to fish, he was good at it. On weekends he would trailer his speedy, 22-foot Lund to compete on the walleye circuit around the Midwest and West. Before long, he was a pro. One of the prime spots he discovered was Lake Oahe.

So Shadwell cashed in his retirement, and he and his wife, Kim, took a second mortgage on their house in Denver. They bought Point of View after a single visit, just before the water started to drop. They made their leap after the 9/11 attack in 2001, a time when people were reevaluating how they lived. "We wanted to get away from conventional society and do something that's fun," says he.

I'm not witnessing much fun at his empty restaurant and bar, where nightly receipts in prime fishing season have plunged from $700 to $25. Nor is there much fun out on the water that drew him to South Dakota. There are no customers, and the low water has exposed the limbs of thousands of cottonwood and ash trees on bottomlands flooded in the 1950s behind Oahe Dam. If there are no fish stories being told, there are plenty of tales about folks who, after figuring how to drop their $40,000 fishing vessels in the water, harpooned them or ruined outdrives on barely submerged treetops. Adding to the gloom, my trip with Shadwell is shortened by a 25 knot wind that forces us to brave ocean-sized waves and execute a harrowing docking at a makeshift ramp.

Drying out with a beer in front of him, Shadwell sounds resilient. But he allows that he's begun renegotiating his payments to keep Point of View afloat. "The rest of the country has no idea what we're going through up here," he says.

HIGH AND DRY ON THE PLAINS

Shadwell is a casualty in the water wars of the last decade of America's twentieth century. South Dakotans—like their water-obsessed neighbors in North Dakota—have always had to worry about water in their semi-arid lands, which are forbidding places where masses of people probably don't belong.

To bring down water, Peter Carrels relates in his book *Uphill Against Water* (1999), nineteenth-century rainmakers bilked residents of the parched communities of the Plains. In the twentieth century, federally funded experiments detonated balloons filled with explosive gas. In the 1950s and 1960s, many South Dakotans fought to get their four dams in hopes of capturing that passing Missouri River water. In the 1970s, they rejected their own version of North Dakota's Garrison Diversion, an irrigation system in the making so big it can be seen from space. By the 1990s, planners and politicians were scheming again, this time to get enough water for the new century.

In fighting for twenty-first century water, South Dakotans were not alone. Tensions were simmering even in regions of the United States accustomed to bountiful rainfall. The hundredth meridian, which runs through the Dakotas and Kansas down to Texas, divides the nation into two distinct categories: the half that averages more than twenty inches of rain every year and the half that doesn't. Until recently, water wars were fought west of the hundredth meridian, where civilization has depended on Promethean quests to capture water, store it behind dams, and transport it vast distances via canal for life's every need. In the late twentieth century, new conflicts began to erupt east of the hundredth meridian.

Robert Hirsch, associate director of the U.S. Geological Survey, confirmed the change when I visited his office in suburban Washington, D.C., where the nation's water is watched and measured. "The level of conflict over water that we usually associate with the West is now occurring around the country. There are many concerns and even jealousy. Everybody worries that somebody's going to steal their water," said Hirsch, the government's chief water scientist.

In each of the emerging water wars, the same forces—farmers, cities, and conservationists—collided as they attempted, usually with little success, to share an increasingly precious resource. Farmers want water from rivers to irrigate. Cities and towns need it so people can drink and factories operate. Conservationists want water for the sake of wildlife. And wherever water wars roil, the Army Corps of Engineers was in the middle of the fight. That was the case in Arkansas, where I traveled while taking the measure of other river struggles.

ARKANSAS'S GRAND PRAIRIE SCHEME

The White River begins in northwest Arkansas, flows east into Missouri, and then meanders on a southerly route back through Arkansas before meeting the Mississippi south of Memphis. In the eastern Arkansas town of Augusta, Gayne Schmidt, a chamber of commerce leader, shared her water worries.

"What God laid out here for us here, they're messing with," she said at the local Methodist church, where she is financial secretary.

In one of America's new trouble spots, farmers are, indeed, intending to mess with what God gave eastern Arkansas. On a long fertile delta known as the Grand Prairie, rice growers and the Army Corps of Engineers devised a plan to divert 1 billion gallons of water a day from the White River for irrigation. When I visited their farms to find out why, the growers had begun a campaign in Congress on behalf of a $300-million-plus pumping project that amounted to subsidies of $300,000 for each of the thousand or so landowners in line to receive the water. Some were well-heeled, none more so than Arkansas's Lieutenant Governor Winthrop P. Rockefeller, a billionaire who owned several thousand acres in a newly formed irrigation district.

Unlike farmers in the Dakotas, the Arkansans who live off the soil are blessed with fifty inches of rain annually. Rice-growing conditions are perfect: eight to ten inches of topsoil above a layer of impermeable clay that holds water like a saucepan. To fill that saucepan as rice growers flooded their fields, the Mississippi alluvial aquifer offered all the water rice could want. Those blessings have made Arkansas the leading rice producer in the nation.

Yet trouble was brewing in Eden. Early twentieth-century farmers could tap rushing water by drilling just fifty feet into the earth. By the middle of the century, drillers found the aquifer dropping a foot or more every year. In the early years of the twenty-first century, what was left of the aquifer might be 120 feet down, and likely will be all but drained by 2015. Arkansas has realized the U.S. Geological Society's worst fear: depleting groundwater that has been around since the Ice Age.

Rice growers might have concluded that irrigation farming couldn't sustain water or prosperity and changed their methods or their crops. In fact, the growers did much the opposite: They tripled their acreage planted in rice over the past three decades. They farmed harder, further draining the alluvial aquifer and punching deeper into the earth to tap the thinner Sparta aquifer, the region's source of drinking water.

Then, with time and water running out, rice farmers turned their eye to the White River, a wildlife paradise that attracts the largest population of wintering mallards in North America. All those waterfowl bring millions of dollars in recreation and tourism to towns around the river. Their plan would pit farmer against farmer, towns against the countryside.

Rice grower Gloria Strohl invited me to her home to hear tales of desperation. Walking the family fields, she'd hear telltale belching and hissing as irrigation wells run dry. "We watch that water not belonging to anyone flowing by us on its way down to the Gulf of Mexico," she said.

On his 1,000-acre spread near the town of Stuttgart, Ray Vester, a fourth-generation rice farmer, put the value of water in different terms. "Rice is about more than farming; it's our culture," he said. "You can get along without a lot of things in life, but you can't get along without water." His lament could be spoken by any combatant in America's new water wars.

Corps officials, too, told me the project they had devised would divert less than 2 percent of the White River, lowering it by just a foot or so. Rice or not, that pump would be turned off if water levels dropped to levels that imperiled the river or its waterfowl.

It seemed to me that Army engineers might be rooting for the project for yet another reason: The White River diversion would expand the Corps' mission to irrigation, which in the West has long been the province of the Bureau of Reclamation. The Grand Prairie was one of three Arkansas Corps projects to irrigate more than 1 million acres of farmland. The other two seek to divert water from the Arkansas River, which cuts through the center of the state. To environmental advocates, the Corps' interest in going into the irrigation business was as worrisome as trouble on the White River.

On a boat ride up the White River, David Carruth, attorney for the town of Clarendon, Arkansas, recounted his community's concerns. Corps dams already have damaged fishing, mussel gathering, and tourism, he said. Now, the people in his town worried that the region's famed duck-hunting trade—a multimillion-dollar industry that drew such notables as Will Rogers and Joseph Pulitzer—would suffer with the White River's flow diminished.

"The problem is, we're getting too many soda straws in the glass. And if they get that big straw in the river you can bet they'll suck out what they want," Carruth said.

APALACHICOLA'S PHANTOM BARGES

Dakotans calculating the odds of halting barge traffic on the Missouri River might consider the case of the phantom barges of the Apalachicola. Locals in Wewahitchka, Florida, told me they can count on one hand the barges that drift by in a few months' time on the Apalachicola River, which slices through the Florida Panhandle on its way to the Gulf of Mexico. Yet the Army Corps of Engineers continues dredging the river, scraping out a channel for barges that seldom arrive, then spewing up sand that chokes the life from swamps. "Stupidity" was how Senator Bob Graham, a Florida Democrat, referred to dredging for naught. A top Army Corps official in the Clinton administration, Assistant Secretary Joseph Westphal, had broken ranks to assert that commercial navigation on the Apalachicola "is not economically justified or environmentally defensible."

Yet when I traveled up the Apalachicola to take stock of another simmering water war, the Army Corps was on the verge of getting even more money for dredging and maintenance plus a tidy bonus: $5 million for studies on correcting the problems it has caused.

Self-described "river rat" Marilyn Blackwell offered a view that was hard to contest. "If somebody wants a picture of mankind's insanity, they ought to come down here and take a picture of this thing," she said from the bow of a johnboat.

The Florida river war suggests a nautical version of a law of physics: Once barges are put in motion by an act of Congress, they stay in motion. Barges on the Apalachicola ferry sand, gravel, coal, and an occasional piece of machinery to and from Georgia and Alabama. Like the Missouri River, the Apalachicola never reached expectations as a commercial corridor. Navigation hangs on because of the abiding relationship between the Corps and Congress, whose members pay attention to their constituents' desires for water back home. In the Apalachicola case, members of Congress from Alabama and Georgia want the navigation to continue, however infrequently.

Florida endures the damage to its longest river but reaps little in the way of benefit from the navigation. The Apalachicola forms at the Georgia border, where the Chattahoochee and Flint rivers meet. Then, it flows 106 miles south to Apalachicola Bay, where it feeds the nation's richest oyster fishery. The swamp-lined Apalachicola is home to the largest number of endangered plants in the state and more reptiles and amphibians than anywhere else in North America. In the swamps at night, I watched tiny red lightbulbs gliding at water level. Best not to pursue those red dots, I was told, since beneath them gape the jaws of alligators.

Along more than one quarter of the Apalachicola shoreline, the light brown sand from Corps dredging rises in stark contrast to the swamp's lush green growth. Among the mounds is so-called Sand Mountain, a sprawling three-story heap that rises like a desert dune. Since navigation work was authorized in 1945, sand and silt have washed into the swamps, clogging sloughs that normally fill the swamps with water. In some places, sand pumping has rerouted the river, cutting off hairpin curves—as the Corps did along the Missouri—to make navigation easier for barges. The Corps manages a dam upstream to open barge navigation windows, quickly raising and lowering water. Fish trapped in the swamps die when the water falls.

David Taunton, a former county judge, wages his anti-dredging crusade in the *Gulf County Breeze*, a monthly tabloid newspaper he has published since retiring from the bench. When you own your own paper, you can write headlines like the one that screamed: *NO MORE CORPS DREDGING!* In one of his stories, he wrote that barge operations "brought sudden death to an age-old intricate, natural ecosystem and wildlife habitat."

Beekeeper L. L. Lanier would agree. Lavernor Laveon Lanier Jr., who was approaching his eightieth birthday when we toured his hives, was the patriarch of a century-old honey operation that relies on the tupelo gum trees that grow along the Apalachicola in greater abundance than anywhere in America. For two weeks in the spring, his family trucks colonies to the riverbank so the bees can partake of tupelo blossoms. The result is an uncommonly smooth and flowery honey.

Lanier shook his head as he examined several dead tupelos fallen in a dry stretch of swamp. It's rare, he said, for the gnarly, long-lived trees to succumb, as these are doing. Flipping butts of Camel filters out his pickup window into the swamp, L. L. Lanier hardly fits the stereotype of an environmentalist. But just before my visit, he had telephoned Senator

Graham to offer encouragement in battling the Corps and its allies in Congress.

"I said, 'Be a man, Bob, be a man. If we're not careful, those Army engineers will mess things up worse than they already are.'"

BIG, THIRSTY ATLANTA

I was beginning to think like Bob Shadwell, the angry e-mailer back on the Missouri. More and more, water is the stake in American's twenty-first-century civil wars that pit state against state and brother against sister. Rivers seldom adhere to political jurisdictions, and solutions bump up against boundaries dividing sides each as intractable in its own interest as a wild river. The pattern held true all the way to Atlanta, where I detoured yet again seeking water war solutions and where I sat in on cease-fire negotiations that embroiled a three-state region.

Metropolitan Atlanta added 1.3 million people to its population in the booming 1990s alone. With all those people came unprecedented demands for water. For three years Georgia, Alabama, and Florida fought over how to slake the young giant's thirst. Finally, the three states called formal negotiations on two interstate compacts that would allocate water from the region's chief rivers for the next thirty years.

Failure would trigger regionwide uncertainty and probably water hoarding—or a court-ordered distribution plan. But if negotiators succeeded—so it seemed to me—their trail-blazing agreements could draw a blueprint for cooperation along the Missouri and across the nation. Following these negotiations had another appeal for me. I'd been on the Apalachicola, and now I would get to know its feeder rivers, the Chattahoochee and the Flint. Waters of all three little-known but much-used rivers would be governed by the pending agreement.

As Atlanta's commissioner of planning and development until 1996, Leon Eplan hadn't charted water on his list of worries. "For a long time, we were in a Garden of Eden," Eplan told me. "Fifty inches of rain, huge hills to the north with wonderful streams. We'd dammed up the Chattahoochee for water. We were in high clover. We didn't even give water a thought. Suddenly there were restrictions, environmental concerns, and legal challenges."

Atlanta had turned on its growth gene. In the 2000 census, the population of the twenty-county metropolitan region surpassed 4.1 million, nearly seven times the count a half century ago. With no natural borders and no end in sight to expansion, a tiny town founded in 1837 as a railroad crossing has the potential of becoming one of the biggest cities on the planet.

No metropolis in the United States depends on such a measly source for its water. Metropolitan Atlanta takes nearly 80 percent of its water from the modest Chattahoochee River, which in places is barely a creek. Flowing for 430 miles, less than one fifth the length of the Missouri, the Chattahoochee does not rank with America's main rivers.

Planning for water shortages carries an extra challenge in Atlanta, because the metro area is a political crazy quilt. Metropolitan Atlanta has more than seventy counties, towns, and various government jurisdictions, all looking out for their own interests—and the interests of their political backers.

Among Atlanta's problems is one that doesn't worry Dakotans: urban sprawl. Until water got scarce, neither had sprawl worried Atlanta area officials, who were enjoying its spoils. As I was told by Wesley Wolf, executive director of the Southern Environmental Law Center, sprawl features in the creation story of Atlanta's water woes and wars. "Sprawl has had a firm grip on our political leaders and how they fund their campaigns," Wolf told me. "Our political leaders are not really seeking out creative ways of getting campaigns funded other than the tried-and-true ways of taking money from developers."

Now riversheds are paying sprawl's price. Among them is the Flint River. Former President Jimmy Carter, who grew up on one of the Flint's tributaries, recommended a trip on the Flint for "anyone who wants to experience the way Georgia was when God made it." Rising meekly from what looks like a drainage ditch near Hartsfield Atlanta International Airport, just south of Atlanta, the Flint widens into a spectacularly scenic river on its 350-mile journey to meet the Chattahoochee at Lake Seminole near the Florida border.

But near Thomaston, sixty miles south of Atlanta, lodge owner Jimmy McDaniel has the same complaint as Bob Shadwell. It's green here rather than sere, but green doesn't make up for low water. Downstream from big users, McDaniel's bookings are down and he hasn't rented many canoes of late. Not even the heartiest paddlers want to endure lengthy portages caused by low flow. Standing in a drying river bottom, McDaniel laments the powerlessness of Georgians downstream from thirsty populations, much as Shadwell complains about the impotence of Missouri River states upstream. "It's like somebody turned off the faucet up yonder. Before too long, this river could be a dead duck," he tells me.

McDaniel's lament suggests still another challenge of water negotiators: Besides worrying about whether there will be enough water to drink, they must consider the health of the rivers that sustain the region. The

Upper Chattahoochee has an advocate—the Upper Chattahoochee Riverkeeper Fund—to make its case. In defining Atlanta's impact, the fund's Matt Kales spoke not only for his river but for many: "First and foremost, this is about a boom town wrestling with issues affecting people all over these days. But these rivers also are the front line of environmental stress in the country as we determine how we grow and where we grow."

Negotiators from Georgia, Florida, and Alabama knew the stakes were high back in early 1997 when they sat down to craft a treaty in the suburban Atlanta office of House Speaker Newt Gingrich. A meeting planned for forty-five minutes ran for almost fourteen hours. With Gingrich pushing, the structure of two novel interstate compacts emerged.

Usually when states set up interstate compacts, their legislatures have the final word. But under this newly negotiated structure, these compacts went to the state legislatures first. All three state legislatures agreed to follow wherever the negotiations led, a remarkable ceding of power. If the negotiators decreed that Atlanta would go dry on Thursdays—or that Alabama or Florida would—the states had to accept it. Only the federal government would have stopping power on the treaty the negotiators wrote. The future belonged to the negotiators.

By 2001, Georgia and Alabama had reached agreement based on that 1997 treaty framework. The last hurdle was satisfying Florida, which was worried about its Panhandle. To assure there'd be water for the Panhandle, Florida had drafted a proposal detailing how the Army Corps of Engineers would operate Lake Lanier, Atlanta's main reservoir, and how much water—about 14 billion gallons—could be withdrawn in a year's time.

In an office stacked with an archive of paper spawned by years of talks, Bob Kerr, Georgia's chief negotiator, reflected on one aspect of the pressure. "Every constituent group is sitting out there listening to you only in terms of what you are doing to them and nobody else," he told me. "It has made the give-and-take difficult."

Still, Kerr was so hopeful of a breakthrough that he stayed away from his beloved mountain getaway the whole summer of 2001. "Whether we do this right or wrong, whether we can come to an agreement or not, I suspect that this is something that will guide future actions elsewhere," he said.

I was hopeful, too, having told the half-million readers of the Sunday *St. Louis Post-Dispatch* that in a meeting in Montgomery, Alabama, on the coming Wednesday, these negotiators might well make history and show states along the troubled Missouri River the way.

But that meeting would be scrubbed because of Florida's eleventh-hour intransigence. For two more years, the negotiations crawled along. Then, in the spring of 2003, the last Ts were ready to be crossed. Luckily, I didn't lead readers astray once more.

Feeling cocky with spring, Georgia said that it just had to have more Chattahoochee River water. At that, Florida balked. Florida governor Jeb Bush threw the decision to the courts. Talks languished until September of '03, when the five-year negotiations ended with a whimper, not a bang. No truce would be signed in this water war.

Bob Shadwell and beleaguered denizens of the Upper Missouri would need to look elsewhere for hope.

SOUTH DAKOTA POINT OF VIEW

At Point of View a year after my first visit, Bob Shadwell's plight has worsened. Lake Oahe is down another four feet, to 1,584.4 feet above sea level. For three prime fishing months, his business had plummeted 70 percent from a year ago, and it stank then. Many of the fishing fellows and their families who had counted Point of View as a favored getaway, Minnesotans especially, are worried about getting their boats onto water. If they can get out, there's no assurance they can get back. On a morning outing, we get caught in the wind tunnel and have to creep through sloppy waters, avoiding cottonwood stump monsters seeking retribution while figuring how to negotiate an ever less safe ramp.

Shadwell, who is missing a bottom tooth or two and has a lean-forward walk like he's in a hurry, has been trying to get his message through to Congress in more direct ways than his barrage of e-mails. He was told by an aide to South Dakota senator Tom Daschle that the senator would personally read his note; but that didn't satisfy Shadwell. "I don't want you to read my fuckin' letter," he told the aide. "I want to address Congress myself!"

Another congressional aide had told him that there might be some relief in the budgetary process in Washington. "I don't give a rat's ass about the fucking budget. I want to know what you're doing to help us on the Missouri River," Shadwell said, relating the story.

His e-mails were getting more aggressive, like this one he sent to several members of Congress:

There's a drought in the upper northern tier of Montana and the Dakota snow pack has been very low with very little runoff. But where the problem lays is how you, the government, that is supposed to represent the people of this country, only represent the affluent people. We know that you depend on votes to get into office, but are all of you on the take with the lobbyists in Missouri?

It's time that you look at the law on navigation on the Missouri

River and how we can keep a business running on a plan that just doesn't work in this day and age [when] trucking and rail service are the better ways to move commerce than by the way of Huck Finn.

In closing, I just want to thank you S.O.B.s for destroying my dream of having that American dream.

Shadwell and upstream interests seemed about to get a break in the dry summer of 2003 in a federal court in Washington. But in a litigation fest that had much longer to run, the court was trumped by an appellate ruling, and, as Yogi Berra might put it, the status quo remained the same. It was e-mail time at the Point of View Lodge.

Well, you guys got another judge to favor you on the river. It just amazes me that every time we go to court over how the river runs, it ends up in good old St. Louis. How much did it run to buy off that judge? . . .

My business is all but dried up and blown away. We are down sixty-five percent and tomorrow I am going to file for bankruptcy and will more than likely lose everything. So thought I would give you the little guy's view of this damn mess and thank you for destroying my business.

Some competitors lowball Oahe's problems and exaggerate the fishing, but Shadwell says he's not wired like that. He says he plans to keep blowing the whistle. But the tension is wearing on him, I can see, and he's hinting about making changes. He remains quick with a laugh, but he says he's feeling old. After a mere five rums the night before, he says he feels like "I got drug through a knothole and had the shit kicked out of me."

When I phoned Bob Shadwell in the fall, the news was worse. He thought I was the bank calling. He had lost his F-350 truck because he couldn't make the payments; that was the vehicle he used to tow his Lund to the lake for fishing. In a week, he said he would be starting full time in the service department of the Ford dealership in town. It was the routine he'd left behind when he followed his dream.

The dream was fading in ways big and small. Shadwell was a professional fisherman, but goddamned if he could catch a fish. A heat wave combined with chronically low water had driven Lake Oahe fish south, where the water is deeper and they could lay low. Shadwell and his pal, professional guide Dennis Bates, had fished for nine hours one day and reeled in nary a walleye. "And it's not like we don't know what we're doing," Shadwell said.

Shadwell was angry at downstream states, at the barge industry, at politicians. But he couldn't fire off any more e-mails because his computer blew. Probably the mother board, a pheasant hunter at the bar had told him. The only way he got a taste of relief was in the little revenge of refusing to stock Budweiser, which is made downstream in St. Louis.

"It's all but fuckin' killed me," he lamented. "Somebody needs to pull their head out of their ass and take a good look at what is happening up here."

Shadwell was down but not out. He and his wife were considering selling their home in Denver. She might even quit her job at a Denver publishing house and move to South Dakota to run the lodge while Bob worked in town. She was going to join him in a few years, anyway. Sometimes dreams take retooling.

Shadwell had something else cooking, too: He wanted to get into politics himself, possibly running for the Campbell County Board of Commissioners. "I know I don't have a college degree. But I think the only way we're gonna get representation is to get people in office who aren't lawyers and big business people. I know a lot of people are tired of hearing me bitch, but I'm not gonna give up the fight," he told me.

The other sliver of hope was the weather report. Sort of a weather report. An old-timer had told him that heavy clover on the riverbanks means a heavy winter full of snow and sweet precipitation. Looking out his window, Shadwell could see that where waters used to lap, fields of clover were flourishing.

~13~

ONE MORE RIVER TO BOSS

When the well's dry, we know the worth of water.

—Benjamin Franklin, 1871

IN WHICH WE LEARN WHY
NORTH DAKOTANS ARE THIRSTY

Cry me a river
Wash my blues all away.

LANDING

WHY NOT MINOT?

AT THE NORTH Dakota State Fair in the town of Minot, thirty miles north of the Missouri River, a visit by Michael Dukakis is about as improbable as a boy's clawing by a tiger at the same fairground years later. In North Dakota, big cat attacks and presidential visits occur with roughly the same frequency.

The weekend after claiming the Democratic presidential nomination in 1988, Dukakis had, curiously, stopped in North Dakota to campaign. No Democrat has won a presidential contest in North Dakota since 1964. In 1988, North Dakota would be offering nothing beyond its usual puny allotment of three electoral votes to either Dukakis or, almost certainly, George H. W. Bush. But the exposition in Minot holds the potential of a visual that melds smartly with Dukakis's theme of the hour: Uniting diverse Americans.

That's the kind of piffle Dukakis's following of political writers was dishing out. The truth was a bit different. Lewis and Clark scholar Dayton Duncan, the campaign press secretary at the time, recalled later that the Dukakis visit had something to do with the North Dakota heritage of his running mate, Texas Senator Lloyd Bentsen. He offered a second, more plausible reason for the visit.

"We had a preposterously small campaign plane, as you may recall, that was incapable of making a transcontinental flight. So whenever we went coast to coast, we had to stop and refuel somewhere along the way. If you've got to refuel anyway, why not turn it into a campaign visit?"

Filling up the tank had to be easier than filling up the Minot fairgrounds. Assembling a crowd in tiny North Dakota, anywhere or anytime, is a challenge for the best advance man. Luckily, someone on the Dukakis team realized that the North Dakota State Fair was playing in Minot, on a Saturday night no less, so here was Dukakis laboring to persuade the Minot Merry Mixers and stiff-legged square dancers in go-to-meetin' blue jeans that he was one of them.

The scene on the dusty fairground contrasted mightily to Dukakis's previous stop, in Modesto, California, where a mosaic of ethnicity greeted him. Hispanics, Greeks, Armenians, Syrians, Scots, and Portuguese crossed the dais to present Dukakis with flowers and gifts. In the emotions of the moment, sometimes they grabbed and hugged the Democrats' diminutive aspirant, making him flinch. Signs read: SIKHS FOR DUKAKIS; ARRIBA EL DUQUE (UP WITH DUKE); and GAMOS MIGUELITO (LET'S GO LITTLE MIKE).

Here in Minot, speaking from a ribbon-bedecked platform near the

Evans Chrome-Vac Grain Vacuum display, Dukakis seems to have forgotten where he is. "We come from dozens and dozens and dozens of strains of ethnic groups, but we are one nation, one community, one family," he says.

I didn't have the patience to parse it. I'd filed my Sunday story from California, a disjointed account of news from campaign stops from Texas to California hung on the theme of Dukakis trying to win back prodigal Democrats. Having worked thirteen straight days and most nights, after enduring uncountable speeches at the Democratic National Convention in Atlanta—among them a 32-minute epic by the ambitious governor of Arkansas, Bill Clinton, twice the time allotted him—and now spending another Saturday night on the road, I had not a sliver of interest in hearing Michael Dukakis prattle on about diversity.

Dipping down into North Dakota on "Sky Pig," the stubby and slow Boeing 737 that ferried the Dukakis campaign circus around the country, all I could think about was a drink. I was not alone. Even the most frazzled, half-bright among the 119 reporters and news techies on the trip could find the spigots beneath huge letters spelling out B-E-E-R on a permanent brick-and-metal edifice. Inside, it smelled of a mix of manure, sweat, and human scrub lotion, and the mood was as foul.

"How ya' doin'," I said, scooting into a table of North Dakotans with my two cups of beer, one half-empty by now. A fellow looked at me and then into his own plastic cup.

"Dry. Dry, man," he said, staring hard at my notebook when I recorded his words.

"No fuckin' rain. Never." He shook his head slowly.

There was more drinking than talking, and when the band took a break, I recognized Dukakis's wafting voice saying something about farmers. I had no intention of topping my story with a Minot dateline or sending along an insert with a latest Dukakis pronouncement. Who cares? Then again, seeing how Dukakis is among farmers, I thought that I had better listen for something absurd, like when he advised Iowa corn farmers to rotate to broccoli.

I kept my notebook out, and my questions about Dukakis brought glazed looks. "Can he bring us water?" asked an Indian with a braid drooping down from the back of his billed cap.

"Who gives a shit about doo-COCK-us," said a fellow from the Cowboys Drum and Bugle Corps with the name WILLISTON (a town) embroidered on his shirt. A woman with pink-blond hair laughed faintly at his words about the time I began hearing yips and howls outside.

Over the loudspeakers, a woman's voice mixed with Dukakis's nasally, clipped notes. It was slurred, but I could make out the words.

"Boring. Boorrrrrrrrring."

Dukakis lost his place, and I moved in for a closer look.

"BOORRRRRRRRING" she shouted. She was Indian, I could see, and she stumbled to the left as she yelled.

Normally, Dukakis was about as spontaneous as an urban affairs lecturer. Two months down the road, when asked at a presidential debate at UCLA how he would feel about the death penalty if his wife, Kitty, were raped and murdered, he replied with a bloodless discourse that all but assured that the White House would never be his home.

But the Duke got off a good line in North Dakota. "Whoever that cheerleader is out there," he said, "don't try to drive home when you leave here."

I listened some more, and I did indeed stuff the phone receiver in a set of rubber couplers, the technology of the day, and transmit an insert for my Sunday story, a Dukakis quote that seemed inessential to the editor on duty but still ended up in the story. It read: "Mike Dukakis and Lloyd Bentsen, with all our strength and all our ability, can't make rain."

Looking back, I understand, at least partly, what was bugging the beery crowd that night. Dukakis had picked up on it right away. The year 1988 marked the second year of a wicked drought in a land that chronically suffers from little water, bad water, or water in the wrong place. The drought not only made folks grumpy but also was about to open a new front in the battle over the Missouri River. It would reverberate down the Missouri for almost half a continent, provoke diplomatic tiffs with Canada, and explode, where water fights wind up, in Congress.

What Dukakis stumbled onto that evening in North Dakota was the rumbling of a great American water war that has carried on for more than a century and probably will last another century. The Missouri River flows tantalizingly through North Dakota, where it is banked for storage behind one of the biggest man-made structures on earth, Garrison Dam. But the North Dakotans can't withdraw enough water to relieve their misery, an irritant nonpareil to their well-being, both physical and mental. In later trips I would learn so much more about North Dakota's water woes that I was grateful when North Dakotans like Keith Farstveet, a rancher from the southwest part of the state, laughed rather than raged.

Farstveet—whose Scandinavian heritage is common in the state—recalled sending a yellowish sample of well water to a state lab for analysis. It came back with a note, which Farstveet read to me.

It said: "Your horse is pregnant."

FIGURE 8. North Dakotan Keith Farstveet displays some of his state's acrid water. The North Dakota delegation in Congress keeps a supply of such water bottles that they cart to committee rooms when pleading for water development. (Photo courtesy Bill Lambrecht)

THE PROMISE

Keith Farstveet's water report only slightly exaggerated the disgust North Dakotans feel toward the water they're cursed with. In the parched Great Plains of North Dakota, the pungent, mineral-laden water in parts of the state is barely fit for even the livestock to drink. Each time I visited, somebody would pull out a plastic bottle with pungent contents that looked more like cream soda than what fish are born to.

Of course, I never knew whether I was being bamboozled; maybe it was cola or stuff from a mud puddle or, perhaps, it really was horse pee. For all I knew, by the time I was climbing in my rental car, those earnest North Dakotans were slapping thighs: "Ha! Fooled us another damn reporter."

Once, in a Fargo hotel lobby outside a meeting room where the topic of the afternoon had been water, a thirtyish woman with red hair came close during the afternoon break to ask, "Do you know why I wear black panties?"

Nothing more than "Uh" sounded from my lips. This was not the Scandinavian reserve for which North Dakotans are known. She laughed at having embarrassed me before explaining that women in her part of North Dakota learned early in life that white underwear didn't stay white long when washed in funky water.

I once snapped a role of film of forlorn people standing by mineral-corroded sinks and toilets. Brown and nasty these fixtures were, pitted and eaten away. One photo is worth way more than a thousand words. Brenda Fox stands alongside an assemblage of cans, jugs, and boxes of water treatment potions, her arsenal to combat the putrid water that eats her sink. "You can't get away from the rotten egg smell," she told me. I saw in the developed photo what I missed on the spot: On the wall is a painting of cowboys on horseback, the leader on a white stallion, heading upstream in haunch-deep flowing water.

I pitied people bereft of so essential a good as clean water. Who would want to slide into a bath of coal-tarred water? Be baptized in a font of stink? Or smell like sulfur for the big ball in cow town on Saturday night?

On the other hand, I also learned not to trust everything that the North Dakotans said, especially in Washington. For more than a century, North Dakotan politicians have hustled, schemed, and crusaded for antidotes. What they have craved, what they can't seem to get done, is to stick a huge straw in the Missouri and start sucking.

It began with John Wesley Powell. In the 1880s, the one-armed Civil War hero, explorer, and son of a traveling minister preached to the

North Dakotans about the salvation of irrigation. Powell was a geologist who had taught at my alma mater, Illinois Wesleyan, and later became director of the U.S. Geological Survey. He was obviously a persuasive man, so persuasive that the Army let him take along his wife, Emma Dean, onto the Civil War battlefield to function as the right arm that he had lost.

In 1889, during the North Dakota Constitutional Convention, framers heard the gospel according to Powell. "All other wealth falls into insignificance compared with that which is to come from these lands from the pouring on them of the running streams of the country," Powell advised them. "You should provide in the constitution which you are making that the water which falls from the heavens and rolls to the sea, down your great rivers—that water should be under the control of people, subject always to the will of the people."

The North Dakotans followed Powell nearly verbatim, adding a provision in their constitution that read: "All flowing streams and natural water courses shall forever remain the property of the state for mining, irrigating, and manufacturing purposes."

But almost immediately, Powell's gospel became twisted. North Dakota's fathers drafted a formal letter asking Congress to build them a canal across North Dakota to transport Missouri River water. That quest for the means to pump Missouri River water and spread it around the state became no less than an obsession that persists in the twenty-first century.

Of course, Powell would say that irrigation is greatly desirable, but moving water between basins is not—nor is dunning the federal government for assistance rather than arriving at solutions independently. It was Powell who had warned Congress that it was foolhardy, "almost a criminal act," to support and even encourage settlement in dry lands.

But Powell, that old Battle of Shiloh survivor, had planted the seeds for a great battle for water, and ever since, the North Dakotans, like guerrilla fighters, have waged war for water against Congress, other Missouri River basin states, and even the nation of Canada. North Dakotan leaders become primed early on for their mission. Water is the raison d'être of the state's political leaders, the single issue that turned them into Capitol Hill warriors plotting ceaselessly to divert vast amounts of Missouri River water and bleed American taxpayers for the plumbing to do it.

I have come to believe that it's either coded in their DNA or gets in their system at a young age. Bill Guy, who was North Dakota's governor from 1960 to 1972 and among the elders of his state who proudly wears the term "water buffaloes," recalled to me how, in the 1930s, he would long to get clean after showing his purebred sheep at the 4-H fair in Fargo. But there were nights he'd stink like wool and sweat because, back at the YMCA, when he turned on the showers, nothing came out . . . *not even foul water, for Christ's sake!*

"We have looked at the Missouri River as our only saviour, the only way to keep people in this state," Guy, who was in his early eighties when we spoke, told me.

In the waters of Big Muddy, the North Dakotans see the antidote to forbidding land and putrid water. Schoolchildren were taught the Great Dream: pumping water to lure industries and settlers to a state of such tiny population that it rates a single seat in the U.S. House of Representatives. When those kids grew up to vote and write newspaper editorials, they graded politicians on the boldness of their water proposals and the government cash brought home to advance them.

Embedded in the North Dakota collective consciousness is the certainty that water is the reason nobody goes there and many flee. In 1920,

North Dakota's population was 620,000; in 2000, it was 642,200. In the 1990s, forty-seven of North Dakota's fifty-three counties lost population.

The North Dakotans have another motivator, a powerful sense of having been wronged. In building Garrison Dam, the Army Corps of Engineers acquired 550,000 acres of land, about one third of it belonging to the Mandan, Hidatsa, and Arikara tribes that had helped Lewis and Clark survive the first grueling winter of their journey. Politicians say that in return, they were promised virtually unlimited access to the Missouri: enough water to irrigate over 1 million acres.

"The promise" is what they call it. When North Dakota politicians like Senator Byron Dorgan remind people of the promise and what is known as "the permanent flood," his words bespeak the regional rivalry that has evolved.

"It floods in St. Louis, so they can't play softball in the parks in the spring. So they want to harness the river. They say, 'We'll give you a deal. We'll give you a big permanent flood, then you take water from behind the flood and move it around for your own purposes to benefit your state.' We say, 'That sounds like a pretty good deal.' So we got the flood, and we protect St. Louis," Dorgan told me at his Washington office.

He added a little jab to newspaper readers of St. Louis: "Is Missouri the Show-Me State? North Dakota is the state where, when you make a deal with somebody, you keep your end of the deal."

Out of that potent mix of pique and deprivation, North Dakotans have achieved an engineering feat that rivals most anything on earth. Their success is the Garrison Diversion, an unabashed plan backed up by massive plumbing for which American taxpayers already have spent $800 million. That's not all: an additional $700 million was authorized

FIGURE 9. Thirsty North Dakota planned to divert massive quantities of water from the Missouri in this canal but angered environmental advocates and stirred up a water war with states downriver. (Photo courtesy Bill Lambrecht)

for water remedies by legislation I watched escape from Congress under peculiar circumstances in 2000.

Numbers alone don't begin to describe a construction adventure of unbounded grandiosity that a century of thirsty plotting hath wrought. What I was about to witness across North Dakota's semi-arid plains sprawled beyond the simple excess of public maneuvering. Jon Lindgren, the ex-mayor of Fargo, put his finger on it for me over coffee.

"Garrison Diversion is not a water project, it's a religion," he said.

BOONDOGGLE VISIBLE FROM SPACE

Instead of "Sky Pig," I looked down fifteen years later from a Cessna at prairie potholes, the strange, circular bowls created by glaciers that dot

North Dakota's landscape. The undulating land is full of these depressions. Perfect little natural reservoirs they are—or were, given that the same compunction that drives North Dakotans to search for water also led farmers to farm or drain them, destroying some of North America's richest ecological treasures.

Nothing in the way of altered landscape compares to what humans have done in the north-central part of the state, along Lake Sakakawea, the impoundment perversely named, though misspelled, for the young Shoshone celebrated for her role in Lewis and Clark's journey.

Garrison Dam itself is the planet's biggest rolled-earth dam, 12,000 feet long, 210 feet high, and a half-mile wide at its base. It took 70 million yards of earth and 1.5 million yards of concrete to build. The mighty dam came into existence as part of the 1944 Flood Control Act, that fateful piece of legislation won with promises of wondrous rewards for all. Now, North Dakotans demanded their payoff for deeding over all those river bottoms to be flooded. The 1944 law also authorized a plan called the Missouri-Souris Diversion Unit, which would carry water in a canal all the way from Fort Peck Dam, the Missouri River impoundment in Montana, to irrigate 1 million North Dakota acres.

In 1957, the Bureau of Reclamation retooled the plan, naming it the Garrison Diversion Unit of the Pick–Sloan Missouri River Basin Project, and began shopping for a million acres of land. Finally, in 1965, Congress authorized what would be henceforth called Garrison Diversion and financed the Garrison Principal Supply Works.

The straw in the Missouri the North Dakotans demanded is huge indeed: a four-story-high concrete structure called the Snake Creek Pumping Station, with three pumps, each with 8,000-horsepower electric motors and the capacity to draw 2,000 cubic feet of water per second.

Run those pumps all day long and it would add up to 1.3 billion gallons of water: enough to fill 4,000 football fields a foot deep from end zone to end zone.

Snake Creek is just part of the plumbing. The North Dakotans dug most of 150 miles of open canals, some as deep as 114 feet, for the purpose of transferring the water from Lake Sakakawea eastward first to Lake Audubon and then to the Red River basin for the watering of eastern North Dakota.

From the air, the canal looks like a surgical slice across the land in need of stitches. Initially, the plan called for nearly 7,000 miles of main and lateral canals crisscrossing the state, eight reservoirs, hundreds of smaller pumping stations, and over 9,000 miles of drains.

But by the 1970s, with just twenty-two miles of connections unmade, the audacious plan would run into trouble. By any yardstick, the cost was a scandal: the equivalent of $1,250 for each person of the state and a $300,000 subsidy for every farm family that might partake of the irrigation. The destruction of wetlands and wildlife was yet another disaster in waiting.

To budget hawks and conservationists who came to understand the ultimate ecological damage, it was a boondoggle deluxe, a rip-off visible from outer space. Even a few people residing in North Dakota questioned the wisdom of Garrison Diversion. Among them was Gary Pearson.

~14~

LEARNING TO LOVE
DR. STRANGELOVE'S CANAL

The river runs crooked through the valley, and just the same way the channel runs crooked through the river ... The crookedness you see ain't half the crookedness there is.

—Charles Stewart, *Century Magazine*, 1907

IN WHICH WE LEARN WHAT NORTH DAKOTANS WILL DO FOR A DRINK

She's rolling down from the Rocky Mountains
Carrying the Great Plains news.

LANDING
JAMESTOWN, NORTH DAKOTA

THERE IS DOG ENTRANCE and cat entrance at Gary Pearson's Prairie Veterinary Hospital, which is situated on the outskirts of Jamestown, North Dakota, just down the road from the Buffalo Museum and across the street from a display of snowmobiles at the Harley-Davidson dealership. The choice of doors gives visitors pause. When I came years ago to see Pearson, my old yellow Lab, Max, was still among us, and I entered Pearson's hospital accordingly. This time, I pass through the cat entrance, reflecting the species of the remaining creatures who claim me back home in Maryland.

Pearson clearly has more important business than mine. A tom cat, a big-headed yellow stray, was in a holy-hell fight and sported an abscess to show for it. He didn't have a home, but he had a patron who looked out for him and, among his triumphs, he'd passed his feline leukemia test.

Worse, a woman on a riding mower had run over her German Shepherd, a sweetheart of a dog named Bailey, darn near cutting off a back leg. Pearson is speaking with the mortified owner, who has come to visit her hospitalized pet. Waiting in Pearson's office, I have time to notice plaques bestowed on him by the National Wildlife Federation and the National Audubon Society. I gaze respectfully at a bank of file cabinets, knowing that in them he has collected the most complete account in existence of the tortured history of Garrison Diversion, a trove of irreplaceable documents relied on over the years by congressional panels, the government of Canada, several states, and conservationists aplenty. The contents tell the story of how North Dakota politicians pursued water so zealously that they followed it no matter what got in the way.

Before Pearson opened his hospital, he was a waterfowl disease expert in the Fish and Wildlife Service's Northern Prairie Wildlife Research Center. He'd arrived at the center with an M.S. in microbiology on top of his degree in veterinary medicine, both from Ohio State University. He was among a handful of government experts devoted to avian disease, the government's principal waterfowl disease diagnostician for the central United States. If ducks turned up sick, Pearson got the call.

Along the Illinois River near the city of Peoria, an outbreak in duck populations in 1974 had baffled experts. "Botulism," Pearson declared soon after arriving in central Illinois. Up to then, pathologists from the region hadn't tested for botulism. The afflicted birds were not displaying a classic symptom of the poisoning seen thereabouts mainly in chickens and pheasants: a limber neck. So why bother with the botulism tests? But Pearson, having plenty of experience with waterfowl in the Dakotas, knew that ducks do not develop droopy necks until late in the course of the disease. Within twenty-four hours after Pearson made his preliminary diagnosis, the Illinois labs confirmed botulism.

Pearson, who was born in 1939, is among the linear thinkers able to chart a life course early (and to preserve documents and studies from several decades in perfect order so they're instantly retrievable). He'd grown up in northern Ohio near the then-pristine Sandusky Bay marshes, the grandson of a devoted waterfowl hunter and the nephew of a veterinarian. By the age of four, he had settled on a career as a vet; soon thereafter he concluded that he would live his life in a place where the bird life is rich. By the early 1970s, he was living his life precisely as he planned, "with fascinating birds that had been my lifelong passion." Quite likely, he would have remained in the government employ his entire career— were it not for a vengeful senator, timid, deceitful bosses, and a compunction to tell the truth.

Garrison Diversion had nothing to do with Pearson's job. But by the early 1970s, the environmental consequences of carving up the North Dakota landscape were waking up a few people. Even pointing out the trade-offs of Garrison Diversion amounted to heresy in a state where pursuit of gargantuan water projects had become state-sponsored religion: *This is what our fathers and grandfathers thirsted for, a straw in the Missouri River. How dare you criticize!* Grumblings were especially unwelcome by the North Dakota delegation to Congress, which had maneuvered *real* money out of the federal treasury to pay for all this plumbing.

One day, a senior government biologist mentioned to Pearson that vast wetlands would be eliminated during the construction of McClusky

Canal, the principal proposed conduit of Missouri River water. "I was aghast that there were these guys who knew what the public didn't," recalled Pearson, who back then was a case study in naivete. "I didn't understand why someone wasn't talking about what this was going to do. That is not how I was taught in my government classes that things were supposed to operate."

Pearson knew it would be imprudent for a Fish and Wildlife Service researcher to blow the whistle. His agency had even approved the project before later backing away. When a government biologist Pearson knew had gently criticized Garrison Diversion at an Earth Day event, the biologist found a letter of reprimand on his desk.

Perhaps foolishly, Pearson began speaking publicly about the environmental costs of Garrison Diversion—as a member of the local chapter of the Audubon Society rather than a Fish and Wildlife Service researcher. *Yes, North Dakota needs water. And by the way, Garrison Diversion will destroy 62,000 acres of prairie wetlands and roughly that much grasslands, including 43,000 acres of native prairies. A dozen national wildlife refuges will be harmed, one of them inundated altogether.* Just a few facts.

Pearson traveled to Canada in 1973 to speak at the request of the Manitoba Naturalists Society, who decided that they needed to know more about this plan to move water from the Missouri basin to the Red River basin and then into Canada's Hudson Bay. Soon after Pearson returned to North Dakota, he was summoned to the office of the Northern Prairie center's assistant director and told to shut the door. The meeting would be the first indication that higher-ups were paying attention to Pearson's extracurricular activities. Among them was North Dakota senator Milton Young, who had fought for Garrison Diversion.

On November 13, 1973, Young wrote to Harvey Nelson, the director of the Fish and Wildlife Service research center in Jamestown, North Dakota, inquiring about Pearson. "I would be interested in knowing what his assignment is at the Northern Prairie Wildlife Research Center," the senator asked.

Young's letter and others would come to light later in Civil Service Commission proceedings. Nelson replied eight days later that Pearson did excellent work but had begun dabbling in environmental issues unrelated to veterinary medicine and microbiology. The letter added that the agency had a plan for Pearson: reassigning him to a Fish and Wildlife outpost in Utah.

Permanently.

"Present plans are to transfer Dr. Pearson to the Bear River Station some time this fiscal year, preferably as soon as possible."

Senator Young was pleased. "I like your letter of November 21!" he wrote back.

"RUMBLINGS ON THE DITCH"

Other lives were changing, too, as a result of Garrison Diversion, as the Farmers Union found out. If it's not about water in North Dakota, it's probably about farming, and farmers along the corridor of canals that began slicing the prairie swapped tales about what was happening to their land and to their lives. So the board of directors of the Farmers Union, the state's most potent farm organization, assigned the twenty-three-year-old assistant editor of its tabloid newspaper, North Dakota Union Farmer, to take a look. Later, the Farmers Union president would wish they hadn't.

What the assistant, Rich Madson, and his editor, Karl Limveer, discovered ran as an article in the July 1972 *Union Farmer*. Amid photographs of farm families, a calendar of events, and news on grain prices, a bomb was hidden: a remarkable, fifteen-page exposé, titled "Rumblings on the Ditch," capturing the seeds of a prairie rebellion. The diversion was designed to bring irrigation to more than 1 million acres of underachieving ground of the parched Great Plains. North Dakota farmers were to be the primary recipients of the great payback for giving up all that land for Garrison Dam.

But with pain in their words, farmers reported being squeezed and brutalized by government agents buying land. Harold Nordwall, who had lost his first farm for construction of Garrison Dam, told of his despair in losing still another farm for Garrison Diversion. "I'm too old to try a third time," he said.

Leo Reiser, photographed sitting forlornly on a hay bale, lamented that he had nowhere to turn. "I either have to go buy some expensive farmstead or just give up. It's just like you took someone away from what he owned and put him in prison, because there's no place to go and you can't do anything about it. I'm wondering why we took it away from the Indians in the first place."

Later, Reiser's friends and neighbors linked arms to keep the bulldozer away from his door. Another dozer would knock down his clothesline while building a massive berm near his house.

Ben Shatz, who had fought with Patton's Tankers in World War II, recalled being told by government real estate men that his farm was just a dot on the map. "I get so mad, all I can do is cuss," Shatz told the *Union Farmer*. "They hire appraisers that are psychiatrists. They work on you and work on you until you give in."

The coup de grâce was a poem, "Ode to Diversion," by McLean

County Farmers Union president Don Sondrol, featured in a two-page center spread with a photo of a farmer walking along a ravaged prairie resembling a moonscape. The poem read:

My generation saw the "dam vision"
We were awed by the earthen wall
And cheered when the ribbon was cut
The Mighty Missouri harnessed
Irrigation and recreation at last
HURRAH AND HALLELUJA!

Today I view the final rape of Mother Nature.
Did we envision this?
Could we but see this ragged gorge
Winding its way through the meadows
And across the field?
Nothing will stop its relentless path,
Aquifer or hill, home, wildlife or farm.
The relentless march goes on.

My generation is shocked!
This is my native land so crudely handled
Where is that vision for the future
My children's children's children,
I fear for them.
Will no one plan for them?

Rich Madson's board members thanked him for his digging but the Farmers Union president, Ed Smith, turned livid on hearing from Washington about the little newspaper's effrontery. He declared that the *Union Farmer* would not be standing in the way of Garrison Diversion and fired the young assistant editor during a stormy meeting in which he yanked Madson's telephone cord from the wall and ordered him from the building. Smith himself would later be ousted by members angry about Garrison Diversion.

If promoters could replay history, they might not be so swift with retribution. The young idealist Madson, who years later would become a Fish and Wildlife Service biologist, had become outraged during his reporting. "I didn't think that this country would treat its own citizens that way," he said years later. With $310, he founded the Committee to Save North Dakota to fight Garrison Diversion and ran newspaper ads in the state's daily newspapers listing by township the names of hundreds of farmers whose land was being disrupted by Garrison. The project's vengeful backers had unleashed a warrior with the freedom to fight them to the death. Now they were about to repeat that mistake.

SOME KIND OF NUT

By early 1974, Gary Pearson's position as a government waterfowl expert was looking tenuous as his public profile grew, albeit unofficially, in the expanding opposition to Garrison Diversion. As the young investigative reporter documented the social failings of the project, Pearson illuminated the environmental consequences. Meanwhile Senator Milton Young was writing more letters, to the Fish and Wildlife Service complaining of Pearson's presence in a facility that the senator himself was responsible for locating in North Dakota. "It has been responsible for bringing in several people who are some kind of nuts on the Garrison Diversion issue. This really is none of their business," the letter from Young read.

Young wrote again to Harvey Nelson, Pearson's boss, implying that

Pearson should be moved to a job where he could play no further role in the widening controversy: "Harvey, he may be exceptionally well-qualified and deserving of a promotion!"

Continuing his one-man education campaign, later that month Young wrote more letters, stamped "Personal and Confidential," to editors at five North Dakota newspapers. In them he tucked copies of letters Pearson had mailed as a private citizen to Young. "I thought they would be of help to you in better understanding the determination, zeal, and strategy of these people," Young addressed the editors.

Pearson lost his job after refusing a transfer not to Utah but Wisconsin, where he was told to report no later than March 31, 1975. The purpose of the reassignment and its value, either to the Fish and Wildlife Service or to him, was never spelled out. But Pearson knew instinctively that political interference from Washington was behind the transfer and he said as much to Fish and Wildlife Service officials in Washington in letters questioning the transfer.

On June 16, 1975, Pearson received a letter from O. V. Schmidt, acting deputy director, notifying him that his employment at the Fish and Wildlife Service had come to an end. Schmidt wrote: "I reject your contention that your proposed reassignment is politically motivated due to your environmental activities. While the conduct of your outside activities may have been disturbing to some officials within the Service, the decision to reassign you was made for no other reason than to satisfy a legitimate research program need. I find no connection between your outside involvements and the decision to reassign."

Pearson fought to no avail to get his job back. His lawyer lacked the subpoena power to force Senator Young to testify at a Civil Service Commission but asked him to show up voluntarily. Young declined. "I don't know of any business I would have in testifying at such a hearing. I am a totally disinterested party," he wrote.

TRUTH OUTED

It would take twenty-three years for the truth that Gary Pearson had suspected to emerge. In 1998, out of the blue, he opened a letter from Nathaniel Pryor Reed, who had been assistant secretary at the Interior Department in both the Nixon and Ford administrations. Reed, a former Air Force officer, was a throwback to the day of Republicans as ardent conservationists, sensibilities that later would lead him to become an officer with several environmental organizations.

Reed had something to get off his chest. Pearson's transfer indeed was rooted in Garrison Diversion and pressure from North Dakotans in Congress, Reed wrote, recalling the sequence of events leading up to Pearson's dismissal.

"One of the sad moments of my service as assistant secretary was the confrontation over the orders to transfer you out of North Dakota. The Service leadership felt that their continuing efforts to acquire land for refuges and waterfowl production areas would be thwarted by the congressional delegation if you stayed and continued to raise holy hell," he stated.

"I took the side of the angels—you were to stay. But then the director signed your transfer orders and informed me that it was a *fait accompli* and that I could not reverse the order. I should have marched right into the secretary's office and told him we could not afford to lose you. I will go to my grave with the knowledge that I should have defended you more vigorously."

Reed told me later that his failure to take extraordinary steps to save Pearson's job was one of two transgressions that haunt him from his years in government, the other one being his failure to assist an outspoken senior fisheries biologist. "I made a terrible mistake, and it was something that I absolutely couldn't forget," Reed said when we spoke.

Reed leaped into the Garrison Diversion fray himself, working from inside the Interior Department to kill the project. His efforts brought death threats when he visited North Dakota. "It was one of the greatest lemons ever produced, and I was constantly amazed that it got as far as it did. And all for a relatively small group of farmers, at vast public expense and with great damage to national wildlife refuges and thousands of acres," he told me.

RETHINKING THE DEAL

How does Congress undo such a grievous error? as Congressman Wayne Aspinall of Colorado, chairman of the House Interior and Insular Affairs Committee, put it as early 1965.

Referring to wording in the Pick-Sloan Missouri River Plan, Aspinall observed that "in a single subsection comprising seven lines in that act, the Congress authorized works which today carry a cost of almost $5 billion. As I have said so many times before, this was a serious mistake and has been the cause of untold problems ever since."

In the early 1970s, while Gary Pearson and Rich Madson sowed seeds of dissent in North Dakota, the President's Council on Environmental Quality and the recently established Environmental Protection Agency declared the Bureau of Reclamation's environmental studies inadequate. Canada turned up the heat diplomatically, fearing the impurities coming its way when the Missouri's water was pumped into the Red River basin. Add determined work by the National Wildlife Federation and the National Audubon Society, and support in Congress for finishing the Garrison Diversion diminished steadily into the 1980s.

Many Americans first learned about this obscure Missouri River battle in a 1985 *Reader's Digest* article by James Nathan Miller beneath the title "Half a Billion Dollars Down the Drain."

An outraged Byron Dorgan, then a North Dakota congressman, wrote letters to colleagues on Capitol Hill accusing Miller of distortions and challenging the depiction of Garrison Diversion as "an environmental holocaust."

With support eroding and the prospect of never seeing another federal nickel to finish all that plumbing, the North Dakotans consented in 1986 to reformulating their dream. Legislation passed that year axed the allowable irrigation down to 130,940 acres and shifted the project's emphasis to the development of drinking water supply systems for cities, towns, industries, and farmers.

Even so, justifying more spending on the mammoth project became a chore. The administration of George H. W. Bush wanted to eliminate it, as did just about everyone outside North Dakota.

But the North Dakotans wouldn't quit. They pushed more schemes to divert Missouri River water by pipeline and to complete Garrison Diversion's principal supply works. It became clear to the state's political leaders that they needed more authority and more money. They went after both in what, after decades of efforts, could be do-or-die for their grand Garrison Diversion plan.

Back in 1955, the North Dakota Legislative Assembly had set up the twenty-four-county Garrison Diversion Conservancy District with the power to levy a one-mill tax to keep hustling for water. In the town of Carrington, I saw what the tax had built: a sprawling brick edifice and a lake.

"Top of the day to ya," I hear. The speaker is Warren Jamison, who is the project manager for Garrison Diversion and therefore is chief strategist of North Dakota's quest for water. He is a dapper, cheerful man in fine loafers in a land where boots are favored. He's also an experienced bureaucrat; before taking the job, he pushed water development in many Bureau of Reclamation positions.

Times have changed; so has the commitment to the ideal of irrigating vast swaths of land. I hear his words, but I don't believe for a moment that the Dakotans have spurned the water religion that has driven them for a century.

Jamison is preparing for a new and potentially fateful skirmish and he has one lament: the tenor of this water war, the shrillness as both sides gird for the next round. Once more, the Missourians stand in the way.

THE GARRISON COMPROMISE

Taunya McClarty was working late on Capitol Hill one November evening in 1999 when she heard a familiar beeping from the Senate cloakroom. It signaled a fresh batch of presumably noncontroversial bills that would be lumped together and passed on a voice vote the next day. The Senate was technically in session, but the Capitol had long since emptied. McClarty, an aide to Senator John Ashcroft, a Republican from Missouri, had the task of monitoring routine business. Amid the beeping, she scribbled numbers of the bills, trying to keep up. She didn't recognize most of them, but one stood out; Senate Bill 623, the Dakota Water Resources Act.

That evening, battle lines were drawn for yet another siege. For the people of North Dakota, Senate Bill 623 offered new hope. It was intended to bring new life to Garrison Diversion and that century-long drive to pump billions of gallons of water from the Missouri River. North Dakota's grand plan had seemingly run out of steam—until SB 623 found its way onto the Senate's fast track.

Well honed is North Dakota's artful maneuvering in the name of water. Senators are fond of waiting for the right moment, often late in the session in the dead of night, to append requests for more Garrison money onto other bills. The rules allow it.

In 1980, after President Jimmy Carter had put the North Dakota scheme on his hit list of projects to be killed, Senator Milton Young demonstrated North Dakota hardball. He succeeded in adding Garrison Diversion construction money to an appropriation crafted for emergency reasons: for people suffering from the Mount St. Helens eruption; for Cuban refugees landing in Florida; and for suffering coal miners afflicted with black lung. In the Senate, one member can filibuster to block the most worthwhile initiatives.

"Hell, if it wasn't for the Senate, it would have died years ago," North Dakota senator Quentin Burdick observed a few years later.

On this November night in 1999, it was unclear to McClarty and the Missouri senators whether the North Dakotans were being devious or whether a clerical error had been made.

Whatever the reason, the bill shouldn't have been on the "hot-lined" list of agreed legislation. Senator Christopher Bond ordered a "hold," the

Senate term for blocking legislation until disagreements can be worked out or concessions made. After reaching a Bond legislative aide at home, McClarty phoned the Senate cloakroom with instructions to strike 623 from the list of agreed-on bills.

The next morning, North Dakota senators Kent Conrad and Byron Dorgan retaliated. They slapped holds of their own on fifty-two other hot-lined water projects, generating a torrent of phone calls to Bond's office from irked senators. Bond stormed to the Senate floor with that look about him that prompts staff members to get out of the way.

"I serve notice on my colleagues, if they have a problem because their bills are being held up in an attempt to blackmail me, it is not going to work," he declared. "We cannot and will not tolerate the diversion of water."

The North Dakotans were in a rage. In a meeting in the office of Majority Leader Trent Lott, a Mississippi Republican, the unassuming Conrad banged the wooden conference table so violently that it left a dent, Lott joked afterward. Conrad had regained his cool by the time he took to the Senate floor.

"Yesterday, we were told that North Dakota is seeking somehow to steal water from our neighbors to the south. That is factually incorrect," he said.

"We have people who are turning on their tap right now in North Dakota, and what comes out looks filthy. It looks filthy because it is filthy."

Fighting Missouri is one thing, but taking on a legion of aggravated senators eager to get the hell out of Washington required more nerve than Conrad and Dorgan could summon. They backed off, agreeing in yet another high-level confab to drop their holds on those fifty-two bills.

They got something in return: agreement to hold a Missouri–North Dakota summit about Missouri River water.

On May 15, 2000, the summit convened a block from the Capitol in the Senate office building named for Everett McKinley Dirksen, the Illinois Republican who recognized a boondoggle when he saw one. ("A billion here and a billion there and pretty soon you're talking about *real* money," Dirksen once said.) Even in the Capitol Hill world of secret hideaways and unspoken codes, the gathering in Dirksen 366 was unusual.

Like seconds at a prizefight, advisers stood behind elected officials seated at a round table. Sure enough, somebody brought along one of their jars of cola-colored water. I wondered if Senator Conrad, the likely culprit, had dispatched an aide curbside along Constitution Avenue to scoop from a puddle. But I knew better; North Dakotans keep an assortment of funky water at the ready in all manner of glass and plastic containers for occasions like this.

For this meeting, they'd brought with them an additional prop and perched it on a tripod: a blown-up photo of two children bathing in water the color of mud.

"This is what the people in my state drink," Conrad declared.

Senators aren't known as patient listeners; they're the ones accustomed to doing the talking. But they sat for over two hours, Bond and Ashcroft from Missouri; and Dorgan and Conrad from North Dakota, listening to one another, to North Dakota governor Edward Schafer and to Missouri Department of Natural Resources director Stephen Mahfood, sitting in for Missouri governor Mel Carnahan, who at that moment had more on his mind than thirsty North Dakotans.

By the spring of 2000, Carnahan and John Ashcroft were deeply into their explosive Senate race, and no one knew what, if anything, they might agree to as far as the Missouri River. After listening to the others, Bond spoke. He had kept a wary eye on Garrison Diversion since his years as Missouri governor, and he surprised some in the room when he said that Missouri might agree to authorizing the hundreds of millions of dollars in water projects that the North Dakotans wanted.

But Bond added these important caveats: No diversions could take place unless a new government study of alternatives endorsed taking Missouri River water. Even then, North Dakota would have to return to Congress for approval to divert water.

"We're not going to buy a pig in a poke," Bond said.

It sounded like the makings of a deal, but a deal the public wouldn't be able to evaluate because, like the meeting itself, participants kept the results secret. In the months that followed, few outside the tight circles of Missouri and North Dakota officials knew what was in the new version of Senate Bill 623 or how it got there. There would be no committee hearings airing the revised legislation and therefore no opportunity for opponents of Garrison Diversion, such as the government of Canada and the National Wildlife Federation, to have their say.

Despite what the civics books say, Senate Bill 623 offered a lesson in how a bill *really* becomes a law.

Fearing they might end up with nothing, the North Dakota senators consented to the guts of Bond's proposal. There would be an Interior Department study of water needs in the Red River Valley of eastern North Dakota, where the North Dakotans want Missouri River water to flow. If the study recommended diversions from the Missouri River, the North Dakotans still would need the go-ahead from Congress.

There was spending authority and lots of it: $631 million, contingent on future appropriations. To pass SB 623 so late in the session, the North Dakotans needed a formal endorsement from Missouri. That would prove tricky because of hostilities between Ashcroft and Carnahan; by all accounts, trust had died in their bitter contest.

Ashcroft had slapped his own hold on the bill. If he lifted it, Carnahan might skewer him publicly for opening the door to diversions. By the same token, if Carnahan endorsed the legislation, Ashcroft might score points back home, accusing his Democratic challenger of selling out to the North Dakotans.

What was needed was a device to let Carnahan and Ashcroft act simultaneously, thereby giving neither political advantage. By early October, time was growing short for the North Dakotans. Dorgan and Conrad phoned fellow Democrat Carnahan several times trying to persuade him to endorse 623. Carnahan worried on about an Ashcroft double-cross.

The North Dakotans wouldn't quit; they never do. They recruited a powerful South Dakota ally, Senate Minority Leader Tom Daschle, to their cause. Now Carnahan was getting calls from the man who had something to say about late Democratic Party contributions to Senate aspirants and everything to say about Carnahan's committee assignments if he became a senator.

Recalling the dealings with Missourians, Conrad told me: "I have never been through such a painstaking, difficult, rancorous negotiation. I've been through a lot of negotiations, and nothing can match this."

Finally, Carnahan softened, and the North Dakotans came up with a peculiar plan that would get them their Missouri endorsement—and keep Carnahan and Ashcroft from each other's throats. It was a device absent not only from the civics books but also from any freshman orientation sessions in Washington instructing the newly elected how to serve.

Carnahan would address a letter to Conrad, a Democrat, expressing support. But the letter would be held by the Republican-led Senate Energy and Resources Committee so that it could not leak or be used for otherwise nefarious purposes.

On October 10, Carnahan submitted to this peculiar plan, an indication of mistrust in every quarter when it comes to the Missouri River. It read: "Based on Senator Bond's assurances, the state of Missouri does not object to this proposal. . . . Nonetheless, I must reiterate that Missouri will continue to steadfastly oppose out of basin transfer of water now or in the future."

That day, Ashcroft sent a letter lifting his hold on 623 and it was "hot-lined" anew.

It happened just in time: Six days later, Carnahan died in a plane crash in Missouri, setting up the bizarre scenario of Ashcroft losing the election to a dead man. Carnahan's wife, Jean, later was appointed to the seat.

Of course the public knew nothing about the North Dakota maneuvering because parties on all sides had been sworn to secrecy. On Friday the 13th, I took the day off. I knew a few of the details, but this story had long ago become too complex a serial to sell to editors. The schedule in Congress that day was light because of the funeral in St. Paul, Minnesota, of Representative Bruce Vento. Many members had left after being assured that little would happen.

My cell phone rang in the cabin of a dream boat at the Annapolis Boat Show. It was a Canadian diplomat calling to say that the Dakota Water Resources Act passed the Senate. With no debate.

Even so, the House of Representatives wanted nothing to do with the notorious Garrison Diversion. "Bad policy" and "an end run" by North

Dakota was how California Republican representative John Doolittle described the legislation in a letter to House Speaker Dennis Hastert. A House analysis concluded that Senate Bill 623 canceled repayment of $600 million in the state's debt to the federal government in connection with the project, raising the ultimate cost of the bill to $1.5 billion.

After Carnahan's death, Missouri officials expressed qualms of their own. State attorney general Jay Nixon worried about his state giving any ground to the North Dakotans. The heads of Missouri's conservation and transportation departments sent letters to Congress asking to stop Senate Bill 623, fearing fine print that one day could allow seemingly unlimited use of Missouri River water to replenish groundwater and increase the flow of streams.

It wouldn't matter. On the night of December 15, the North Dakotans watched both the Senate and House approve catch-all spending legislation that was as close as it comes to the proverbial Christmas Tree Bill with something for everyone. Among the goodies: $1.5 million for sunflower research and $176,000 for the Reindeer Herders Association. Tucked into the legislation, the last bill passed on the final day of the 106th Congress, was the Dakota Water Resources Act.

The North Dakotans' dream may be diminished, but the revised legislation still authorizes 58,000 acres of irrigation. It instructs the government to maintain that pumping plant and those canals through which Missouri River water would flow.

Of course, Warren Jamison and the North Dakotans were thinking ahead. Even before the legislation passed, they secured an arrangement that gave supporters of Garrison Diversion control of the study.

When I asked Gary Pearson, the veterinarian long since drummed out of government, what he thought of the arrangement, he likened it to "the foxes guarding the henhouse."

Manitoba premier Gary Doer asked the pertinent question when I phoned him. "Did North Dakota pull one over on Missouri?"

Senator Bond, who acceded to the North Dakotans' power play, said not to worry. "We'll be here," he told me, alluding to future fights in Congress. "We're not going to let Big Muddy turn into mud."

EPILOGUE

North Dakotans don't take kindly to outsiders nosing around in their water business. In 2003, as the state's water warriors labored to shape a study proving the need to suck from the Missouri River, the state legislature also went on the offensive. It passed a resolution vowing unspecified "aggressive action against individuals, organizations, and entities interfering with the development and progress of state water projects."

That is broad enough to include the U.S. Congress, other states, and me. I decide to stay out of North Dakota at least until the Dakotans signal its next bold stroke. Unfortunately for them, it would have to be carried out with less skill because of the death of chief water strategist Warren Jamison, of pancreatic cancer at age sixty-four.

But being dead didn't mean that Jamison was out of the picture totally, at least right away. His zeal to tap into the Missouri continued with his memorial fund, which collected donations in Jamison's memory for the North Dakota Water Education Foundation.

~15~

AT THE HEADWATERS:
CHOOSING A NEW FORK

*The country opens suddenly to extensive and beatifull plains
and meadows which appear to be surrounded in every direction
with distant and lofty mountains; supposing this to be the three
forks of the Missouri I halted the party . . .*

—Meriwether Lewis, July 27, 1805, upon
arrival at the headwaters of the Missouri
River

IN WHICH AFTER A LONG JOURNEY WE PARTAKE
OF A LIVING RIVER AND THE WISDOM OF BUD

*"I've got peace like a river in my soul. I've got a river in my
soul."*

LANDING
THREE FORKS, MONTANA

FOURTEEN MONTHS AND 438 DAYS into their voyage, the Corps
of Discovery reached the three-forked headwaters of the Missouri
River. There, Meriwether Lewis physicked the ailing William Clark with
Dr. Benjamin Rush's all-purpose pills. Then Lewis climbed a limestone
bluff to its top. Looking down over the vast country, he conferred Euro-
American names on "these noble streams" that formed the Missouri

River. One he named for President Jefferson; one for the secretary of state, Madison; and the last for the secretary of the treasury, Gallatin.

Were Lewis to reprise those exertions today, after he quenched his thirst he might himself be taking some of those all-purpose pills. For when my quest brings me beneath Lewis Rock, I find a boil-water order posted at the very beginning of the river, not far from a children's grave-yard dating from the 1870s.

"Recent bacteriological testing has confirmed the presence of fecal coliform bacteria in the water supply," the sign reads, warning that *E. coli* has been determined to be a serious health concern by the Environmental Protection Agency, a governmental office that didn't arrive until 167 years after the celebrated voyagers reached Montana.

Lewis, a man of some literary skills, surely would approve of the name given to an industrial plant just upriver and within sight of the three forks: Trident, a cement plant operated by a company with a fine-sounding name of its own, Holcim. But the efficient captain surely would not have admired an enterprise so beset by equipment failures that it violated air emission levels for five hundred hours in 2002. And he might wrinkle his nose in disdain were he to learn that the company had applied to burn scrap tires—75 per hour, 1,800 per day, 657,000 per year—thereby polluting the air of the Gallatin Valley.

At the other end of the river, Lewis and Clark's Camp Dubois has been reconstructed—only to be deconstructed when undermined by bank erosion—just across the highway from a Superfund toxic waste pile leaching heavy metals. Two hundred years after Euro-Americans "discovered" it, America's river west begins and ends at pollution.

THE WISDOM OF BUD

From the Missouri River headwaters, Montana is blessed for hundreds of miles with a clear, wild river snaking through soaring buttes and rich with trout that outwitted Corps of Discovery voyageurs accustomed to catfish and other easily fooled fish. Long stretches of the river look much as they did when the explorers fought their way upstream two hundred years ago.

I came to these headwaters to interpret all I had observed in the three years since I first slid down a raw embankment to the river in Kansas City. Environmental destruction compounded by water wars made for problems that daunted even presidents. Congress continued to argue over who owns the water. Finally, the courts entered deliberations with no better charts than those the Corps of Discovery followed through *terra incognita*.

For me, too, the Missouri had become all work and no fun. I'd dragged along a fly rod on most of these reporting trips to the Missouri River, but I'd handled it less than airline security folks alarmed by the long, thin case I carried it in. Newspaper reporters, at least at my shop, are expected to work much like those beavers that brought nineteenth-century fur trappers west. Besides, fishing in much of the Lower Missouri River is geared more these days to Wicked Sticky cheese bait than to the cycles of hatching flies.

In the Upper Missouri, upstream (oddly, that is south) from Great Falls, the story is considerably prettier: rainbow trout; German browns; native cutthroats and some of those pucker-mouthed little mountain whitefish that Lewis referred to in his journal as "bottlenose fish" abound in idyllic waters that have escaped ferocious engineering.

No one knows these species more intimately than the fellow at Three Forks I had come to see: Waymen "Bud" Lilly, fly-fishing guru, fourth-generation Montanan, and a principal architect of a western fly-fishing industry that beckons anglers from around the world to the Upper Missouri and the idyllic rivers of Montana. At Montana State University in Bozeman, Lilly assembled a 15,000-volume library to support the Bud Lilly Chair in Trout and Salmonid Bibliography. He's guided politicians, diplomats, and sports heroes on these Montana waters and presided over many meetings between fat cats and fat trout. A lifetime of seeking those sporting fish has ripened the wisdom of this native son.

I anticipated no trout myself; I had come to see Bud about business other than flipping barbed bits of feathers and fuzz into swirling waters for the purpose of tricking pretty fish. I'd heard that in addition to mastering the art of fly-fishing, Bud Lilly, who was born in 1925, had pioneered some solutions for the travails of rivers. He'd made headway in mastering the tricky balance between commerce and the environment, a feat elusive on most of the Missouri. On the lower river, commerce is king, and the business of recreation fights stiff odds and artificial flows. In Montana, Bud had lessons to teach, among them the development of trout-fishing ranches.

On pilgrimages a year apart, I sat with my host, a former redhead now gray, just beyond the sun's reach on a bench outside Bud Lilly's Angler's Retreat, which was built in Three Forks in 1908 as the last in a string of railroad hotels along the old Milwaukee line. Except for vast hanging pots of bright petunias, the Angler's Retreat puts on few airs. We're perched just a few hundred yards away from a cottonwood grove along the Missouri River where Sacajawea, then a Shoshone girl of nine or ten years, was snatched by the Minatarees and propelled on her odyssey.

Bud Lilly dresses in soft, deerskin shoes and, mornings before the summer heat sets in, corduroys. The professional fishing guide spurns the color white because it reflects the sun and spooks trout. At any time of the day, he might want to uncase a rod at a trout ranch down the road where he lives with his wife, Esther, and where Bud and his partners are creating a fly-fishing community on restored streams nourished with native trout.

Starting with his cratered, sun-scarred face, everything about Bud Lilly is worn but fine. His movements remain fluid, with a deceptive, insouciant precision like fly line arcing from a bamboo rod. He is tall and athletic, and he might have become a professional baseball player rather than a fishing pro had World War II not interfered.

Once, when a traveling team of Negro all-stars came through town, the kid they called Bud stroked a single off legendary pitcher Satchel Paige. Perhaps Paige was just toying with young Bud. But Paige, who later would pitch in the major leagues, whirled around and fired the ball in plenty of time to prevent the precocious teen from stealing second base.

Lilly sits erect and speaks in a measured voice, delivering his stories with the same control as he presents a woolly bugger.

"The Missouri is like an artery system that carries the blood of the entire nation, and if we delay in restoring it, we eventually will pay a high price," he says.

That is Bud's conservationist side talking, and his own transformation needs some explaining. His father, Waymen "Bud" Sr., taught him the fishing arts, but with a rule: Every fish caught had to be eaten. Nothing was to be wasted, a dictate that served America in the depression years just as it did in its pioneer days. By his ninth or tenth year, young Bud was a proficient angler. Back when the fly-fishers of the region could be counted on one hand, he learned how to handle a fly rod. But catching fish was his ultimate aim, and he deployed baits ranging from sucker meat to elegant flies.

Many nights, he'd venture down to the Missouri River with the proprietor of a local grocery, Roy Vaughn, a man of generous spirit willing to extend credit in the scrambling 1930s. Vaughn was also a man with an appetite for drink. Bud found these regular outings desirable on several fronts; he was especially keen on the grocer's habit of toting a bag bulging with larder from his shelves—along with a fifth of whiskey. From about ten o'clock through much of the night, they'd perch themselves on Ling Rock, at the headwaters across from 200-foot-high bluffs. Bud would eat and fish, fish and eat, hauling up burbot, a tasty specimen referred to back then as bullheads. While Bud tended to the fishing, Roy handled the whiskey. Not long before dawn, Bud would clean the fish and help the grocer home.

To live up to Bud Senior's never-bending rule, young Bud had to either eat all his fish or give them away before he could wet his line anew. It got so that his well-stocked neighbors no longer answered their doors when Bud, bearing filets, came calling.

As long ago as the mid-1950s, while he was developing a flourishing fly-fishing business in his tackle store in West Yellowstone, Lilly concluded that his father's rule was flawed. Fish populations were declining in the Upper Missouri River basin. The solution becoming too acceptable to suit Lilly and a few other progressive thinkers was hatchery—

raised fish. Lilly knew that the release of all these alien fry threatened the native species, western-slope cutthroats.

The loss of natives had begun much earlier. In the late nineteenth century, settlers started hauling in brook, rainbow, and German brown trout by the barrel and stocking them in any water that moved. Unaware, they were beginning the threat to the wild trout in the Missouri and its tributaries. Nearly a hundred years later, Lilly measured the consequences and resolved to correct them. He vowed to return to the waters every trout he and his parties caught. His solution, catch-and-release fishing, did not meet ready acceptance in this land peopled by the ancestors of self-reliant pioneers who sheltered, fed, and clothed themselves from nature's storehouse.

"We grew up thinking it was going to last forever," Lilly said. It didn't, but old ways change hard.

Bud's oldest son, Greg, who at the time operated the Healing Waters Lodge nearby on the Ruby River, recalls the reaction of guides, bar owners, and hoteliers who believed in the religion of bulging creels. "They thought that for people to feel like they were successful, they had to take home a whole bunch of fish. It was very difficult to overcome their resistance to being told that they couldn't take a lot of fish out of the rivers," he told me.

Bud Lilly persisted, becoming a leading advocate in the West for the formerly radical ethos of catch-and-release fishing. He worked to spread his conservation vision as he guided Japanese bankers, Idaho potato magnates, and New York entrepreneurs on behalf of the state of Montana.

In his words, "Since Lewis and Clark's day, the Missouri River has evolved into a major trout fishery, attracting people from all over the world."

FIGURE 10. Fly-fishing guru and conservationist Waymen "Bud" Lilly, who operates at the Missouri's headwaters in Montana, likens the Missouri River and its tributaries to "an artery system that carries the blood of the entire nation." (Photo courtesy Bill Lambrecht)

Before long, fly-fishers would not have found fishing on the entire 2,400 miles of the Missouri River to match what they discovered on the stretch they visited with Bud Lilly. He persuaded not by fuzzy environmental aphorism or by preaching morals. Rather, he argued the economics of the equation. "That trout has more value in the river than out of the river. Put it back in the river and you can keep catching it," he would say.

To this day, Bud Lilly witnesses for catch-and-release. One of America's best-known trout fishermen hasn't eaten a trout in more than thirty years.

ON A LIVING RIVER

Before Fort Peck, the first of the Missouri's six mainstream dams, largely pristine waters support a vibrant recreation industry that's a sharp contrast to the downstream, channelized Missouri. Outfitters beckon adventurists to Montana for several river pleasures, setting a standard for what could happen downstream if flow changes allow recreational entrepreneurs to operate commercially.

Wolf Creek Outfitters, on the Missouri one hundred miles from the headwaters, offers one such tale of the successful life enterprising people can build along a clean, undisturbed river. In 1995, Dan and Danielle Kelly started their boat rental and livery service on a single credit card. They retired that credit card debt two years later, and when I rented from them in 2002, their hard-earned prosperity was such that they owned a fleet of canoes and $6,000 dories and had opened a fly-fishing store.

"I was a vegetarian tree-hugger and Dan was a gun-toting, meat-eating mountain man," Danielle told me of a marriage that proves what odd partnerships the Missouri can support. "We're living the life we created."

The Kellys have staked their claim along a world-class, hatchery-supported trout fishery set amidst rising foothills.

Farther upriver just after Fort Benton, the river turns decisively east to flow through the 377,346-acre Upper Missouri River Breaks National Monument. That designation, proclaimed by Bill Clinton shortly before his presidency ended, was the first link forged between land preservation and the Lewis and Clark Bicentennial.

This is wild country. "Breaks" are the geological upheavals that have broken the highlands surrounding the river here into the fantastical forms that amazed the Corps of Discovery and provoked Lewis beyond scientific description to flights of literary fancy. "The hills and river Clifts which we passed today exhibit a most romantic appearance," he wrote on May 31, 1805. "The bluffs of the river rise to hight of from 2 to 300 feet and in most places nearly perpendicular; they are formed of remarkable white sandstone which is sufficiently soft to give way readily to the impression of water. The water in the course of time . . . has trickled down the soft sand clifts and woarn it into a thousand grotesque figures. . . ."

Paddlers today see nearly the same sights in the 149-mile stretch of river further protected since 1976, another bicentennial, as a National Wild and Scenic River. Along the White Cliffs and into the Badlands, the Bureau of Land Management has mapped water trails to correspond to the voyage of discovery and laid very primitive campgrounds (read privies) and occasional landings. Guidebooks contribute thick chapters on history, geology, and wildlife. Around Fort Benton, outfitters, livery services, and guides support the burgeoning recreational industry.

Such uses don't suit everybody. Critics in Congress continue efforts to scale back the monument's reach. Landowners objected to both the eleventh-hour methods of the former president and the restrictions on what they might do with their land. Among them is Don Lundy of Fort Benton, who has some choice land to protect. His property includes the site of the former Fort McKenzie, the nineteenth-century fur-trading post where beaver pelts were collected to be floated downriver to St. Louis.

FIGURE 11. Meriwether Lewis said his Corps of Discovery had encountered "a thousand grotesque figures" in some of the most poetic lines in his journal when he found scenery such as this at the White Cliffs of Montana. (Photo courtesy Bill Lambrecht)

"They just kind of shoved it down our throats," Lundy complained to me. "I don't think anybody has the right to say that you can't build on your own property."

A DYNAMITE SOLUTION

In the broader Missouri River debate, disputes over the fate of unspoiled stretches are rarer. That's because the vast majority of the river has been altered by dams.

Dams are like faucets; they turn rivers on and off. They are operated for peak power production without regard to the rhythms of the river or its wildlife. They make habitat disappear and alter what is left by subjecting aquatic life to changes in temperature and oxygen levels. They trap millions of tons of sediment, removing from the river flow carbon and minerals that support plant and animal life.

The first dam on the Missouri was built at Great Falls in the late nineteenth century. Six mainstem dams followed, from Fort Peck, Montana, in the 1930s, to Gavins Point Dam at Yankton, South Dakota. The great dams were built before the emergence of environmental values and consequent federal protections for conservation and wildlife. In 1976, such values and protections saved those 149 miles of wild and scenic Missouri in Montana from a dam at Cow Creek.

It took until the waning months of the twentieth century for communities to begin coming to grips with the damage from so many dams in the United States—some 77,000 over six feet high, only 3 percent of which generated electricity. Then Americans unpacked the dynamite. Since the breaching of Edwards Dam on the Kennebunk River in Maine in 1999, roughly 150 dams were removed by late 2004.

Of course, there is no reason to think that the Missouri River dams that provide hydropower, flood control, and a bit of barge navigation will be removed any time soon. They stand as monuments to the era of gigantism in our public works and our bold thinking. It's hard to imagine how the political will could be summoned to erase these indelible marks on our civilization, as has been done with dynamite on nearly a dozen rivers since the mid-1990s.

Environmental advocates don't dare make the case for removing the massive dams along the Missouri lest they be marginalized as reckless. When downstream politicians offer the specter of killer floods to rebuff proposals for a carefully orchestrated, two-week spring rise for wildlife, imagine the big guns they'd drag out to greet plans to remove whole dams.

The dams will be gone in time, of course. There is no doubt in the minds of tribal members along the river that the Missouri one day will unchain itself to resume its incorrigible wandering, its life-giving perfidy.

Geologists, too, see the Dam Era of America in fleeting terms; in the hundreds of years, not the thousands. For behind those dams are rising millions of tons of earth, the river's lifeblood sediment coagulating in a finite space.

At nine hundred years, the life expectancy of Montana's Fort Peck Dam is the longest of any along the Missouri. But at the lower end of the string of dams, the reservoir at Gavins Point in South Dakota could, by 2025, be too sediment-filled to be effective. By then, Army engineers will need to have figured how to perform the engineering marvel of removing sediment—or be forced to let the river there run free again.

At stake is more than the intrinsic value of rivers running free, according to those who argue for dam removal. To these heretics—and the late Stephen Ambrose was among them—dams lose the cost-benefit analysis to the environment and the rhythms of life they disrupt.

In terms of navigation, hardly anyone besides barge operators, farmers, and their political supporters argues in favor of the enduring value of transporting less than 2 million tons of grain and goods each year. Faring little better is the argument that dams are needed to prevent flooding. That argument is given the lie by the floods of the Dam Era: the Flood of '60; the Flood of '71; the Flood of '84; the Great Flood of '93; and lesser floods that bespeak the river's caprice.

The dynamite throwers support their case with less visible costs and benefits. Rivers scholar Robert Kelley Schneiders builds his pro-removal argument on the need to restore democracy to the Missouri basin. The corporate interests and their allies in Congress and the federal government "are directly draining the power from people through those dams," he says.

Schneiders, who was born in 1965, grew up near the Missouri River in Sioux City, Iowa. With six brothers and seven sisters, it was easy for him to get lost, and he often ended up along the sped-up, perilous waterway six blocks from his home. Always he has been drawn to that river and to rivers. When not on one or prowling its shoreline, he has written two authoritative books, *The Unruly River*, about the Missouri, and *Big Sky Rivers*, about the Yellowstone and the Upper Missouri.

Schneiders had recently canoed 550 miles of the Missouri when we met, requiring plenty of aspirin after keeping his six-foot seven-inch frame folded into paddling position day after day. His recollection after 130 miles of Fort Peck Reservoir matched my own.

"It was like a caged animal beneath us that wanted to buck us right off," he said.

Schneiders not only says take down the dams, he prescribes an order. Begin, he says, with the southernmost, Gavins Point, given its approaching uselessness. Move next, he says, to the Fort Peck Dam, a Dirty Thirties make-work project that returns little recreation and no navigation. Then Big Bend, a dam the Corps didn't want in the first place, followed by Garrison, Oahe, and Fort Randall.

He measures the potential benefits in human terms. "We all live our lives inside a box," he says. "The Missouri River, in the thirties and forties, was placed in a box. Standing in or alongside that box now, you don't have hifallutin' thoughts, spiritual thoughts. But you might have negative thoughts.

"I believe if you let the dams fall," Schneiders argues, "the shackles are not going to come off the Missouri River. They're going to come off of humanity."

A FLORIDA SOLUTION

I had to detour far from the Missouri to set eyes on how rivers can be restored. I am startled at the radical solution I see, but no one can hear my reaction over the racket of the airboat careening near the Florida Everglades.

"UNBELIEVABLE!" I yell.

I am shouting at flocks of waterfowl along the Kissimmee River which, like the Missouri, was devastated by reengineering. After hearing sad songs about the Kissimmee's fate, I hadn't expected what is rising and scattering before me: gawky herons, white ibises, marsh hens, and those freakish black-neck stilts, their tiny bodies riding on spindliest of legs. The birds have returned after a bold and expensive restoration that may hold lessons for the degraded Missouri. That is why I came to this remote stretch of restored river, traveling first on a helicopter, pods of alligators snapping at our shadow, and now on this swamp dragster.

The birds appear less troubled by the roar than I am. We're back and we're not leaving, they seem to be saying by refusing to take flight despite the unholy rumble of a 350-cubic-inch V-8 and the shouts of possibly a madman.

If ever there's a call for a how-to manual on killing a river, the Army Corps of Engineers has one on the shelf. In the 1960s, before the Corps began to dredge, channelize, and resculpt the Kissimmee River, it snaked 103 miles from the Kissimmee Chain of Lakes south to Lake Okeechobee. It was a meandering artery, spreading out like the Nile across Florida's interior, a mile and sometimes two miles wide, and carrying fresh water toward the Everglades. The birds were part of an ecosystem rich with three hundred species.

But like many of our great rivers, the Kissimmee would spread too far and too swiftly for locals with secure development on their minds. Much as the Great Flood of 1943 led to the taming of the Missouri River, Florida floods of the early twentieth century created the climate for transforming the Kissimmee into 56-mile canal running straight as a highway.

Divorced from its floodplain, the Kissimmee deconstruction was a miniature version of Missouri River engineering that turned a natural system into a ditch in the name of flood control and navigation. In a final insult, the Corps and its collaborators dropped the name Kissimmee altogether: Henceforth, the river that bore the name of an Indian tribe was to be called Canal 38, with its impounded reservoirs given the equally lifeless appellations of Pools A through E.

"It was an environmental catastrophe by any measure," says Gary

Williams, a biologist with the South Florida Water Management District, once he turns off his noisy airboat.

His vessel, mercifully quieted, perches on swampy land that just four years ago was the middle of a thirty-foot-deep canal. But this stretch of Canal 38 no longer exists, thanks to a machine that makes even more noise, a 72-foot-long, 370-horsepower "Dragon" dredge, which is backfilling 22 miles of the canals that supplanted the river forty years ago.

Fixing the Kissimmee is part of the controversial, $8.4 billion Everglades restoration, the most far-reaching and expensive environmental restoration attempted anywhere.

Decades ago, the Army Corps of Engineers was the agent of destruction for many rivers. Now, along the Kissimmee and other rivers where the political will can be mustered, Army engineers are dispatched to undo the earlier damage. Besides filling in the canals that replaced stretches of the river, the Corps and its partner, the South Florida Water Management District, are recarving nine miles of river channel, demolishing two dams, and buying 110,000 acres of buffer land.

It took the Corps nine years to channelize the Kissimmee. It will take longer—thirteen years or so—to fix just part of the damage. Turning the river into a ditch in the 1960s cost $32 million. But $578 million has been authorized for restoring a stretch of the river, and many conservationists say that isn't nearly enough. Half of the money comes from the federal government and half from the state of Florida.

Biologists studying the restored stretch of the Kissimmee were able to swiftly calculate rewards. Before the backfilling of seven and a half miles of canals, they counted thirty-three wading birds per mile. The first phase of the project was finished in 2001; three years later, the number of birds had quadrupled. Ducks that had disappeared magically returned:

northern pintails; northern shovelers; American wigeons; ring-necked ducks; and the fulvous whistling duck. Likewise, eight species of shore-birds returned.

Sitting with Williams along another stretch of Kissimmee, I hear the splat of a largemouth bass making lunch of a mosquito fish. A few years ago, it would have been hard to find anything but rough fish like bowfin and gar.

Williams, a fifth-generation Floridian, has seen his state's population nearly triple, to 17 million people, since he was born in 1964. He understands that pressures from people—and developers—probably wouldn't allow such a project in heavily populated portions elsewhere in the state.

"I see this restoration project as catching something in the nick of time and trying to put things back the way old Florida used to be," he says.

Before the airboat engine roars again, I ask Williams if people still call the Kissimmee the C-38 Canal. His reply suggests one more benefit not calculated by feathers and fins, the restoration of a river's integrity. "I think it's an even bigger insult to call the C-38 Canal the Kissimmee River," he answers, suggesting that the restored Kissimmee shouldn't share its name with an unsightly ditch.

BUD'S BRAND OF RECOVERY

Economics drove Thomas Jefferson's decision to dispatch Lewis and Clark like traveling salesmen with scissors, kettles, and beads to lure trading partners. He imagined the Northwest Passage and its channel of commerce as the lifeblood for his American empire.

The fur traders followed the Corps' westward path along the Missouri in search of pelts bringing high dollar in New York and London until beavers, like the bison before them, were used up. Later, the calculated destruction of the natural river was justified by the dream of a flourishing barge industry and the imperative of protecting the most important American commerce of all: farming.

Human decisions about rivers always are calculated in economic terms. For two centuries, no one argued for preserving a river that routinely rose up to consume valuable land, kill people, and even snatch the dead from their graves. In consequence, for a river of such history and size, the Missouri is uncommonly devoid of recreation and related commerce.

That's why I could find no kayak to rent in St. Louis. That's why Jeff McFadden's *MorningStar* charter remains mostly at its dock near Kansas City. And it's why Robert Shadwell is watching his dreams dry up along with the shoreline at the Point of View Lodge in South Dakota.

But there are unexplored intersections where economics and conservation could meet. There are river-long lessons in the experience of Bud Lilly and the new Montana conservationists.

Lilly pioneered in fly-fishing, and now his family is in the forefront of an effort at the headwaters of the Missouri River to save land and restore streams. There's a payoff for conservation, which much of the river has yet to understand. Greg Lilly's Healing Waters Lodge was booked from May to October with patrons who pay $400 to $500 a day to be on the water. When I asked Greg why his customers were willing to travel far and part with so much cash, he replied: "Many people are under a lot of stress in their lives, and with fly-fishing you can put everything else out of your mind because you need to focus."

The generation of Montana conservationists that came after Bud

Lilly is finding ways to approach river saving. Greg Lilly is among the fishing pros allied with environmental advocates in the Jefferson River Watershed Council, which has achieved remarkable success.

In the drought of the late 1980s, the Jefferson, one of the Missouri's three forks, was down to wet rocks. No water flowed between pools, and you could walk across the river Meriwether Lewis named for his benefactor without getting your feet wet. Along the shoreline, stately cottonwoods fell over dead, wells ran dry, and irrigators were vilified for their exploitation of a scarce resource. Those years were a sickening reminder of the consequences when drought and greed are teamed up with bad communications.

Cattle ranchers control the vast majority of the water in the Montana streams that feed the Missouri. Like landowners and bargers downstream, the Montanans enjoy water legislated for their use, typically to irrigate the alfalfa to feed their animals. Nagged by fear that someone else will get the water if they don't, many ranchers use every drop to which they are entitled and perhaps then some. Relinquishing their water is unnatural; this pioneer stock does not cede away what they've fought for.

One-sided river management is most apparent in drought, but even in the rainy years of the mid-1990s, the local Lewis and Clark Trout Unlimited chapter noticed a continuing loss of fish in "the Jeff." The health of rivers is measured by what swims in them, and in 1995, a fish count found just 279 brown trout per mile, less than half the number of a decade before. Whole generations of fish had been lost.

Water planning is hardest when the drought ends because rain washes the immediate threat away, seemingly never to return. But the sportsmen understood that the next drought could devastate the fishery and all who depend on it. In 1998, the Trout Unlimited chapter brought together ranchers, business leaders, outfitters, and government agencies in the Jefferson River Watershed Council, which they modeled after other such organizations they'd heard about. They had no clue, of course, that the new millennium would deliver a king-hell drought—or that they'd succeed in surviving it.

Jerry Kustich, an architect of the Watershed Council, told me that ranchers on the council gradually agreed to give up water for the greater good. They came to understand the value of lining their ditches and installing soil moisture monitors in their fields to prevent over-irrigating. By some accounts, farmers reduced their water use by 20 percent, an achievement that has saved the river and earned them lavish praise.

"The water in that river right now comes from the good hearts of the agriculturists who were willing to sit down at the table," Kustich said.

Kustich has a job that keyboard slaves like me dream about. He makes bamboo fly rods—with prices starting at over $2,000—for a famous manufacturer, the R.L. Winston Rod Co. And, of course, he fishes. And fishes. He also has written two books, and in an op-ed article he describes vividly what happens to the Jefferson when it gets squeezed into the diversion ditches of the irrigators: "What is normally a proud river of peaceful gentleness then slips into a state of emaciation—a skin-and-bones flow barely able to sustain life so dependent on the water that should be pumping through its veins."

Four years after one of Montana's worst droughts began, Kustich called what he was seeing in the Jefferson as miraculous. "There shouldn't be any water in this river at all," he said.

But water had remained plentiful. Indeed, it's floating my canoe to Three Forks and another meeting with Bud Lilly, who puts the phenomenon into historical perspective.

"There is now a dialogue between the farmers and ranchers and the sportsmen and the recreationists, with the growing understanding that there's more value to that water in the river than out. If we don't change, we're going to lose a lot of the value of the river. And I don't just mean aesthetics," he said.

Approaching his eightieth birthday, Bud was still involved with the Montana Trout Trust, the Montana River Action Network, and American Wildlands. He and Esther Lilly work to preserve land as well as water; she sells riverfront parcels and together they're advancing the concept of trout-fishing ranches. You could say they're an ideal match.

When they met in the early 1980s—before she divorced and Bud's first wife, Patricia, died—Esther Miller was executive director of the national organizations of both Trout Unlimited and the Federation of Fly Fishers. She was organizing the International Fly Fishing Center in West Yellowstone. To be its first chairman, the center needed not just a legendary fisherman but also a well-spoken ambassador for the sport: Bud Lilly.

Today, the Lillys are partners in Baker Springs, a former cattle ranch being converted into a 250-acre fly-fishing development. Biologists, hydrologists, and experts in stream restoration have mapped out a fly-fishing heaven along two miles of Baker Creek, which ultimately flows into the Missouri River.

First, fences, debris, and nitrogen-saturated soils from the manure of a feedlot operation were removed. Decades of silt were scooped out of streams to uncover gravel beds, the better for both spawning and clean-flowing water. Underground springs were dammed to create ponds; three were stocked with German and brown trout and another with the native westslopes.

The last time I visited, the Lilly partnership had sold nine of eleven waterfront parcels—for prices up to $800,000—primarily to people not planning on building any time soon. Baker Springs' sole residents were the Lilly family and many fish. Such was the success that they were purchasing an expanse of degraded land next door for another restoration.

Another swath of eroding, denuded earth was on its way to becoming a lush ecosystem, already drawing wildlife and an array of birds from golden eagles to red-tailed hawks to killdeer.

"Sooner or later," Bud said between sips of lemonade served on his porch, "it will look like it did two hundred years ago."

⌢ PADDLING ⌣

PIONEER STOCK

Bud Lilly springs from ancestors who followed Lewis and Clark west. Grand-mother Mary Wells would have fit into the Corps of Discovery—had Lewis included women among his recruits.

Granny Yates, as Wells came to be known across the middle of the conti-nent, organized wagon trains from St. Louis to Montana and was singularly responsible for populating the West with thousands of people. The Virginia-born Wells, the daughter of a Welsh father and an Irish mother, had eleven children. After her husband died of typhoid fever, she became one of the most adventuresome single mothers in American history. All told, she crossed the Great Plains from Missouri to Montana thirteen times, accord-ing to the family records. On one trip, a son, Zachariah, was wounded in an Indian attack. He survived but later drowned driving cattle across the Yel-lowstone River. Still another son died at the hands of the Sioux at Little Big Horn.

On one crossing, as an Indian war party surrounded the wagons, Granny Yates stuffed another of her small boys, Tom, in a flour barrel in hopes he might survive. Then she grabbed her rifle and started firing, helping to fi-nally repel the attackers. She was not only strong of will but, at a solid 160 pounds, strong physically. She traveled with similarly fearless women; ac-cording to family records, one of her sister pioneers pulled out a butcher knife and scalped an Indian as he attacked. She cut the warrior from his eye-brows to the top of his spine, then rolled up the hair and flesh for a souvenir.

Granny Yates was a Bible-spouting Baptist who practiced a devoted mercantilism that would enable her to set up each of her children in homesteads near the Missouri River. Riding sidesaddle, she drove cattle and horses westward along with her wagons, and she rarely lost an animal amid skirmishes with Indians and that era's many other vicissitudes of travel. Travel was hazardous, but safe arrival paid well. Gold miners paid one dollar each for apples she transported for resale. She sold her featherbed to a French boatman for a fifty-dollar gold piece and his assistance in carrying her wagons across a river. Being illiterate didn't stop her from mapping whole towns or directing the construction of cabins for settlers.

In 1901, Granny Yates might have been amused at finding herself included in a compilation entitled Progressive Men of Montana. During the last years of her life, she retired to her rocking chair to spin the tales of her life. When she died in 1915, at age ninety-two, she left behind sixty grandchildren and ninety great-grandchildren.

That was on Bud's mother's side. On his father's side, two uncles were professional outdoorsmen and guides, and his father, Waymen "Bud" Lilly Sr., had been a market shooter as a young man, bringing in prairie chickens and whatever game he could sell. The senior Bud became the town barber, and, when he married, enabled Bud's mother, Violet, to revel the rest of her life in a two-flower name: Violet Lilly. "The first one, it was given to me. The last one, I had to go find," she said.

There were bad actors in the family, too. In 1915, a cousin shot town marshal Jack Dolan as the marshal rousted him from a Three Forks bawdy house. The Three Forks News reported what happened before and after the fatal bullet struck down the lawman. Dolan's body, the account read, "was removed after the arrival of the coroner, Dr. Seitz, of Bozeman, to the undertaking parlor of N. M. Kvalnes, where Dr. Gaertner, in the presence of the coroner and a few others, probed for the bullet, which was found to have entered the body about one and one-half inches below and an equal distance to the left of the left nipple, and passed through the thorax, penetrating a number of large organs.

"As nearly as the facts can be determined," the newspaper account continued, the shooter "and a woman named Pearl Wells were in a room of Bess Miller in the red-light district when Marshal Dolan made his usual visit to the place, as he does in the line of his duty at some hour almost every night, and Jack ordered them to leave the place. [Bud's cousin] did not want to go."

What happened in the trial demonstrated further the resilience of Bud Lilly's family. Never was there a shred of doubt that the cousin had shot the town lawman dead. But he was acquitted of murder and set free when the jury sympathized with a silver-tongued lawyer's portrayal of his client as a devout family man wrongly interrupted during a rare dalliance.

~16~

THE SHIFTING BALANCE

*When Kansas and Colorado have a quarrel over water in the
Arkansas River, they don't call out the National Guard in each
state and go to war over it. They bring a suit in the Supreme
Court of the United States and abide by the decision.*

—President Harry S Truman, 1945

IN WHICH, CALLED BY COURTS ON CARPET
THE CORPS REWRITES THE BIBLE

*Take me to the river
Wash me down
Cleanse my soul
With my feet on the ground.*

LANDING
U.S. DISTRICT COURT, WASHINGTON, D.C.

U.S. DISTRICT JUDGE GLADYS KESSLER is steaming like the July
day in Washington, D.C., where my Big Muddy quest has returned
me. She looks mad enough to climb down from the bench and throttle a
government lawyer.

"The Army general counsel didn't think this was a significant enough
matter to attend himself?" she asks one of the half-dozen lawyers frying
on her griddle.

Worse, the Army's acting secretary, Les Brownlee, hasn't showed either. Brownlee had to be overseas, his staff had told her. Now, Kessler hears that he's busy at Fort Leavenworth. Which is it?

"I think that what was reported to my office was that he was in Europe, not Kansas. Kansas is a little closer than Europe," she snaps.

The fuming judge could fairly be called a liberal. Kessler had been a founder of the activist Women's Legal Defense Fund before her appointment to the federal bench by President Bill Clinton. Kessler had also been a notable defender of civil liberties. "Secret arrests are a concept odious to a democratic society," she had written.

Despite her personal views, on the bench Kessler had a reputation for fairness if not for warmth. She was viewed as high-strung and, occasionally, harsh. "Not a relaxed person," in one lawyer's description.

Of course Kessler had seen things that would make even a judge nervous. Once, when she was handling felony criminal cases, a witness stabbed his ex-girlfriend as he left the stand; he had hidden a knife in his wheelchair. The victim was not seriously injured, but the rolling attacker was found guilty of multiple crimes.

Now Kessler was taking on a whole federal agency, a branch of the military to boot. On a June Saturday ten nights before, Kessler had ordered the Missouri River to fall. Today's action resulted from that decision. Judges don't like to work summer weekends any more than you or I do, but Kessler's disinclination was overridden by her determination to save the protected young of 2003 while there was still time. Piping plovers and least terns were about to hatch in their nests on sandbars—unless the rising water drowned them. Kessler intended the Corps to follow the law and drop the river.

Her injunction ordering the Corps to drop water levels to protect endangered species was the first ever such court ruling on the Missouri.

Suddenly, the Corps' mission of river navigation—of keeping those barges running—had been trumped by those two protected birds and one endangered fish, the pallid sturgeon.

"There is no dollar value that can be placed on the extinction of an animal species—the loss is to our planet, our children and future generations," the judge wrote in a passage that might have been worded by the advocates from American Rivers.

Kessler called the rise or fall "an immensely difficult case with great ramifications for the Missouri River." No one would disagree. She was so sure that the lawsuit brought by American Rivers and their brethren advocates would prevail that she had ordered the Corps to lower the flows in advance of formal victory. There is no question, she wrote, that the species would be harmed if the government followed through with its annual operating plan.

The angry judge ignored the government's argument that barge companies would suffer. In her ruling, she recalled the damning testimony of Justice Department lawyer James Maysonett on whether the Army Engineers could in the future operate the river in accordance with the Endangered Species Act.

KESSLER: What kind of commitments is the Corps offering so as to give any credibility to its promise that it will not take a similar position in 2004. . . .

MAYSONETT: "Well, I think the Corps . . . [is] working through revisions to the *Master Manual*, and they are engaged in consultation with the Fish and Wildlife Service for the *Master Manual*. . . .

KESSLER: Well, I guess I certainly got an answer by silence to my question, which was, what commitments and assurances is the Corps prepared to offer to establish that next year it will comply with the 2000 biological opinion, and your answer, in effect, was none. Isn't that right?

MAYSONETT: Well, I'm not certain what assurances the Corps could offer.

TRUMPING THE JUDGE

I missed Judge Kessler's unusual Saturday night decision, for I was far away in Montana, camped along the river whose ripples were stirring up such a fuss. By the time I returned the next week, the ruling's seismic impact on future operations of the river was being felt.

The earth had suddenly shifted, yanking decision-making power away from the Corps, which had run Big Muddy since the Pick-Sloan Plan in 1944. There was a second trembler underlying her ruling: If Kessler's logic held, the balance of control over the river might shift to upper basin states for the first time in decades. And her logic might well apply to other river wars across the country.

Among recorders of the shock waves was a *New York Times* editorial writer, who observed: "On the eve of the two-hundredth anniversary of Lewis and Clark's historic journey, Americans can begin to hope for a better future for the river that carried the expedition westward."

The government's reaction to Kessler's injunction was as unexpected as the order itself, and that's what brings lawyers back in front of Kessler's bench on this steamy July morning in 2003. At Gavins Point Dam on the Missouri just above South Dakota's border with Nebraska, the Corps initially dialed the flow back slightly, to 25,000 cubic feet per second. But the move was a mere feint toward compliance. The government refused to heed the injunction to lower the flow to 21,000, a level that would miss inundating least tern and piping plover chicks and nests.

In the Corps' defense, Justice Department lawyers hauled out an earlier injunction from a Nebraska court. Those judges had affirmed the Corps' responsibility to provide water in sufficient quantities to float barges no matter how few barges plied the river. This Nebraska court had entered the debate to resolve a Nebraska-Dakotas water war: The Dakotas had sued to prevent the Corps from releasing water from their sinking reservoirs, saving the water for Dakotans like unfortunate Robert Shadwell at the Point of View Lodge.

Nebraska countered the Dakota suit by seeking an injunction to keep the water flowing for barges. Two months before Kessler's ruling in this sudden explosion of litigation, the Eighth Circuit Court of Appeals in St. Louis had upheld the Nebraska injunction. Kessler knew that, and she faulted her St. Louis counterparts for failing to factor in the Endangered Species Act.

Now, the Justice Department sought to shelter the Corps behind the Nebraska and St. Louis decision. "These orders are mutually exclusive, and the Corps can't comply with both," Samuel Rauch, assistant chief of the Justice Department's wildlife and marine resources section, told Kessler.

The conflict boiled down to this: Would the Corps follow its *Master Manual*—that document around which all things swirled—giving the water to commerce? Or would it forsake its bible for the Endangered Species Act, as Kessler ordered?

Meanwhile, time and nature are speeding by. Kessler's precedent-setting order applies for a month only, just long enough for the protected terns and plovers to finish nesting on sandbars found in the last wild segments of the middle third of the river. For that whole month, Kessler wants to give the Fish and Wildlife Service a drawdown that would not only protect the birds but also begin restoring habitat for the pallid sturgeon.

The bargers and lower basin water worriers are apoplectic at the prospect of change. To them, it's radical, even though no less a mainstream organization than the National Academy of Sciences had warned that failure to make such changes risks "irreversible extinction of species."

DOWN THE MOUNTAIN

David Hayes, the lead counsel for the environmental coalition, hadn't expected to find himself in Kessler's blond-wood courtroom on this July day. The deputy secretary of the Interior Department in the Clinton administration had been mountain climbing in Grand Teton National Park when he got word that Kessler was taking the Corps back to court.

Hayes makes it back in court in time to tell Kessler that the government's intransigence is "a complete defiance of your injunction and a direct violation of the Endangered Species Act."

"Certainly refusal to comply with a federal judge's order is an extraordinarily serious matter," Kessler adds, raising the stakes.

Since the judge has brought Hayes so far, she asks his opinion on what the Corps' intransigence should cost them. Hayes figures $50,000 in fines. That's $50,000 a day. But it's nothing compared to the fine Kessler quietly has in mind.

Kessler's courtroom, No. 19, on the sixth floor of the E. Barrett Prettyman Building in the United States District Court for the District of Columbia, has become the epicenter of furious legal wrangling. In a month's time, six separate court battles will be waged over these plovers, terns, and sturgeon—and through those creatures, the river's future.

ONE ANGRY JUDGE

It's not only the Army Corps of Engineers but also President George W. Bush's White House that is taking fire for its dawdling in this United States District Court for the District of Columbia.

After three days of defying Judge Kessler's ruling, the Corps of Engineers has announced that the president's budget office has committed an additional $42 million to help restore the river's ecosystem. (The Corps later scaled its promise back to $22 million after being pressured from allies in Congress whose own projects were being diminished to find money for the Missouri.)

A day later, the Corps details for me its plan to spend nearly $200 million over the next five years. Those efforts would de-engineer in small ways some of the "improvements" made over the years. The money would pay for setting back levees, removing dikes, and creating chutes into the floodplain to create more shallow water for the pallid sturgeon. The feds will do even more for that odd prehistoric sturgeon, they say, by giving new money to Fish and Wildlife hatcheries to breed sturgeon to forestall extinction.

Judge Kessler is not impressed. She fits her description as "not a relaxed person" the afternoon she declares the Corps in contempt for refusing to lower water in the Missouri River. She's in a hurry, but she gives the government one last chance and a few more days to do as she orders.

Now if the Army Engineers refuse, she promises to impose a $500,000 fine. That's $500,000 a day for every new day the court defies her. That's ten times more than even plaintiff Hayes proposed. What's more, Kessler vows she will consider "more draconian" steps if her terms weren't met within three days.

I'm not immediately sure what could be more draconian than a half-million-dollar-a-day fine, but it sounds to me like the judge is pondering jail time for a few Army officers.

Kessler makes short work of the government assertion it is making a good-faith effort by moving to clear up the issue in other courts.

"The Corps' actions demonstrate the exact opposite," she writes. "Moving to stay an order does not represent a good-faith effort to comply with that order. Rather, it represents an effort to postpone compliance with that order in the hope that it will be overturned on appeal."

"This is one angry judge," says Hayes, when I reach him that evening on his cell phone.

A few minutes later, I call a Corps official and read the judge's words. Silence lingers on the line. Then he says, "I'm glad my name isn't on there anywhere."

COURTROOMS COMPOUNDED

Despite Judge Kessler's threats, the Corps refuses to budge. But for the government and barge operators, relief comes from unexpected quarters. What happens next is the judicial equivalent of the Major League Baseball commissioner stepping in with a scheduling change during the World Series. It's a classic deus ex machina.

Kessler never gets to drag the Corps into her courtroom again, or levy her fine, or get draconian.

On the afternoon before Kessler's latest deadline, the Judicial Panel on Multidistrict Litigation, which I'd never heard of, transfers six Missouri River cases—among them the litigation in front of Kessler—to the courtroom of a Minnesota judge. The panel, I quickly learn, was set up in the 1960s to help federal courts run more smoothly. Coincidentally, it was meeting in Portland, Maine, that very July week. And it looks as though victory has been snatched from environmental advocates at the eleventh hour.

Henceforth, the panel ruled, the conservation groups, the barge industry, and states trying to secure water from the river would be making their cases in St. Paul in front of U.S. District Judge Paul Magnuson, a senior jurist who had been around since the administration of Ronald Reagan.

Tim Searchinger of the New York–based advocate group Environmental Defense is stunned at both the ruling and its timing. "Our main concern is that it disrupts the flow of the case given the fact that we have endangered species threatened right now," he tells me. On the other side, Chris Brescia, president of the trade association representing the navigation industry, sounds thrilled. "Maybe the legal system will work now and the right hand will know what the left hand is doing," he says.

The Justice Department wastes no time requesting a stay in the $500,000-a-day fine about to be levied on the Army Corps of Engineers. Nor is there much time to waste, for the fine is set to begin the next day. Up in St. Paul, the new judge is just as fast in granting the Corps' request.

For the St. Louis Post-Dispatch I write: "The legal merry-go-round over Missouri River water has slowed for the time being in favor of the Army Corps of Engineers—but in a threatening spot for federally protected birds." Indeed, thirty tern and plover nests with unhatched eggs, and more than one hundred chicks too young to fly are nesting happily along the 59-mile stretch of relatively undisturbed river bordering South Dakota and Nebraska where the endangered species still build nests. If the Corps begins increasing the flow to make up for low rainfall and keep barges flowing, those are dead birds.

On the barge side of the equation, during these hot and heated days, only four towboats are operating on the 732-mile stretch of river between St. Louis and Sioux City, Iowa, according to the Corps daily boat report. Never during these legal proceedings fought by the government to protect the barge industry are there more than a handful of tows pushing barges on the Missouri River.

But in this braided channel of litigation, sandbars, and snags, the Corps is not getting everything it wants. Government lawyers lose motions in Nebraska and the District of Columbia appellate court. Then the appellate court in St. Louis rules that the Nebraska injunction on which the Corps was relying wasn't even in effect. Finally, after a two-week delay, up in Minnesota, Judge Magnuson, who has jurisdiction now, agrees: Judge Kessler's injunction back in the District of Columbia is to be followed, he says. The Corps is boxed in.

In a four-paragraph news release nearly four weeks after Judge Kessler's ruling, the Corps agrees to lower the water in the Missouri on behalf of endangered species. It is reluctant compliance. In the following week, for fifty hours, the Corps ratchets the flow down to the 21,000 cubic feet per second that had been prescribed by the Fish and Wildlife Service and ordered by the judge.

This time, in the dry summer of 2003, dam operations miss killing a multitude of little terns and plovers. Over the years thousands have perished. But by Corps count, only about two dozen of the protected birds are known to have been killed in 2003 in violation of the Endangered Species Act designed to protect them.

SHIFTING BALANCE

Battles over the flows of American rivers are typically fleeting skirmishes with outcomes tipped in advance to the side closest to the political persuasion of the White House. In this round along the Missouri, the opponents of changing the river's flow—barge interests, farm groups, and downstream states avid to protect water supplies—believed that in President George W. Bush they had an ally able to rein in the crusading U.S. Fish and Wildlife Service and put a pesky United States District Court judge in her place.

But seismic shifts rise from forces deeper than politics and out of its reach. The forces that move rivers and mountains rumble along for eons or decades without amounting to anything much. Then, suddenly, they heave up and reshape the world. Kessler's ruling seemed to be part of something that big.

Five days after her ruling, a federal judge in Oakland declared that the Bush administration's plan for distributing water in the Klamath River in Oregon and California violated the Endangered Species Act by threatening coho salmon.

A month earlier, the silvery minnow of the Rio Grande had a panel of judges on its side: The U.S. Tenth Circuit Court of Appeals ruled that the Bureau of Reclamation could take water away from farmers and municipalities to give the tiny fish a better chance to survive. Just before that, a U.S. district judge in Oregon had ordered more diligent efforts to recover endangered and threatened salmon in the Columbia and Snake rivers.

In each high-profile case, judges rebuked government bureaucrats and demanded dramatic actions to protect species. When the history of the Endangered Species Act is written, 2003 might be recalled as the year federal judges gave fish and birds a chance.

Like many waterways, the Missouri River has been managed for a water elite—big farming, big ranching, and big boat operators, a development the egalitarian Jefferson likely would not have abided. For the foreseeable future, decisions about running the river will favor those with political clout to bring the flow their way. Perhaps that's as it should be, considering that the population of the Missouri River Valley lies heavily in the lower river region from Sioux City to St. Louis.

But denizens of the Missouri, as in other basins, clamor for more public participation in these decisions. In the last half century, the decision making—if not the decisions themselves—has been flawed, even in the judgment of the water elite, who now recognize a shifting balance. But from now on, politics along the Missouri may not play out so traditionally.

Six decades ago, it didn't take the governors along the Missouri long to realize what Pick-Sloan hath wrought. In the late 1940s, they fully expected a Missouri basin interagency committee made up of states and federal departments working hand in hand to chart the river's future development. Nebraska governor Val Peterson had the temerity to inquire when the committee would get moving with a plan to sort through projects the governors had in mind.

Committee chairman W. G. Sloan, the Bureau of Reclamation half of the Pick-Sloan Plan, reminded Peterson bluntly that the panel on which the governors sat had neither authority to present projects nor means to carry them out.

"Now the truth comes out," *Denver Post* columnist Roscoe Fleming wrote in 1949. "The little governors supposedly on the committee to look out for their states are just along for the ride. Let them twitch the reins, and Pa will slap their hands down. And what a ride. It isn't just them, it is the people of the basin being taken for a ride, too."

Likewise, the interagency committee's modern successor, the Missouri River Basin Association, has had opportunities—but never the cohesiveness—to chart changes in the Army Corps of Engineers operation of the river.

Larry Hesse—the Nebraska biologist, National Academy of Sciences member, and irritant to the status quo protectorate—proposes a Missouri River Adaptive Management Council to run the show. He sees the river run like a democracy with the Corps of Engineers holding no bigger chair at the decision-making table than farmers, recreationists, and environmentalists.

Hesse's adaptation of New England town hall–style governing seems idyllic indeed. People of a largely forgotten geographical subset, the Missouri River basin, would decide the river's future, perhaps even by plebiscite. But having watched Washington operate over three decades, I know how rarely power gets relinquished and how difficult it will be to move toward such pluralism any time soon.

Missouri, where 2 million people drink from the river—more than the combined populations of North Dakota, South Dakota, and Montana—and which has the largest congressional delegation in the basin, remains too obsessively worried about the river's water to submit to risky new political structures. Politicians holding the reins of power argue that we've got plenty of democracy right now: We were chosen in democratic elections, weren't we?

The shoot-'em-up mentality of western water wars likely will gun down every effort to look into the future. Until states determine how to manage a water commonwealth in a mature way, I'm betting that decisions will be made by a riverine politics that have changed far less than the Missouri itself.

But it is the Corps of Discovery Bicentennial, and the time is ripe for examining how we proceed and how we make amends. That is why I am intrigued by a planning exercise for the future—even though I'm unwelcome at the secret session.

As Judge Kessler and federal courts struggled to decide the river's future, representatives from the Corps, the Fish and Wildlife Service, and other federal agencies, along with tribal leaders and representatives from six basin states, gathered in South Sioux City, Nebraska, for a five-day lesson in what was called "collaborative resource management."

I smell a hustle when managers throw in with focus groups and consultants to share visions. But the praise of participants and past successes in other river disputes are winning me over. I'm voting for more such gatherings with their new way of approaching natural resources management. If government agencies are persuaded to give up their old ways, they will have paid for the privilege. The Interior Department, the Environmental Protection Agency, and the Corps itself bankrolled the Nebraska gathering, which was run by the University of Michigan Collaborative Resource Management office.

Promoters of similar collaborative ventures say they've drummed up more understanding, less name-calling, and a path to congressional funding, always a carrot to ceasing hostilities. The Nisqually River Council in Puget Sound, the Upper Colorado River Endangered Fish Recovery Program, and the Glen Canyon Adaptive Management Program all have reported successes.

The prospect of federal money is a powerful inducement to break bread together; the $8 billion restoration of the Florida Everglades is the gold standard for ecosystem planners. For groups seeking similar largesse, I advise becoming a swing state in the presidential election with a cache of electoral votes. If you can't do that, at least have the political wisdom to move your primary election early in the calendar, and you'll enjoy a quadrennial burst of clout.

Steven Yaffee, the Theodore Roosevelt Professor of Ecosystem Management at Michigan and the lead trainer, described his methods in Sioux City. What I recall most was his having the good sense to send the parties out to a Missouri River sandbar in boats. What transpired on the outing might have had more effect than months of e-mails and conference calls; at the moment federal courts weighed life-and-death decisions about least terns, a tern rose from a sandbar in front of resource managers who will carry out whatever decision seals its fate.

Yaffee and his team might be accused of planting that bird, given their many calculations. In bringing people together on the sandbar, at a state park, and at Gavins Point Dam, they were, he told me, "trying to simply get people walking on the land together. It changes the dynamic from people arguing across the table to sharing the experience."

I still had my doubts. For years, the Missouri River Basin Association—the alliance of Big Muddy states and tribes—has worked to bring its members together in ways that might generate understanding and a semblance of peace. But always, politics get in the way. Yaffee told me he has a vision of a new Missouri era. "It has the potential to shift the energy that's going into the decision-making process to make it more of a problem-solving process where you're getting people to talk about the interests they have and some creative ways to meet those interests," he said. "In the existing process, you don't allow this conversation to take place. The traditional process encourages stereotypes and people cast in the extremes. Media contributes to that; black and white are more easily understood than gray."

I see why I wasn't invited.

Going to the scene "humanizes the process, allows building of relationships and the development of understanding so that you can solve problems," Yaffee added.

I wanted specifics, and Yaffee had a few. Oddly, the "shared perspectives" of the government planners and tribes sounded like what advocacy groups might say.

Number one finding: Change is needed. "The current decision-making system for managing the river and its ecosystem is not working. Decision making is increasingly bound up in stalemate. Some groups, notably the tribes, feel that they continue to be shut out of key processes."

Unfettered and tieless, resource managers peeled the hide off the system. A summary of the proceedings put it this way: "A number of participants felt that the current plans and laws underlying river management were framed in a very different time in the history of the basin and America. This means that guiding principles underlying Pick-Sloan and the 1944 Flood Control Act need to be updated to reflect today's demands and possibilities. . . . We need to look at the Missouri River through our 2003 mindset."

Yaffee told me something I already knew about the scope of a water war complicated by endangered species fought over one sixth of the nation's landmass by all branches of the federal government and eight states.

"It is hard for people to think at this scale, and the amount of political fragmentation between so many states and so many tribes as well as stakeholders and federal agencies makes it hard for people to see that it can work another way," Yaffe said.

Soon, the search for a new way would grow more urgent as the old way, finally, fails.

A RECKONING

When the Army Corps of Engineers started revising its Missouri River *Master Manual*, the first George Bush was commander in chief and the Internet existed only in theory.

The barge industry had visions of thriving. Thousands of birds on the watch list for extinction would never be born because the Corps operated Big Muddy for navigation.

During the revision, enough time passed in the basin for one five-year drought to end, the second-worst flood in a century to inundate the river basin, and a new drought to take hold.

So it was a natural reaction when the Corps finally completed its *Master Manual*, on the eve of the 2004 spring equinox, to inquire why it had taken so damn long. Why, fourteen years ago, couldn't the nation's largest water management agency have adjusted to reflect the contemporary needs of the 10 million people in the basin?

Army assistant secretary John Paul Woodley, who had traveled to Omaha to sign the record-of-decision formalizing the new document, answered my question in a peculiarly off-handed fashion.

He said the Corps' motto is, "We're expensive, but we're slow."

Indeed, over the agonizing time it had taken to change a few pages in its manual, the Corps had spent $29 million, by its count, on studies and paper shuffling. So why not spend a few bucks on a cake for the signing ceremony?

An appealing treat it was, this white sheet cake emblazoned with the shape of the Missouri basin and the Corps' castle logo. But as the details of what the Corps had done became clear, wonderment grew as to what they were celebrating in Omaha.

For after fourteen years of being told that the flows on the Missouri River had to change, after hearing from both the U.S. Fish and Wildlife Service and a federal judge that it was breaking the law, the Corps put off decisive action once more.

The new *Master Manual* revision delayed until 2006 the spring rise of life-giving pulses to recreate backwaters sacrificed to barges and flood control. The Corps also avoided the second pill in the U.S. Fish and Wildlife prescription for river health: shallower summer water for terns, plovers, and the fingerling fish that fought the fast current to survive. Instead, Army engineers promised to create shallow water habitat for endangered species, 1,200 acres in three months and thousands more in coming years.

In a shift of water in the basin, the Corps imposed a drought plan that promised to hold more water in three of those upstream reservoirs: Lake Oahe, Lake Sakakawea, and Fort Peck. But the plan did little to slake the insatiable thirst for more water up and down the river.

"Nothing short of abysmal," said Senate Minority Leader Tom Daschle of South Dakota.

"Significant problems," Kit Bond told me.

"Appalling lack of leadership," concluded an alliance of ten environmental groups.

Woodley, a Virginian known for his folksy ways, feigned shock. "I'm taken aback," he said over the telephone when advised of full-throated denunciations from every quarter.

There are three things the Corps can't do, he remarked: Number one, make it rain; and number two, make the rain stop.

"The third thing that the Corps of Engineers cannot do," Woodley added, "is make everybody happy, and I'm beginning to think that we can't make anybody happy."

I would agree. The Corps is reputed to be an environmental criminal for its destruction of river ecosystems and branded an agency bent on expanding its domain no matter the cost. But I would remind the critics that the Corps is an agent of the federal government, albeit one with an unusual alliance with the pork-loving officials of the legislative branch. The 2004 *Master Manual* revision was produced in an election year under a White House whose master was struggling in his quest to keep his job and who had targeted Missouri, the most populous state in the basin, as a key battleground.

Good politics hinges on timing, and given the unrelieved drought, the timing for the *Master Manual* revision could scarcely have been worse. As the document was being sent to the presses, two of the Mandan-Hidatsa-Arikara communities in North Dakota that drink from the river had run dry.

In South Dakota, Lake Oahe was nearly twenty-eight feet below normal, and the state was fearful of losing its spawn of rainbow smelt, the foodfish for its valuable walleye fishery. That prospect had set off Governor Mike Rounds during a meeting with the Corps in Pierre two days before release of the *Master Manual.*

The mild-mannered Rounds pounded his desk when told that on a river that would continue to be maintained for navigation when his state desperately needed water, the only large boats might well be Corps vessels building habitat.

"I guess you can say that I was more than mildly agitated," Rounds told me. "It struck me as extremely inappropriate to be releasing stored water just so the Corps could float their own boats."

By spring 2004, it was hard to know who in the Missouri River is being forthright and who is positioning themselves for court. But the cries from lower basin politicians looking out for their states' futures were as anguished as Rounds's. Missouri governor Bob Holden, another politician fighting for his political life, said that the new Corps plan "would reduce the commitment to downstream drinking water supplies, power plant cooling, and river commerce."

Next came complaints about further delaying the protection of endangered species. "It's like spending fourteen years to create a new way to play music, and then deciding in the end to use eight-track tapes," Tim Searchinger, the Environmental Defense lawyer, told me.

Woodley argued that the Corps of Engineers and therefore the Army had complied with the Endangered Species Act. But I'd already seen a letter from the Interior Department sent to the Corps just two days before asserting that without flow changes recommended by the Fish and Wildlife Service, the *Master Manual* "does not achieve the desired goal of avoiding jeopardy to the listed species."

It was not lost on some of the complaining parties that as part of its solution, the Corps, famously vigilant about growing its budget and domain, was calling for $1.3 billion over the next twenty years. Already, the nation's biggest civil works agency had begun punching holes in dikes, plowing into the floodplain, and ever so slightly undoing the straitjacket it began strapping on the river with bank stabilization in the late 1800s.

Brigadier General William Grisoli, the commander of the Corps' Northwestern Division and therefore the boss of the Missouri River, observed that he was "pleased and proud" to be part of the announcement. Grisoli had more on the line than most people knew.

In a ground-floor nook of the Corps' Omaha building was a photograph of Grisoli's immediate predecessor, General David Fastabend, bearing a diagonal slash. Also slashed were the photos of nine other Northwestern Division commanders: Brigadier General Bob Ryan; Brigadier General Eugene Witherspoon; Colonel Don Hazen; Colonel John Schauffelberger; Colonel Michael Thuss; Colonel John Craig; Colonel Michael Meuleners; Brigadier General Robert Griffin; and Brigadier General Carl Strock. The defacements did not suggest service in any but the best Corps tradition for these Army officers, who went on to other assignments and promotions.

The inside joke indicated was that all ten shared a common failure: Completion of that elusive new bible of river operations.

But in affixing his signature to a completed *Master Manual*, Grisoli avoided the dubious distinction of so many predecessors. His photo—or so the wags said—would hang undefaced in the Omaha District headquarters.

Sixty years had gone by since that 1944 law that ordered the dams built and turned the Missouri River over to the Army Corps of Engineers. It had all been the plan of Colonel Lewis Pick, the master salesman who would become general and who, in a way, still bosses Big Muddy after all these years.

Grisoli signed the *Master Manual* on Pick's desk.

If the Missouri River ruckus were to show the way for other river flow fights around the country, it seemed that America could look to half-solutions—and to the courts to sort matters out.

A "GREAT STATE OF MISERY"

For the final chapter in this slice of Big Muddy history, the players gathered far from where the river flows. All of the basin states where I had traveled were represented, as were the farmers, the bargers, the environmentalists, the recreationists, and the Indian tribes. Those dueling bureaucrats Lewis Pick and Glenn Sloan, who set the Missouri on its tortured course, made an appearance. Even Lewis and Clark showed up. They all have come together in a federal court, and it is not that of Gladys Kessler, the judge who had so little patience with the Army Corps of Engineers that she was about to dispatch an officer or two to jail.

This time, the parties convene not in Washington, D.C., but in St. Paul. In the court of Federal Judge Paul Magnuson, lawsuits contesting the river's flow, and the debate over the sanctity of its fish and birds, have been transferred. This ruling could be the most momentous for the Missouri River in decades, and I wonder if Reagan's death on the eve of the decision will make any difference. As I ponder, I have no inkling that Magnuson's ruling will be of such import that another president, George W. Bush, will talk about it while traveling in Europe.

Coincidentally, much is happening at the moment in the lives of many who depend on the river. Robert Shadwell, the South Dakota lodge owner prone to tirades, e-mailed to say that he filed for bankruptcy protection. When I phoned him, he told me that water levels along the Lake Oahe stretch of the Upper Missouri had continued to drop. Cottonwoods submerged for a half century protruded like a forest graveyard, he said, and getting on the river was spooky as well as dangerous. A state biologist had torn off his propeller the day before.

I couldn't believe the water could drop any lower in South Dakota than I'd seen it, with the cove in front of Shadwell's Point of View Lodge a half-mile away from water. So I checked with the Corps of Engineers. Sure enough, the river was eleven feet lower than a year ago, when I had visited last, and it was scheduled to drop another three feet in coming months.

Shadwell sounded remarkably cheerful for a man on the brink. He and his wife, Kim, had recalibrated their life plan, selling their house in Denver early and moving into a Point of View cabin while working to restructure payments on the lodge. Robert planned to open a body shop in nearby Harriett, South Dakota. That's the life he had fled in Denver, but he needed income, and when we spoke, he was seeking to buy a painting booth. Despite the low water, Point of View had gotten some new bookings recently, and some Illinois fellows had hauled up lunker walleye twenty-eight and thirty inches in length. Shadwell was proud of the catch, and he even managed a kind word for the Army Corps of Engineers, which had held back some water to help save a smelt spawn rather than releasing it downstream.

A resort nearby had closed, a victim of drought and water allocation policy favoring downstream. But despite disastrous conditions, Shadwell insisted that he would not abandon his dream of running a fishing lodge with his family. "I can't give up on this. I'm going to hang on until the fat lady sings or the bank shuts me down," he said.

Government policy kept the water flowing downstream for barges at the expense of the Shadwells of the basin. But something had gone wrong with this calculation, too, I discovered at the other end of the river. One of the lawsuits in front of Judge Magnuson had been filed by Roger Blaske, a third-generation barge operator based in Alton, Illinois, near the confluence of the Missouri and Mississippi rivers. Blaske operated the *Lauren D*, the towboat on which I had ridden upstream along with a load of fertilizer.

I'd heard that the bargers downstream, like the recreationists upstream, were suffering and that only a couple were operating. For the towboat operators, it wasn't just the drought but the uncertainties of not knowing what river policy would be six months in the future that kept them from booking business. Blaske, a lanky, genial man and a fishing fanatic, had been ducking me for a while. I knew he resented being cast by environmentalists as a villain in newspaper stories, and I presumed that was why he had been hard to reach.

When I finally got him on the phone, I found out he'd had other things on his mind. He and his brother, Stanley, were closing the business that their grandfather had started as Alton Barge Service more than a half century ago. He had sold the *Lauren D* and put up for sale *Omaha*, the vessel whose barges had hung up on a shoal, ruining a load of soybeans and costing the company $50,000.

We spoke three days before he shuttered his office on Broadway, a few doors down from the *Alton Telegraph* newspaper, where I had begun my career thirty years before. After running his own business, Blaske was preparing to go to work for another barge line that did most of its business on the Mississippi.

"They finally broke us after all the junk that has gone on. It just got down to where we couldn't make any money. To this day, I don't understand why you can't have some kind of a system that does a fair job for both the industry and the environment," he said.

That had been a question in my mind about the Corps-run river. I wondered if the new judge would take it upon himself to fix the governing system or let things continue as they were.

The run-up to the ruling had turned ugly in other ways that involved me. The state of Missouri, ever vigilant about protecting its water, had discovered some inflammatory e-mails in court exhibits and was using them to persuade the judge that the Fish and Wildlife Service was biased against Missourians. I found them mostly funny. Others didn't when they ended up on the front page of the *St. Louis Post-Dispatch* under my by-line.

Dismissing Missouri's worries utterly, one electronic missive sent internally by a Fish and Wildlife biologist and not meant to become public referred to "chicken little stories emanating from the great state of Misery."

It added: "I guess that is a reflection of the education system in the Mississippi of the North." Missourians in Congress didn't appreciate that line.

Another government biologist who luckily had just retired managed to insult Army engineers, elected officials, and the town fathers of Jefferson City, Missouri, in a single message when he reflected on efforts to protect water intake pipes during low water the previous summer.

"Never mind the fact that the river gets much, much lower in January and they never have a problem. Goes to show how the Corps media machine and self-serving politicians can instill fear in people who should know better," the e-mail read.

As best I could determine, the judge paid little heed to Missouri's e-mails or, for that matter, the arguments of any party in the case but one.

For the first big Missouri River court ruling in Washington, D.C., I was far from civilization in a canoe on the river itself. This time, when Judge Magnuson finally speaks, I'm fooling around somewhere in the Florida outback where cell phones can't reach.

Libby Quaid, an Associated Press reporter in Washington who has been yanked into this story inconveniently on many occasions, summed things up in her first two sentences:

> The Missouri River can operate without changes sought by environmentalists to save endangered fish and birds, a federal judge ruled Monday. U.S. District Judge Paul Magnuson ruled in favor of the Army Corps of Engineers on Monday on all counts.

One by one, Magnuson dismisses every notion, point, or pleading of any party other than the Corps of Engineers. To South Dakota and all the Shadwells without water, the judge said simply that the law is not designed to protect against "these kind of difficulties."

He noted that the state of Missouri disagrees with the Corps, but so what? Former barge owner Roger Blaske's name shows up liberally as a plaintiff. So does the levee protection group headed by Tom Waters, the Missouri farmer who had described to me his fear of that two-faced, mean river that runs by his land. Waters doesn't want that river to rise and Blaske doesn't want it sink. Neither came away from this judge with more than faint praise for "vigorously advocating their positions."

Nobody in the litigation got the back of the hand like the Indian tribes. Chairman Tex Hall and his Mandan-Hidatsa-Arikara Tribe, who had hosted me in my travels, had argued that they needed a plan that took into consideration their fishing and economic needs. They wanted the river operated so as not to wash away their sacred sites and the graves of their dead, their brief said. They wanted no more traumas like the Sioux in South Dakota had endured seeing the bones of their ancestors exposed by the ebb-and-flow of the water.

At that moment, receding waters on Lake Oahe had started to reveal what would expand to an eleven-acre island piled with the bones of bison and the scattered remains of Indians. Tribal members gazing dumbstruck from the bank at their heritage would glimpse fluttering in the stillness: terns and plovers, other players in the litigation in front of Judge Magnuson, building nests amid the skeletons. It took only a moment for the Army engineers racing to seal the island to solve the mystery of batteries amid the bones. They'd been dropped by midnight looters draping themselves with blankets to shield their crimes.

To the Indians' concerns about the river, the judge didn't speak: He dismissed everything the tribes had argued by saying simply they lacked standing to make their claims. In other words, the people who had been on the Missouri the longest couldn't determine the future of the river because, the judge said, they had demonstrated no injury. I noted that he had misspelled "Hidatsa."

American Rivers, Environmental Defense, and the green plaintiffs got nothing in the short run. The judge barely considered that the Corps might be acting arbitrarily, capriciously, immorally, politically, or stupidly. But within his words lay perhaps a major victory for the pro-conservation crew: The judge said that he expects the Corps by 2006, rain permitting, to begin those spring rises of water to rescue wildlife. That's roughly half of what the Corps and its nemesis, the Fish and Wildlife Service, had fought over for fifteen years.

It looked to me like the judge had taken a rather elementary view of matters: The Army Corps of Engineers was the boss; all others were yelping special interests. The Corps must listen to what they say and try to strike a balance, he allowed, but the Army runs the river by order of Congress. That's how it has been since the Pick-Sloan Plan, and that's how it is today.

It was a pro-establishment ruling in every regard, a ruling that not only preserved the status quo but did nothing to widen participation in the future of the Missouri by the people in its basin. In that the ruling postponed change beyond the November election, it was a triumph for President Bush and fodder for the politics of the season.

Soon afterward, Senator John Kerry, Bush's Democratic challenger, and I were sitting on metal folding chairs beneath a maple tree, not far from the river. Kerry was weary from campaigning, looking downward with his elbows resting on his knees, but he perked up when I asked him about the Missouri.

That *Master Manual* that the judge endorsed would not stand in his administration, he said. "What I want to do is sit down anew with the parties and see if we can't bring people together in an effective way that balances the interests here," he told me. He wouldn't get the chance.

Bush was not far from the Shannon River, Ireland's longest river, during a United States–European Union summit when his office issued a statement about the longest river back home. On that day, a few days after Judge Magnuson's ruling, the Corps and the Fish and Wildlife Service, agencies in his charge that had feuded since the first George Bush occupied the White House, declared that they had agreed on a means to preserve endangered wildlife by creating 1,200 acres of habitat for them along a 2,341-mile river.

I don't know if the president glimpsed the Shannon, which the Irish have allowed to run free. But I do know that in every quarter of the once-great Missouri, it took faith to accept his words about the days ahead for America's river west.

"The citizens who call the Missouri River home can now better plan for their future," the president said, "as they enjoy the many benefits and abundant wildlife that this extraordinary natural resource provides."

WHERE THIS JOURNEY ENDS

Bud Lilly had been ailing; a lung embolism had laid him low and he hadn't fished the Missouri or any river for weeks. Then pneumonia had been the barrier between Bud and the waters he loved so dearly. Nonetheless, he invited me out to the ex-cattle farm where he and his partners are carving out their trout ranch, and he asks me a question instead of vice versa.

"You don't happen to have a rod with you, do you?"

I did.

Truth be told, I had bought the reel twenty years ago for two dollars at an antique shop along the Chesapeake Bay in Maryland, where I live. It was the same reel I'd taken wishfully on many other Missouri River reporting trips along with a slightly better rod. But never had I unpacked them.

And now Bud Lilly, possessor of a king's ransom of bamboo and graphite rods, is using my junky outfit to whip fly line into the Montana sunset.

"You could use a new reel about any time," he says matter-of-factly, while talking about balancing the economy with saving the river's environment.

It's my turn to manipulate the line, and I notice that the fly on the end lands only about two thirds as far into the stream as the casts by a fellow approaching eighty years of age who has been under the weather.

"Can you put a little more oomph in it?" he asks.

I try, fearful of flinging myself into the stream. That's when Lilly recommends some newer gear, and reaches into his pocket.

He carries with him a wallet-sized leather case with a selection of flies, I presume, for any fish on any water in any weather.

"Tie this one on," he says.

I flung Lilly's furry little bug toward the home of many trout hoping that if, by accident, I snagged one, it wouldn't be big enough (or smart enough) to untie his fly.

Lilly talked about patience, whether in fishing or environmental damage. "It's going to be a long time before the river can change back to anywhere near how it was when Lewis and Clark saw it. But there's a glimmer of hope," he said of the Missouri.

As he spoke, the line from my two-dollar reel grew as tight as the ribbon on a store-wrapped package.

"Well, pull it in," he said, of the boot-sized trout that soon would be flopping at my feet.

I think Bud Lilly was right. Hope for the Missouri rode on the passion of the people who looked past its chains and saw beauty. Hope rode on the belief that one day soon the river would be run as a commonwealth with people up and down its banks committed to its revival and deciding how its riches will be shared.

With a glimmer of hope, as Bud put it. That's where this Missouri River journey ended.

APPENDIX A

EARLY JOURNEYS

Log Book of the American Fur Company's Antelope

The log books of the American Fur Company's steamboat *Antelope,* a supply boat servicing other steamers on the river, recorded its annual trips along the Missouri from St. Louis to Montana in the 1840s. The river trip was full of dangers—hull-busting snags; fierce winds; balky crews; wood shortages; sandbars where none had been before; and unpredictability all around—and all were recorded by the master of the boat, Captain Joseph A. Sire. The log books were given to the Missouri Historical Society, in St. Louis, by H. M. Chittenden, a former Army Corps of Engineers employee. Some excerpts follow.

1841

APRIL 7: Took ten cords of wood at Widow Massey's. Took more wood at the entrance of the Gasconade. Going slow, bad wood.

APRIL 12: Our large cable, which was caught on a snag, cannot hold; it breaks and we have to let the boat be nearly swallowed up. We lose three-fourths of the day.

APRIL 15: The water keeps getting lower; the farther we go, the more difficulties we encounter.

APRIL 16: Francis is going to sound and finds five scant feet. Took eight and a half cords, which I have not paid for.

APRIL 19: Acquired some wood for which I had to pay the savages.

1845

JUNE 11: This is a day of delay, of accidents, and of misfortunes. The piece we had put in our boiler was lined with lead and melted. One of our men, named Edouard Mani, is crushed by a tree and two hours after our departure the unfortunate fellow exists no longer. Stopped at Fort Mitchell but there is no longer any trees to cut.

JUNE 15: We have a bad trip today. First at Three Islands, we cannot get out at the head of the middle channel. We therefore have to go back at least three miles to take the left channel.

JUNE 16: It seems that everything is against us. We cannot pass at the end of John's banks nor at the head of the island across from the banks. We have to go back at least five miles. We find only four scant feet of water at the left. As no boats have ever passed in this channel we find plenty of ash there; I stop two hours to cut some because we have already burned the cedar which we took such pains to obtain yesterday afternoon. We have much trouble in getting out of the channel where we are blocked in.

JUNE 17: We are lucky enough to be able to land on the grand isle of the Old Cedar Fort, where we can cut excellent dry cedar. We lose about an hour and a half in forcing ourselves in three and a half feet of water. Saw several savages a little farther on Deslauriers Island.

JUNE 23: We experience a frightful gust of wind accompanied by hail of extraordinary size. All the panes of our lookout as well as those of the pilot house and our cabin and several of our staterooms are submerged. This lasts at least ten minutes and I believe at each instant that our smokestacks will fall.

JULY 11: The wind continues to blow. Hardly are we en route when we fall among the animals. We kill several and have on board two buffalo cows and a calf. Meet a war party of Yanktons whom we take aboard and set on land below the river at Bazille. They are going to war with the Pawnees.

1846

JULY 1: We soon arrive at the village of the Gros Ventres (presently Fort Berthold Reservation). We lose a good five hours in making a feast with the savages and in holding council. Left and grounded immediately on the floor of the sandbar across from the village. The wind bothers us to such a degree that we are stuck to the sandbar. Killed a roebuck.

JULY 24: We ground so often today that I do not remember how often. Much trouble in cutting a little wood. Meet the steamboat *Clermont II* of the opposition.

JULY 26: I am seriously disappointed at not finding fourteen cords of wood that I left on the island. The *Clermont II*, it seems, took everything, in spite of the fact that the persons at the fort pointed out to them that the wood belongs to the company. We are obliged to fall back and to cut some snags. This place has become impassable.

1847

APRIL 21: Here begin our tribulations. We hit a snag, which would not have made the old *Antelope* tremble, but which knocks in five or six knees and two planks of these damned false sides. We put to shore as soon as possible, unload the whole boat with the exception of one aisle in order to hold it aslant, and get rid of the water which filled the false side. This was not vexation enough; we also had the misfortune to break two flanges. To repair all this will take us at least two days. It really is a pity.

APRIL 22: We believe that Peterson and William Dutchman, who have not appeared during the day, have deserted.

APRIL 23: It is certain that the two men have deserted.

Two decades later, the successor to *Antelope* would be destroyed by fire near Yankton, South Dakota, killing two passengers. *Antelope* pilot Joseph LaBarge became a famous captain in his own right. In 1876, his steamer, *John M. Chambers*, happened on to the sinking *Damsel*. The passengers that LaBarge and his crew rescued were not the typical steamboat adventurers: They saved an entire circus that had been summoned to the West to perform.

APPENDIX B

*Selected Law, Court Rulings, and Political Pronouncements
Regarding Tribal Land*

1803: Letter from Thomas Jefferson to Meriwether Lewis: "In all your intercourse with the natives, treat them in the most friendly and conciliatory manner which their own conduct will admit; allay all jealousies as to the object of your journey; satisfy them of its innocence; make them acquainted with the position, extent, character, peaceable, and commercial dispositions of the United States; of our wish to be neighbourly, friendly, and useful to them; and of our dispositions to a commercial intercourse with them."

1785–1871: The United States and tribes enter into more than 600 treaties in which Indians are promised a place to live and protection in exchange for vast tracts of land.

1831: In Cherokee Nation v. Georgia, the U.S. Supreme Court defines a trust responsibility between the federal government and tribes that "resembles that of a ward to his guardian."

1877: The General Allotment Act allocates land for reservations and names the U.S. government trustee over the land with the task of maintaining its value.

1886: In U.S. v. Kagama, the Supreme Court further spells out that Indians are legally dependent on the United States. "From their very weakness and helplessness . . . there arises the duty of protection."

1921: The Snyder Act directs the Bureau of Indian Affairs to spend money "for the relief of distress and the conservation of health" on Indian reservations.

1935: The Supreme Court, in U.S. v. Creek Nation, awards damages to Creek Indians and tells the government they also need to protect Indian land from injury caused by federal projects.

1942: In Seminole Nation v. the United States, the Supreme Court emphasizes the government's obligation in dealing with a "dependent and sometimes exploited people."

1964: Congress orders the government to consider "the needs and best interest of the Indian owner and his heirs" when it comes to tribal land.

1970: President Richard M. Nixon declares that the relationship between the government and tribes "continues to carry immense moral and legal force."

1987: In Blue Legs v. the United States, a U.S. District Court judge finds the government liable for open dumps on the Pine Ridge Reservation in South Dakota, and orders federal agencies to pay for most of the cleanup.

1991: President George H. W. Bush decrees that the government will do nothing "that will adversely affect or destroy those physical assets that the federal government holds in trust for tribes."

1999: In the first visit to Indian country by a sitting chief executive since Franklin Roosevelt, President Bill Clinton describes the relationship between government and tribes as "imperfect," while speaking at South Dakota's Pine Ridge Reservation. He adds, "But I have seen today not only poverty but promise, and I have seen enormous courage."

1999: U.S. District Judge Royce Lamberth in Washington rules that the government must account for more than a century of royalties from oil, gas, mining, and timber operations that it has collected on 47 million acres of tribal land mainly in the Dakotas, Montana, New Mexico, and Arizona after tribes sued in federal court, charging that they have been cheated out of billions of dollars.

2004: After learning that the Bureau of Indian Affairs had cut off federal checks to Indians suing the government, an angry Judge Lamberth asked whether Interior Secretary Gale Norton had "decided to declare war on the Indians."

INDEX

INDEX

Three Affiliated Tribes, 163–68, 182–86,
224, 303
Three Forks News, 275
Thuss, Michael, 297
Truman, Harry S, 81
Twain, Mark, 45, 194

U.S. Fish and Wildlife Service, *xx*, 49, 93,
139–40, 147, 282, 301
and Army Corps of Engineers, 15,
121–23, 123–25, 126–28, 143
environmental considerations,
economic advantages of, 143
See also Endangered Species Act
Uhl, R. S., 55
Undaunted Courage (Ambrose), 4, 146,
149–50
Unruly River, The (Schneider), 37–38, 264
Uphill Against Water (Carrels), 198
Upper Colorado River Endangered Fish
Recovery Program, 291
Upper Missouri River Breaks National
Monument, 259–60

Van Der Kamp, Jerry, 61
Vaughn, Roy, 256
Vento, Bruce, 247
Vestal, Stanley, 7–8, 42
Vester, Ray, 201
Virginian-Pilot, 131

Washington Post, 130
water wars
Apalachicola River (FL), 202–5
Arkansas rice growers, 199–202
Atlanta and, 205–9
Garrison Diversion, 231–33, 233–36,
236–38, 238–39, 239–41, 241–49

North Dakota, 168, 215–19, 220–25,
225–27, 229–33, 233–36, 236–38,
238–39, 239–41, 241–69
politics of, 193–94, 194–97, 198–99,
199–202, 202–5, 205–9, 209–13,
215–19, 220–25, 225–27
South Dakota, 168, 193–97, 198–99,
209–13
Waters, Tom, 28, 29–33, 302
Waverly Cats Catfish Tournament, 103–6
Wells, Mary, 274
Wells, Pearl, 276
Westphal, Joseph, 202
White Cliffs, 5–6, 259–61, **261**
White Lodge, Chief, 174
White River diversion, 199–202
Wilkerson, Beverly, 169–70
William the Traveler, 84–85
Williams, Gary, 266–68
Witherspoon, Eugene, 297
Wodder, Rebecca, 145
Wolf, Drags, 167
Wolf, Wesley, 206–7
Wolf Creek Outfitters, 258
Wolfe, Malcolm, 170
Woodley, John Paul, 294–95, 296
Woodsworth, William, 27
Wounded Knee, 173
Wright, Julia, 173

Yaffee, Steven, 291–93
Yates, Granny, 274–75
Yazoo Pumps, 130
Yellow Bird, Pemina, 182–86
Young, Milton, 232–33, 236–38, 242
Yowell, Jim "Doc," 105–6

Zahn, Paula, 30